HIS STORY
THE RESCUE

The Bible message from
Genesis to Christ in easy English

ACCESSTRUTH

His Story: The Rescue
The Bible message from Genesis to Christ in easy English

Copyright © 2016 AccessTruth
1st Printing

ISBN: 978-0-9944270-4-5

All Rights Reserved. Except as may be permitted by the Copyright Act, no part of this publication may be reproduced in any form or by any means without prior permission from the publisher. Requests for permission should be made to info@accesstruth.com

Scripture quotations are taken from the Holy Bible, New Living Translation, copyright ©1996, 2004, 2007, 2013, 2015 by Tyndale House Foundation. Used by permission of Tyndale House Publishers, Inc., Carol Stream, Illinois 60188. All rights reserved.

Written by Paul and Linda Mac
General editor: Matthew Hillier
Illustrations: Maxwell Hillier

AccessTruth gratefully acknowledges the pioneering work of Trevor McIlwain and others in developing foundational Bible teaching resources. Their resources have been a foundational inspiration for this book.

Published by AccessTruth
PO Box 8087
Baulkham Hills NSW 2153
Australia

Email: info@accesstruth.com
Web: accesstruth.com

CONTENTS

5	Introduction
9	SESSION 1 In the beginning
17	SESSION 2 God created the first man and woman
25	SESSION 3 Adam and his wife disobeyed God
33	SESSION 4 God put Adam and his wife out of the garden
41	SESSION 5 Cain and Abel were born outside of the garden
47	SESSION 6 God destroyed the earth with a flood
57	SESSION 7 God took Abram to Canaan
67	SESSION 8 God rescued Lot. God saved Abraham's son, Isaac
77	SESSION 9 God chose Jacob. God sent Jacob's son, Joseph, to Egypt
89	SESSION 10 God sent ten disasters to Egypt
103	SESSION 11 God rescued the Israelites and made an agreement with them
117	SESSION 12 God told the Israelites how to worship him

127	SESSION 13 God took the Israelites into Canaan
139	SESSION 14 God sent John to get Israel ready for the Rescuer
149	SESSION 15 Jesus was born and grew up. Jesus was baptized
161	SESSION 16 Jesus started his work
171	SESSION 17 Jesus said that people must be born again
183	SESSION 18 Jesus showed his great power
193	SESSION 19 Jesus is the only door to eternal life
201	SESSION 20 Jesus brought a man back to life
211	SESSION 21 Jesus came into Jerusalem and was arrested by his enemies
225	SESSION 22 Jesus was crucified, buried and raised from the dead
237	Our place in His Story
245	Definitions for some words used in this book

INTRODUCTION

God tells us his story in the Bible. He tells us the true story of how the world began. He tells us the things that he has said and done since the start of time. He tells us what he is like and what he is doing today. God wants every person to know this story of what he has said and done. He wants you to know the true story of your world. It is an amazing story.

God's story is about a rescue. It is about God saving people from death. It is the greatest rescue that has ever happened and will ever happen. But this is not a made-up story, like you would see in a movie or read in a book. This story is true. It started at the beginning of time and it is still going on today. You and your family and friends are part of this story. God wants you to know the truth about the rescue. He wants you to know what he did to save people who were going to die.

God wants everyone to know his story, so he made sure that it was written down clearly[1] in the Bible. We will start at the very beginning of the Bible. Then, we will follow the story through the Bible. We will follow it until we reach the time that God's Son came to live on the earth. We will not look at every part of God's story here. Instead, we will look at the parts of the story that will help you to understand the main message. God wants every person to understand this message of who he is and what he has done.

---

1. **clearly** - so it is easy to understand

HIS STORY: THE RESCUE

All of us have tried to think about what God is like. But how can we find out? We can find out by reading the Bible. We can find out what he is like because we can read about the things he has made, the things he has done, and the things he has said. God made sure that those things were written down for us to read in the Bible. God wants everyone to know what he is like.

When we spend time with other people, we can learn what kinds of people they are from the things that they do and say. We can see if they are friendly people or happy people. We can know them by the way that they speak and by the things that they do. We can learn what God is like too. We can find out what he cares about. We can find out how he thinks. God wants us to find out about him and to get to know him. That is why he made sure that his story was written down clearly for us to read. He knows us very well, and he wants us to know him very well, too.

There are some things you need to know about God before we start the story. These things are important to help you understand the beginning of the story. These are things that God says about himself later in the story. There are many more things that you will find out about God later in the story as well.

God doesn't live in time like we do. We only live at one point in time and then we move on to the next point in time. We can see the minutes passing and the days passing and the weeks passing. We could not go into the future[2] or go back into the past if we wanted to. But God exists at all points of time all at once. God is in the past and the present and the future at the same time.

God doesn't have a body and he isn't in one place. We only live in one place at one time in our bodies. But God doesn't have a body. He is a real person, but he doesn't live in a body like we do. We can only be in one place at one time but God is everywhere at once. He is free to be wherever he wants, whenever he wants.

---

2. **future** - the time after now

INTRODUCTION

About this book

As we go through God's story in this book, we will read many verses from the Bible. Take your time and read these verses carefully. You can read the verses from a Bible written in your own language. When you read these verses from the Bible or when you hear someone else read these verses, listen carefully. This is the story that God wanted to tell you and that he wants you to understand. The other things we have written in this book are to help you to understand what God is saying in the Bible.

GENESIS 1:1

When you see this picture of a book, it means that what is written beside it is from the Bible. The Bible chapter and verse is written there. You can find the verses and read them in your own English Bible, or in a Bible written in your own language.

The English version of the Bible we have used is the *New Living Translation*. This Bible is also available online.

We have written this book in easy English. Many people are learning to read and speak English. If you are learning English, we hope that you will be able to understand the words we have used. Some words are hard to understand in English so we have explained them – these explanations can be found at the bottom of each page. We have also made a list of these words at the end of this book. If there are other words that you don't know, you can find a translation of them in your language in a dictionary or online. Or, you could ask someone to help you to understand what those words mean.

At the end of each part, you will see this question mark. There you will find some questions to think about or to talk about with other people.

7

SESSION 1

IN THE BEGINNING

¹In the beginning God created the heavens and the earth.

GENESIS 1:1

God wants us to know the true story about how things began. So he started his story with *in the beginning*. His story starts at the very beginning of time.

It says that *in the beginning God* was already there. So that means God was there before the beginning of time.

Then God's story says that *God created the heavens and the earth*. The word *create* means to make something out of nothing. Only God can make something out of nothing. Nobody else can do that. When people make things, they have to make them out of something. But God can make new things out of nothing. He didn't need anything else to exist[3] so he could make the heavens and the earth. He could do that because he is God. Only God can make something out of nothing.

---

3. **exist** - for something to be there

HIS STORY: THE RESCUE

God knows more than can be found in all the books and on all the websites in the world. God's power is much greater than all the power in the world that people use. God is not just a little bit more powerful, he is much more powerful. All the knowledge[4] and all the power in the world could not create something when there was nothing before. But God can do that. In the beginning, God created the heavens and the earth when there was nothing before.

GENESIS 1:2

² The earth was formless and empty, and darkness covered the deep waters. And the Spirit of God was hovering over the surface of the waters.

God's story tells us what the earth was like when God first made it. It says that the earth was *formless and empty*. Formless means that it didn't have a shape and it was not in order. It also says that the earth was empty. It says the earth was empty because there was no life there yet – no people, plants, or animals. Deep water covered[5] the whole world and it was dark. So God had made the earth, but it was not a place where anyone or anything could live.

Then God's story says that the Spirit of God was there. It says *the Spirit of God was hovering over the surface of the waters*. Hovering means that he was waiting[6] there. He was waiting above the deep water.

But who or what is the Spirit of God? God's story tells us much more about the Spirit later. He is a real person who is part of God. He is not a different person or another person. God is one person but he is made up of three - the Father, the Son and the Spirit. Sometimes people call God the 'Trinity'. Trinity means 'three in one'. Later in the story, you will hear more about the Father, the Son and the Spirit and find out more about them.

So God's Spirit was waiting over the waters of the dark, empty earth. He was waiting to do something.

GENESIS 1:3

³ Then God said, "Let there be light," and there was light.

Now God's story tells us what God did next. It tells us that God said something. He said *"Let there be light."* The very next thing it says is that *there was light.*

---

4. **knowledge** - all the things that people know
5. **covered** - the water was on top of all the earth
6. **waiting** - to stay somewhere until a later time

SESSION 1: IN THE BEGINNING

So God made light just by speaking. He did not have to go to get anything or go and do anything. All he did was say what he wanted. He said it and then it happened. He wanted to make light so he just said that there should be light and then light was there.

Light is the first thing God made after he made the heavens and the earth. At first, the earth was dark, but then God made light. Light brings energy[7] and helps things to live and to grow. God made light because he was going to make things later that would need light. God knew he would make things that would need light to see, and to get warm, and to live and to grow.

GENESIS 1:4

[4] And God saw that the light was good. Then he separated the light from the darkness.

God tells us in his story that he saw that the light that he had made *was good*. Everything God makes is good. When God says something is good, it means that there is nothing bad in it at all. It is perfect. Perfect means that there is nothing bad or wrong with it. God makes things perfect every time. Everything that God does is perfect.

The next thing God did was to separate[8] the light from the darkness. He moved the darkness and light away from one another. There was no sun or moon or stars. But God made light and he put it in the place he wanted it. Part of the earth was dark and part of the earth was light. God made light without a sun or moon or anything that the light came from. Only God can do that.

GENESIS 1:5

[5] God called the light "day" and the darkness "night."

And evening passed and morning came, marking the first day.

God had separated the darkness from the light. He was making things the way he wanted them. He was bringing order to the earth. He was fixing it up so it was the way he wanted it to be. He was putting everything in its place. He named the light *day* and the darkness *night*. He had made the first day. We can still see the days passing now, going from morning to night. God started that at the very beginning of time.

---

7. **energy** - power that makes things happen
8. **separate** - to move one thing away from another thing

HIS STORY: THE RESCUE

GENESIS 1:6-8

⁶ Then God said, "Let there be a space between the waters, to separate the waters of the heavens from the waters of the earth." ⁷ And that is what happened. God made this space to separate the waters of the earth from the waters of the heavens. ⁸ God called the space "sky."

And evening passed and morning came, marking the second day.

God was putting things in order on the earth. The next thing he did was to put *a space between the waters*. God said that there would be a space between these waters and that is what happened. There was water below that covered the earth, and a layer⁹ of water above. So there were waters above the earth and waters on the earth. God named the space he had made *sky*. That is what he did on the second day.

GENESIS 1:9,10

⁹ Then God said, "Let the waters beneath the sky flow together into one place, so dry ground may appear." And that is what happened. ¹⁰ God called the dry ground "land" and the waters "seas." And God saw that it was good.

On the third day, he put the waters on the earth into place. He just said he wanted this to happen and it happened. He said it and then the water moved into the place God wanted it to be. The water moved into its place and so there was dry land where some of the water had been. God named the dry ground *land* and the waters on the earth he named *seas*.

Now the earth was starting to look more like a place where people or animals could live. There were seas and there was dry ground and there was sky. And there was day and night. God said that everything was good. Everything was perfect just like God wanted it to be.

GENESIS 1:11-13

¹¹ Then God said, "Let the land sprout with vegetation—every sort of seed-bearing plant, and trees that grow seed-bearing fruit. These seeds will then produce the kinds of plants and trees from which they came." And that is what happened. ¹² The land produced vegetation—all sorts of seed-bearing plants, and trees with seed-bearing fruit. Their seeds

---

9. **layer** – a sheet of something that can be thick or thin

SESSION 1: IN THE BEGINNING

produced plants and trees of the same kind. And God saw that it was good.

¹³ And evening passed and morning came, marking the third day.

God said that the earth should *sprout with vegetation*. Vegetation is plants and trees. He said that every kind of plant and tree should grow. God said that it should happen, and then it did happen. The earth grew plants and trees, with flowers and fruit and seeds. All the kinds of plants and trees we see today grew up at the beginning when God said. God made many kinds of plants. He made each kind of tree or plant with its own kind of seed. He made it so that the seeds could grow into the same kind of tree or plant that they came from. God made each seed so that it had life in it and it could grow into another plant of the same kind. Only God could do that.

Only God can make life. He is the only one who could make plants with seeds that could grow into new plants. God makes things very carefully and he plans each thing that he makes. God saw all the plants with seeds and fruit that he had made, and he saw that it was all good. Everything that he had made was perfect. That is what he did on the third day.

GENESIS 1:14-19

¹⁴ Then God said, "Let lights appear in the sky to separate the day from the night. Let them be signs to mark the seasons, days, and years. ¹⁵ Let these lights in the sky shine down on the earth." And that is what happened. ¹⁶ God made two great lights—the larger one to govern the day, and the smaller one to govern the night. He also made the stars. ¹⁷ God set these lights in the sky to light the earth, ¹⁸ to govern the day and night, and to separate the light from the darkness. And God saw that it was good.

¹⁹ And evening passed and morning came, marking the fourth day.

On the fourth day, God made all the things in the sky that shine at night. He made the two great lights, which are the sun and the moon. He also made the stars. These things that God made on the fourth day are in the universe.¹⁰ The universe is so big that we cannot see the edge of it, even with very big

---

10. **universe** – all of outer space; all the stars and all the planets

HIS STORY: THE RESCUE

telescopes.[11] God made so many stars that we cannot see them all. We could never count them all. The universe is huge[12]. But God made all the stars and the sun and moon. He knows each one because he made them all.

God said that he made the sun and moon and stars and put them in the sky. The sky is the space between the waters above and the waters below that God made on the second day. His story says that he put the sun, moon and stars in the sky to light the earth. The earth was a special place in the universe that God wanted to light. God was getting the earth ready for people. He wanted to make a place for people to live. He wanted it to be a perfect home for us to live in.

GENESIS 1:20-23

[20] Then God said, "Let the waters swarm with fish and other life. Let the skies be filled with birds of every kind." [21] So God created great sea creatures and every living thing that scurries and swarms in the water, and every sort of bird—each producing offspring of the same kind. And God saw that it was good. [22] Then God blessed them, saying, "Be fruitful and multiply. Let the fish fill the seas, and let the birds multiply on the earth."

[23] And evening passed and morning came, marking the fifth day.

On the fifth day, God filled the oceans and rivers and lakes with fish and all the creatures[13] that live in the water. He also made birds that fly above the earth. He made every different kind of bird and every different kind of fish and water creature. He made them like he made everything else – he just spoke and then it happened. And he made them so that they could have young[14] that would grow to be the same type of bird or fish. He said that they should have young and fill the seas.

GENESIS 1:24,25

[24] Then God said, "Let the earth produce every sort of animal, each producing offspring of the same kind—livestock, small animals that scurry along the ground, and wild animals." And that is what happened. [25] God made all sorts of wild animals, livestock, and small animals, each able to produce offspring of the same kind. And God saw that it was good.

---

11. **telescope** - a thing to look through so we can see very, very far away
12. **huge** - very, very big
13. **creatures** - living things that God made
14. **young** - babies or offspring

SESSION 1: IN THE BEGINNING

On the sixth day, God made all the animals just by speaking. He made every kind of animal that has ever been on the earth. He made them to have young that would grow to be the same kind of animal. God made a wonderful[15] world of creatures that came in all shapes and sizes. And God saw that what he had made was perfect.

This first part of God's story tells us the beginning of many of the things we can see around us today. We can see the seas, the sky, the sun, moon and stars. We can see the plants, trees, flowers, fruit, birds, fish and animals. God created them in the beginning. We can see all the things God made today. The morning still comes and the night still comes. The sun, moon and stars are in the sky. Plants and trees still grow from a seed of the same kind of plant or tree. And each kind of bird, fish, or animal still has young that grow to be the same kind. This happens all over the world. It happens where people can see it and it happens where there are no people. It is like a story being told each day around the world about the great knowledge and the amazing power of God.

God made all of these things on the earth. He did all of that to get ready for what he was going to do next. God was going to make people. And now the earth was ready for them.

---

15. **wonderful** - something very good that makes us very happy when we see it

HIS STORY: THE RESCUE

1. Why did God make sure his story was written down in the Bible?
2. Have you ever studied the Bible before? Did you follow it through from the beginning?
3. Is God's story like a movie or like a made-up story in a book?
4. What are some things you can see that God made?
5. How did God make things?
6. What do the things that God made tell you about what God is like?

SESSION 2

GOD CREATED THE FIRST MAN AND WOMAN

Now we have come to a very important part of the story of when God created the earth. He had made a beautiful home for people, but there were no people yet. The plants, animals, birds and fish were there. God had given life to each one of them. But now God was going to do something different. He was going to create a different kind of living thing – people.

GENESIS 1:26

> ²⁶ Then God said, "Let us make human beings in our image, to be like us. They will reign over the fish in the sea, the birds in the sky, the livestock, all the wild animals on the earth, and the small animals that scurry along the ground."

God said *"Let us make human beings..."* Why did he say *let us* and not *let me*? Remember that God is a three-in-one God. He is one God, but he is the Father, the Son and the Spirit. The Father, the Son and the Spirit work together and plan things together. God tells us here in his story how the three planned together to make human beings. Human beings means men and women - people.

God said he would make people *"...in our image, to be like us."* These people would be different from the rest of the living things that God had made. They

HIS STORY: THE RESCUE

would be like God. That is what it means when it says *in our image*. They would be like God because they would be able to think about God and they would be able to know God.

God wanted to make people who could think about him. They would be able to speak to him. He would be able to speak to them and they could listen to him when he spoke. They would be able to thank him for the beautiful things he had made. They would be able to love him and obey[16] him. They would know that God loved them.

God says that these people would reign over the other living things that he had made. Reign means to rule over something. He would give these people important work to do for him. God wanted them to take care of the earth and to take care of the other living things that he had made.

God said he would make people and so that is what he did.

GENESIS 1:27-31

> 27 So God created human beings in his own image.
> In the image of God he created them;
> male and female he created them.
>
> 28 Then God blessed them and said, "Be fruitful and multiply. Fill the earth and govern it. Reign over the fish in the sea, the birds in the sky, and all the animals that scurry along the ground."
>
> 29 Then God said, "Look! I have given you every seed-bearing plant throughout the earth and all the fruit trees for your food. 30 And I have given every green plant as food for all the wild animals, the birds in the sky, and the small animals that scurry along the ground—everything that has life." And that is what happened.
>
> 31 Then God looked over all he had made, and he saw that it was very good!
>
> And evening passed and morning came, marking the sixth day.

God created one man and one woman. Part of the work God wanted them to do was to have children. God wanted the earth to have many more people. So he made the man and woman so that they could have children.

---

16. **obey** - to follow what someone says

SESSION 2: GOD CREATED THE FIRST MAN AND WOMAN

God saw that all he had made was very good. The man and woman that God had made were perfect. He had planned to make them and he made them just like he wanted them to be.

God's story tells a bit more about when God made the first man and woman. We will look at what it says in Genesis Chapter 2. It tells more about the time at the beginning when God made everything.

GENESIS 2:1-3

> ¹ So the creation of the heavens and the earth and everything in them was completed. ² On the seventh day God had finished his work of creation, so he rested from all his work. ³ And God blessed the seventh day and declared it holy, because it was the day when he rested from all his work of creation.

God had finished his work of creation. He had finished everything he wanted to do. God always finishes what he plans to do. People start a lot of things but we do not finish all of the things we start. We say that we are going to do things, but we don't always do them. God isn't like that. He doesn't give up and he doesn't go off and do something else. He always finishes the things that he starts. And God always does things right. He plans to do things and he does them just like he planned to do them.

After he finished his work, God rested. God didn't need to rest because he was tired. God does not get tired. He rested because his work was finished. He made the universe and all living things and then he was finished. And so, because his work was finished, God stopped and rested.

GENESIS 2:4-7

> ⁴ This is the account of the creation of the heavens and the earth.
>
> When the Lord God made the earth and the heavens, ⁵ neither wild plants nor grains were growing on the earth. For the Lord God had not yet sent rain to water the earth, and there were no people to cultivate the soil. ⁶ Instead, springs came up from the ground and watered all the land. ⁷ Then the Lord God formed the man from the dust of the ground. He breathed the breath of life into the man's nostrils, and the man became a living person.

HIS STORY: THE RESCUE

Before this part of the story, the name used for God was 'God.' Now, in this part of God's story, he starts to use the name 'Lord.' God started to use this name because there were now people on the earth. There were people and so God could be their Lord. These people would be able to know him and love him. He would be their Lord. He would be the one to take care of them and they would know he would care for them. God made people to know him, to love him and to listen to him. So he started to use the name Lord after people were on the earth. He would be close to them like a father is close to his children.

Genesis 2:7 tells us about how God made the first man. It says that God made him from the earth - *from the dust of the ground*. But the man that God made from the dust of the ground was just an empty body. He had no life yet. He could not move or breathe or work. Then it says that God *breathed the breath of life* into the man. When God put life into him, the man became a living person. He was able to breathe, to work, to speak, to think and to know God. God is the only one who can give life or who can make life begin.

This first man that God made is the ancestor[17] of every person that has ever lived. Later, God's story calls this first man Adam. Adam is a word from the Hebrew[18] language that means 'man.'

GENESIS 2:8

⁸ Then the Lord God planted a garden in Eden in the east, and there he placed the man he had made.

The Lord God now tells us about how he planted a special garden. It was in a place called Eden so we call it 'the garden of Eden.' Then, he put the man he had made into that garden. That garden was an amazing place. It was full of beautiful growing things. There were many plants and trees with flowers and fruit. He put them there for the man to enjoy[19] seeing and for the man to enjoy eating. God made the garden the best place for the man to be. God knew what was best for the man because he is the Lord and he made the man. God made Adam and so he knew what was best for him. God put Adam in the garden and he gave him the work of looking after the living things there. Everything was just like God had planned it to be.

---

17. **ancestor** - person in our family who has lived before us
18. **Hebrew** - people that are descended from Jacob, the grandson of Abraham (we will find out more about them later in the story)
19. **enjoy** - to like doing something or seeing something

SESSION 2: GOD CREATED THE FIRST MAN AND WOMAN

GENESIS 2:9

⁹ The Lord God made all sorts of trees grow up from the ground—trees that were beautiful and that produced delicious fruit. In the middle of the garden he placed the tree of life and the tree of the knowledge of good and evil.

In the garden, there were thousands of different amazing trees, plants and flowers. But there were two special trees that God had put in the garden. In his story, God names these two trees. One tree that was in the middle of the garden was *the tree of life*. The other tree was *the tree of the knowledge of good and evil.*

GENESIS 2:15-17

¹⁵ The Lord God placed the man in the Garden of Eden to tend and watch over it. ¹⁶ But the Lord God warned him, "You may freely eat the fruit of every tree in the garden— ¹⁷ except the tree of the knowledge of good and evil. If you eat its fruit, you are sure to die."

God said that the man was allowed[20] to eat the fruit from every tree in the garden. But God said that the man could not eat the fruit from one of the trees. The man was free to eat the fruit from the tree of life and from all the other trees in the garden. But he could not eat the fruit from the tree of the knowledge of good and evil. God said very clearly that if the man ate the fruit from the tree of the knowledge of good and evil he would die.

The man, Adam, had a choice[21] to make. He could choose to eat the fruit from the tree of the knowledge of good and evil. Or, he could choose not to eat it. Adam was free to decide[22] what he would do. God gave Adam the freedom to do what he wanted to do. Adam could choose to do what God said or he could choose not to listen[23] to God.

The tree of the knowledge of good and evil and its fruit were not evil or bad. God doesn't make anything bad. So why did God tell the man not to eat the fruit from that tree? God just wanted the man to listen to him. God wanted the man to come to him with any questions he had. God knew what would be best for Adam. He put him in a beautiful place with important work to do. And God was right there with Adam. Adam could go to God at any time to ask him

---

20. **allowed** - something that is OK to do and is not wrong to do
21. **choice** - to have to do one thing or another thing, to decide between two things
22. **decide** - to think about what you are going to do
23. **listen** - to choose to agree with someone and follow what they say

HIS STORY: THE RESCUE

a question. Adam didn't need to eat the fruit from the tree of the knowledge of good and evil. He didn't need to know the difference between good and evil himself. Adam could go to God at any time and he could ask God any question he had. The Lord wanted this man to come to him to ask him anything he wanted to ask.

Now God said that the man should not be alone.

GENESIS 2:18

[18] Then the Lord God said, "It is not good for the man to be alone. I will make a helper who is just right for him."

God said the man needed a helper. He said, *"I will make a helper who is just right for him."* God knew Adam in every way. He knew all the things that Adam needed. God had planned to make him and he made him after creating a world for him to live in. God cared about Adam and he wanted Adam to have everything he needed. God didn't have to ask Adam what he needed because God already knew. God wanted Adam to look after the earth and all the living things. He also wanted the earth to be filled with more people. God knew that Adam would need a female helper to do that work.

GENESIS 2:19,20

[19] So the Lord God formed from the ground all the wild animals and all the birds of the sky. He brought them to the man to see what he would call them, and the man chose a name for each one. [20] He gave names to all the livestock, all the birds of the sky, and all the wild animals. But still there was no helper just right for him.

God brought all the animals and birds to Adam for him to name. God gave Adam the work of taking care of the earth and all the living things in it. So God brought all the animals and birds to Adam so that Adam could choose names for all of them. Adam gave a name to each one. Adam was beginning to do the work that God had given him to do.

Adam saw all the amazing animals and birds that God had made. But there was no helper that was just right for him. None of the animals could be a helper for him. The animals were not like him. None of them were made to know and love God. None of them were like Adam. Adam needed a helper that was just right for him. God's story tells us how God made the perfect companion[24] and helper for Adam.

---

24. **companion** - someone who spends time with you, and helps you

SESSION 2: GOD CREATED THE FIRST MAN AND WOMAN

GENESIS 2:21-25

²¹ So the Lord God caused the man to fall into a deep sleep. While the man slept, the Lord God took out one of the man's ribs and closed up the opening. ²² Then the Lord God made a woman from the rib, and he brought her to the man.

²³ "At last!" the man exclaimed.

"This one is bone from my bone,
and flesh from my flesh!
She will be called 'woman,'
because she was taken from 'man.'"

²⁴ This explains why a man leaves his father and mother and is joined to his wife, and the two are united into one.

²⁵ Now the man and his wife were both naked, but they felt no shame.

Adam was very happy with this woman that God had made. He said, *"at last!"* This was the person he had been waiting for. This was the one who could help him and be with him.

God brought this man and woman together.²⁵ God brought them together to live and work together. This was something God did in the beginning. He made the woman to be the helper and companion of the man. This is what we call marriage. God planned it and made it happen when he made the woman as Adam's wife.

The man and woman were both naked – they were not wearing any clothes. They were not ashamed²⁶ of being naked. There was nothing bad in the world, and they were both happy together and did not feel any shame.

---

25. **together** - to be with, or close, to one another
26. **ashamed** - to feel sad about something you have done; to want to hide because you did something wrong

HIS STORY: THE RESCUE

1. Name some of the things that God did for Adam and his wife.
2. God did many things for Adam and his wife. What does that tell us about how God felt about them?
3. Do you think that God created marriage?
4. Do you think that the way the Bible tells the story of creation is true?
5. Have you heard a different story of how the world began?

SESSION 3

ADAM AND HIS WIFE DISOBEYED GOD

Adam and his wife were in the beautiful garden of Eden that God had made for them. Adam and his wife enjoyed being together there. They were free to enjoy all of the beautiful things in the garden that God had made for them. There were many different and very good things to eat. They were doing the work God had given them to do. They were taking care of the earth and the living things that God had made. God was with them, helping them and being with them. He wanted them to know him and to love him.

There was someone else in the garden too. God's story tells us that there was a serpent[27] that spoke to Eve. Serpent is another name for snake.

GENESIS 3:1

> [1] The serpent was the shrewdest of all the wild animals the Lord God had made. One day he asked the woman, "Did God really say you must not eat the fruit from any of the trees in the garden?"

This serpent was not just an animal like the other snakes. It was really another person who had made himself look like a snake. He made himself look like a

---

27. **serpent** - a snake

HIS STORY: THE RESCUE

snake so that he could trick[28] Adam and his wife. In other places in the Bible we can read about who this person is. The Bible tells us who he is and where he came from. We will look at those other places in the Bible now, so that you will know who this person is and why he wanted to trick Adam and his wife. Then, we will return to the story of what happened to Adam and his wife in the garden.

The Book of Job, which comes later in the Bible, tells about the time that God spoke to a man called Job. Job was alive many years after Adam was alive. God talked to Job about the time when he made the earth.

JOB 38:4-7

4 "Where were you when I laid the foundations of the earth?
Tell me, if you know so much.
5 Who determined its dimensions
and stretched out the surveying line?
6 What supports its foundations,
and who laid its cornerstone
7 as the morning stars sang together
and all the angels shouted for joy?

He said that when he created the earth *all the angels shouted for joy*. These angels were there at the beginning of time when God made the earth. Who were these angels? God had not made people yet. These angels were spirit beings. We know from the Bible that they don't have bodies like ours – they are spirits. There are other places in the Bible where it says that angels talked to people and that people saw them in bodies like human bodies. So we know that some angels can be seen in a human shape so that people can see them. We will read some of those stories later.

Just like everything else, the angels were created by God. He made them before he made the earth. We know this because God said the angels were there when he created the heavens and the earth. We know that they were perfect when God made them, because everything that God makes is perfect. The Bible says that there were a huge number of these spirit beings. It says that God gave them work to do and that he gave them great power to do his work. God made them to be his servants[29] and messengers.[30] So, at the beginning of time there were a

---

28. **trick** - a clever act to make someone do something you want them to do
29. **servant** - a person who does work for someone else
30. **messenger** - a person who tells things to people for someone else

SESSION 3: ADAM AND HIS WIFE

huge number of spirit beings there with God. They were very powerful but not as powerful as God, because God had made them.

The Bible says that the greatest of these servant angel beings was called Lucifer. The name Lucifer means 'Morning Star.' He was perfect when God made him. God gave him great authority[31] and power. He was the greatest of all the beings that God had made. He was the closest in power to God himself. But he was not as powerful as God, because God had made him.

The Bible tells us about Lucifer in the Book of Ezekiel. This book tells us about a message sent from God to a man who was a king. He was the king of a place called Tyre. In his message to the King, God talks about Lucifer. The King of Tyre acted just like Lucifer did and so God wanted to tell him about what had happened to Lucifer. We can read what God said about Lucifer in the Book of Ezekiel.

EZEKIEL 28:12-19

¹² "Son of man, sing this funeral song for the king of Tyre. Give him this message from the Sovereign Lord:

"You were the model of perfection,
full of wisdom and exquisite in beauty.
¹³ You were in Eden,
the garden of God.
Your clothing was adorned with every precious stone—
red carnelian, pale-green peridot, white moonstone,
blue-green beryl, onyx, green jasper,
blue lapis lazuli, turquoise, and emerald—
all beautifully crafted for you
and set in the finest gold.
They were given to you
on the day you were created.
¹⁴ I ordained and anointed you
as the mighty angelic guardian.
You had access to the holy mountain of God
and walked among the stones of fire.

¹⁵ "You were blameless in all you did
from the day you were created
until the day evil was found in you.
¹⁶ Your rich commerce led you to violence,
and you sinned.
So I banished you in disgrace

---

31. **authority** - the power or right to give orders and to have other people obey those orders

HIS STORY: THE RESCUE

> from the mountain of God.
> I expelled you, O mighty guardian,
> from your place among the stones of fire.
> [17] Your heart was filled with pride
> because of all your beauty.
> Your wisdom was corrupted
> by your love of splendor.
> So I threw you to the ground
> and exposed you to the curious gaze of kings.
> [18] You defiled your sanctuaries
> with your many sins and your dishonest trade.
> So I brought fire out from within you,
> and it consumed you.
> I reduced you to ashes on the ground
> in the sight of all who were watching.
> [19] All who knew you are appalled at your fate.
> You have come to a terrible end,
> and you will exist no more."

God said that Lucifer was perfect when he was created. God made him perfect and gave him great power and authority. God said that Lucifer was very wise, very powerful and very beautiful. His clothing was made of gold and beautiful stones. God said that Lucifer had very important work to do. Lucifer was free to be with God whenever he wanted. God gave him all of these things: beauty, power, wisdom, freedom, perfection and authority. God made him the wonderful and powerful angel that he was.

Then God tells us what Lucifer did. He tells us that Lucifer turned against God. God said that Lucifer sinned[32] and became evil. Lucifer began to think about how beautiful he was and how powerful he was. He forgot that he was not as powerful as God. He forgot that everything that he had had came from God. Lucifer started to think that he was better than God.

We can read about some of the things that Lucifer was thinking. One of God's human messengers was called Isaiah. He wrote down the thoughts and words of God and his book is in the Bible. He wrote down some of the things that God said about Lucifer and what he thought.

---

32. **sin** - means to go against what God has said, to disobey God

SESSION 3: ADAM AND HIS WIFE

ISAIAH 14:13,14

¹³ For you said to yourself,
'I will ascend to heaven and set my throne above God's stars.
I will preside on the mountain of the gods
far away in the north.
¹⁴ I will climb to the highest heavens
and be like the Most High.'

Like Adam and his wife, God made Lucifer free to decide things and to choose things. Lucifer chose to go against God. He wanted to be the one who ruled all other things. He wanted to take the place of God. The Bible says that many other angels followed Lucifer and also turned against God.

God knows everything. So God knew that Lucifer was going to turn against him. God is the true ruler over everything. Lucifer could not take the place of God. Lucifer's plan would not work. Isaiah wrote the words of God when God said what he would do with Lucifer.

ISAIAH 14:15

¹⁵ Instead, you will be brought down to the place of the dead, down to its lowest depths.

Lucifer was the head of all the spirit beings that God had made. But he turned against God, so God put him out of the high place he was in. God said he would put Lucifer and the other angels who followed him *down to the place of the dead*. God says in the Bible that he would put Lucifer into this very bad place, a place of death. This is a place of punishment[33] for Lucifer and all the other angels who followed him. This place is sometimes called Hell.

From this point on in God's story, Lucifer is called Satan. Satan means 'enemy.' The other angels that followed Lucifer are called demons, devils, unclean spirits or evil spirits.

Satan and his followers are the enemies of God. They have worked against God from the beginning. They are still working against God today. Satan still wants to take the place of God.

Now that we have read about who Satan is, we can go back to the story of Adam and his wife in the garden. Satan hated Adam and the woman that God had made for him. God had given these human beings the work of taking care of the

---

33. **punishment** - something bad done to someone because they did a wrong thing

earth and all the living things. Satan wanted that place for himself, so he hated Adam and the woman.

Satan was there in the Garden. He had made himself look like a snake so Adam and his wife would not know who he really was. He was watching and waiting. He made a plan to try to make Adam and his wife eat the fruit of the tree of the knowledge of good and evil. He wanted them to eat the fruit and to die. God said they would die if they ate that fruit, so Satan wanted them to eat it.

We will go back to Genesis again and read what Satan said to the woman in the garden.

GENESIS 3:1

> [1] The serpent was the shrewdest of all the wild animals the Lord God had made. One day he asked the woman, "Did God really say you must not eat the fruit from any of the trees in the garden?"

Satan made himself look like a snake. The Bible says that the snake *was the shrewdest of all the wild animals*. That means he was the most clever one. Satan always tries to trick people by making himself look like something good. God always tells the truth, but Satan always tells lies and tries to trick people.

Satan asked the woman a question; *"Did God really say you must not eat the fruit from any of the trees in the garden?"* Satan was trying to get her to think bad things about God. He wanted her to think that God was not giving them every good thing that they needed. Satan wanted the woman to start to think about things for herself. He did not want her to listen to God. He wanted her to think that she should start making her own decisions.

We can read all that Satan said to the woman when he spoke to her in the garden.

GENESIS 3:2-5

> [2] "Of course we may eat fruit from the trees in the garden," the woman replied. [3] "It's only the fruit from the tree in the middle of the garden that we are not allowed to eat. God said, 'You must not eat it or even touch it; if you do, you will die.'"
>
> [4] "You won't die!" the serpent replied to the woman. [5] "God knows that your eyes will be opened as soon as you eat it, and you will be like God, knowing both good and evil."

SESSION 3: ADAM AND HIS WIFE

The woman answered Satan's question. She said that they could eat the fruit from the trees in the garden. But she said that there was one tree whose fruit they were not allowed to eat. She said that if they ate that fruit or even touched it that they would die. But this is not what God had said. God said if they ate the fruit they would die. He did not say they would die if they touched it. The woman had changed what God had said.

Satan lied to the woman and told her that they would not die if they ate the fruit from that tree. He said that if they ate that fruit they would know all about what is good and what is evil. He said that God didn't want them to know that because then they would be like God. Satan lied to the woman to make her turn against God.

God wanted the best for Adam and his wife. God wanted them to go to him to ask about anything that they needed to know. He wanted them to do that because he loved them. It was not the best thing for them to start to make decisions on their own without asking God for his help.

God made Adam and his wife so that they were free to make their own choices. We can read now about the choice that they made. Would they listen to God, or would they listen to Satan?

GENESIS 3:6

⁶ The woman was convinced. She saw that the tree was beautiful and its fruit looked delicious, and she wanted the wisdom it would give her. So she took some of the fruit and ate it. Then she gave some to her husband, who was with her, and he ate it, too.

Adam and his wife both ate the fruit from the tree of the knowledge of good and evil. They both made the choice to disobey³⁴ God. They looked at the tree of the knowledge of good and evil. They knew that God had said they should not eat the fruit from this tree. But they looked at it and it was beautiful and the fruit looked very good to eat. The woman wanted the knowledge and wisdom that the fruit would give her if she ate it. So she ate some of the fruit. Then she gave some to Adam. Adam knew it was the fruit that God had told them not to eat. But Adam ate some too.

---

34. **disobey** - not obey; not do what someone says to do

HIS STORY: THE RESCUE

1. Why did Satan want to trick Adam and his wife?

2. God made Adam and Eve so that they could listen to him. Why do you think that God also gave them the freedom to not listen to him?

3. What did Satan say to trick Adam and his wife?

SESSION 4

GOD PUT ADAM AND HIS WIFE OUT OF THE GARDEN

God said that Adam and his wife would die if they ate the fruit of the tree of the knowledge of good and evil. We can read what happened after they ate the fruit.

GENESIS 3:7

⁷ At that moment their eyes were opened, and they suddenly felt shame at their nakedness. So they sewed fig leaves together to cover themselves.

God's story says that *their eyes were opened*. This means that they knew things that they had not known before. Adam and his wife saw everything differently after they ate the fruit. It was a very bad thing that happened to them when they disobeyed God. God's story says that they *felt shame* that they were naked. They wanted to cover their naked bodies. So they sewed fig³⁵ leaves together to cover themselves. Satan told them it would be a good thing for them to eat the fruit. But it was a terrible³⁶ thing. Satan said that they would be like God, but this was not true. Satan had lied to them. They were not happy any more. They did not feel at home in the garden that God had made for them.

---

35. **fig** - a kind of tree
36. **terrible** - a very, very bad thing; something that makes you very afraid

HIS STORY: THE RESCUE

God said that they would die if they ate the fruit. But they were still alive and walking around in their physical[37] bodies. Everything that God says is always true. So what did happen? What did God mean when he said that they would die?

God said that they would die and that was true. When they ate the fruit, they did start to die. Before they ate the fruit there was no death in the world. God was the maker of life and he was there with them so they would stay alive with him. But when they disobeyed God, they cut themselves off from him. Their physical bodies started to die. From this point onward, they would begin to grow old and later their bodies would die.

Adam and his wife had done what Satan wanted them to do. Remember that God said that he would punish Satan and send him to the place of death? He said he would send the demons who had turned against him to that place too. That place is for all of God's enemies. Now that Adam and his wife had turned against God, they would have to go to that place of death too. They had become the enemies of God. So they would have to go to the place of death with God's enemies.

God's story says that Adam and his wife sewed fig leaves together to cover themselves. They felt shame because they were naked. Before they ate the fruit, they were happy and not ashamed. Now they felt that it was bad to be naked. This was because they had turned against God. They hasn't listened to him. God wanted them to be happy and to let him be the one to tell them what was good and what was evil. He wanted them to live together in the garden with him and to be free. But they decided to go against what God wanted. They had made a very bad choice. Now they tried to fix everything and make it better. They tried to cover their naked bodies with leaves. Now they thought that being naked was bad, so they tried to make themselves good again. They went and found a fig tree, and made some clothes from the leaves.

GENESIS 3:8

[8] When the cool evening breezes were blowing, the man and his wife heard the Lord God walking about in the garden. So they hid from the Lord God among the trees.

Adam and his wife heard God walking in the garden. God had been with them there many times before. They had loved being with God and talking with him.

---

37. **physical** - flesh and blood bodies

SESSION 4: GOD PUT ADAM AND HIS WIFE OUT OF THE GARDEN

But this time they hid themselves from God. They were afraid of God so they hid from him. Everything had changed and everything was wrong. God did not want it to be that way. God did not plan it that way.

Adam and his wife were ashamed and they were afraid. That is why they hid from God. They had listened to God's enemy, Satan. They had done what Satan wanted them to do. Because they had followed Satan, they were ashamed.

They were afraid of God. God is always perfect and always good in everything he does. So he could not just ignore[38] what Adam and his wife had done. His way of doing things is the very best way. But Adam and the woman had chosen a different way to do things. God always does the right thing, so he had to do the right thing now that they had disobeyed him. Adam and his wife were afraid of what God was going to do.

GENESIS 3:9-13

⁹ Then the Lord God called to the man, "Where are you?"

¹⁰ He replied, "I heard you walking in the garden, so I hid. I was afraid because I was naked."

¹¹ "Who told you that you were naked?" the Lord God asked. "Have you eaten from the tree whose fruit I commanded you not to eat?"

¹² The man replied, "It was the woman you gave me who gave me the fruit, and I ate it."

¹³ Then the Lord God asked the woman, "What have you done?" "The serpent deceived me," she replied. "That's why I ate it."

God called out to Adam, asking where he was. God knew where Adam was. And he knew that Adam and his wife had eaten the fruit that he had told them not to eat. He knew that they had listened to Satan and that they had disobeyed him. God knows everything. God called out because he knew Adam and the woman needed him. God knew they were afraid of him because they were ashamed. So he called out to them to speak to them. Even though they had disobeyed God, God still wanted to talk to them.

God asked Adam and his wife some questions. God knows everything. So God already knew the answers to his questions. He asked the questions to show Adam and the woman some things. He wanted them to tell him about what

---
38. **ignore** - to act like you don't know about something; to do nothing about something

HIS STORY: THE RESCUE

they had done. He wanted them to tell him that they had done the wrong thing. He loved them and he wanted them to talk to him about what they had done.

God asked if they knew they were naked because they had eaten the fruit. Adam said that it was the woman that God had given him who gave him the fruit to eat. When God asked the woman what she had done, she said it was the serpent who had tricked her. They did not tell God that they had done something wrong. They both tried to blame[39] someone else.

GENESIS 3:14

¹⁴ Then the Lord God said to the serpent,

"Because you have done this, you are cursed
more than all animals, domestic and wild.
You will crawl on your belly,
groveling in the dust as long as you live.

God spoke to the snake. He said that it would now crawl along the ground in the dust. We don't know what snakes looked like before this time. But we do know that God did this to the snakes because Satan used the body of a snake to trick Adam and his wife. When God is talking to the snake here, he is also talking to Satan.

Then God said something else to Satan.

GENESIS 3:15

¹⁵ And I will cause hostility between you and the woman,
and between your offspring and her offspring.
He will strike your head,
and you will strike his heel."

God said that he would *cause hostility between* Satan and the woman. That means that they would be enemies. And God said that *her offspring* would be Satan's enemies. When it says *her offspring* it is talking about a person who would be born later. This person would be an enemy of Satan's.

God said *he will strike your head and you will strike his heel*. God said that a man would be born later who would strike Satan's head, and that Satan would strike his heel. This means that in the future, a man was going to come and fight Satan. God said that Satan would hurt this man in some way. But Satan would not destroy[40] him. That is what God meant when he said that only the man's heel

---

39. **blame** - to say that someone or something else caused something to happen
40. **destroy** - to kill, to ruin, or to end something so that it isn't there any more

SESSION 4: GOD PUT ADAM AND HIS WIFE OUT OF THE GARDEN

would be hurt. But God said that the man was going to hurt Satan's head. God was telling Satan that this man would win the fight. That is what God meant when he said *he will strike your head*. Satan was going to be defeated[41] by him.

Let's see what else God said.

GENESIS 3:16

16 Then he said to the woman,

"I will sharpen the pain of your pregnancy,
and in pain you will give birth.
And you will desire to control your husband,
but he will rule over you."

God told the woman that after this time she would have more pain when her children were born. He also said that she would not be able to decide things for herself. She would have to do what her husband said.

GENESIS 3:17-19

17 And to the man he said,

"Since you listened to your wife and ate from the tree
whose fruit I commanded you not to eat,
the ground is cursed because of you.
All your life you will struggle to scratch a living from it.
18 It will grow thorns and thistles for you,
though you will eat of its grains.
19 By the sweat of your brow
will you have food to eat
until you return to the ground
from which you were made.
For you were made from dust,
and to dust you will return."

God told Adam what was then going to happen. Adam would have to work very hard to get food from the earth. God said that the earth had changed and it would now be a hard place to live. Their lives would be difficult[42] and painful. They would only get food if they did very hard work.

GENESIS 3:20

20 Then the man—Adam—named his wife Eve, because she would be the mother of all who live.

---

41. **defeated** - to be the one to lose in a fight
42. **difficult** - not easy

HIS STORY: THE RESCUE

Then Adam *named his wife Eve*. The name Eve means 'to live' or 'to breathe.' Eve would be the mother and the ancestor of all people who lived after her. God put her name here in his story because he wanted us to know something important. He wanted us to know that now life would be difficult for all people. All people are the ancestors of Adam and Eve. For all people who came after them, there would be pain, and life would be hard. All people who came after Adam and Eve would be the same as they were. They would grow old and die. They would be God's enemies. They would go to the place of death after their bodies died.

GENESIS 3:21

21 And the Lord God made clothing from animal skins for Adam and his wife.

Adam and Eve knew they were naked and they were ashamed. So they made clothes of leaves. But now God made different clothes for them. He made them out of animal *skins*. He gave these new clothes to Adam and Eve to put on.

Adam and Eve wanted to try to fix the bad thing they had done. They made their own clothes. But Adam and Eve could not fix what they had done. Only God could help them.

God made clothes out of animal skins. This means that God had to kill some animals to make the clothes. This is the first time in God's story that animals died. The animals did not do anything wrong. They died because Adam and Eve disobeyed God. Adam was given the work of taking care of the animals. He had given each one a name. Now some animals had died because of what Adam and Eve had done.

God didn't leave Adam and Eve on their own. They had disobeyed him, but he still helped them. God loved them and helped them even after they had disobeyed him. He helped them to cover their shame. He did it in his way, because that is the only right way. Only God knew the clothing that they needed. They could not make their own clothing. Only God could make clothing that would cover what they had done.

GENESIS 3:22-24

22 Then the Lord God said, "Look, the human beings have become like us, knowing both good and evil. What if they reach out, take fruit from the tree of life, and eat it? Then they will live forever!" 23 So the Lord God banished them from the Garden of Eden, and he sent Adam out to cultivate the ground from which he had been made. 24 After sending them

SESSION 4: GOD PUT ADAM AND HIS WIFE OUT OF THE GARDEN

> out, the Lord God stationed mighty cherubim to the east of the Garden of Eden. And he placed a flaming sword that flashed back and forth to guard the way to the tree of life.

Now God's story tells us about what God was thinking. He was thinking about the people he had made. God said *"Look, the human beings have become like us, knowing both good and evil."* God said that the people now knew good and evil. God knew that if Adam and Eve stayed in the garden they would live forever. If they stayed in the garden they could eat from the tree of life and they would not die. Now that they had disobeyed God, he could not let them stay to eat the fruit of the tree of life and live forever.

Adam and Eve chose to go against God. They decided to go their own way, not God's way. They should have asked God what was right and what was wrong. But they did not ask him. God knew that they would keep on making the wrong decisions and that very bad things would happen. Things would get worse[43] and worse. He knew it would not be good for them to live forever like that.

So God sent them out of the garden. He sent them out of the garden and there was no way they could get back in. God put powerful angel servants there to stop Adam and Eve from going back into the garden. Adam and Eve had lost the beautiful home that God had made for them. They could not eat the good things he had made. They could not eat from the tree of life and live forever. They could not enjoy the good work that he had given them to do. They could not be with God or talk to God in the garden. Now in their lives they would have pain and they would grow old and die. They would go to the place of death after their bodies died.

---

43. **worse** - when something is not as good as it was before

HIS STORY: THE RESCUE

1. Why did Adam and Eve hide from God?
2. When God asked them if they ate the fruit, what did they say?
3. How did God make clothes for Adam and Eve?
4. Name all the things that changed after Adam and Eve disobeyed God.

SESSION 5

CAIN AND ABEL WERE BORN OUTSIDE OF THE GARDEN

God's story tells us what happened after Adam and Eve were put outside of the garden.

GENESIS 4:1,2

¹Now Adam had sexual relations with his wife, Eve, and she became pregnant. When she gave birth to Cain, she said, "With the Lord's help, I have produced a man!" ² Later she gave birth to his brother and named him Abel.

Eve became pregnant and had a baby boy called Cain. Later, she had another son called Abel.

God sent Adam and Eve out of the garden, but he still allowed them to have children. He gave them the gift of being able to start new life by having children. God is the one who gives life, and he gave new life to two more people on the earth. They were Cain and Abel.

Life is a gift from God. God is the only one who can give life. He made Adam and Eve, and Cain and Abel, and he made us, too. Another part of God's story tells us that we are God's because he made us. The Book of Psalms in the Bible

HIS STORY: THE RESCUE

is where many songs about God were written down for us to read. This verse is from Psalm 100.

PSALM 100:1-3

¹ Shout with joy to the Lord, all the earth!
² Worship the Lord with gladness.
Come before him, singing with joy.
³ Acknowledge that the Lord is God!
He made us, and we are his.
We are his people, the sheep of his pasture.

Many hundreds of years later, one of God's servants, Paul, spoke the following words about God. His words are written in the Bible in the Acts of the Apostles.

ACTS 17:25

²⁵ and human hands can't serve his needs—for he has no needs. He himself gives life and breath to everything, and he satisfies every need.

Every life comes from God. It is something very important for us to think about. Because God made us, he owns us. We belong to him.

Cain and Abel were born into the world outside of the garden. They did not see the beautiful garden that God wanted them to live in. And they could not just go to God and talk to him like Adam and Eve could. Cain and Abel were born into a world where there was pain and hard work. They were now part of the death that happened when Adam and Eve disobeyed God. They were born as enemies of God. They had the knowledge of good and evil and they wanted to make decisions for themselves. They were born as people who were going to die and they would go to the place of death after their physical bodies died.

God's enemy, Satan, was there too. God said that in the end Satan would be punished. But for now, he was the leader of the people on the earth. They had followed him and they had not listened to God. Satan always tries to trick people. He wants people to listen to him and not to listen to God. Satan is God's enemy and he wants people to be God's enemies too. He makes people think that they are free, but to go against God is always a very bad thing to do. It does not make people free. God loves people and he wants the best for them. Satan always wants to do what is bad for people.

God tells us in his story what happened next to Cain and Abel.

SESSION 5: CAIN AND ABEL WERE BORN OUTSIDE OF THE GARDEN

GENESIS 4:3,4

³ When it was time for the harvest, Cain presented some of his crops as a gift to the Lord. ⁴ Abel also brought a gift—the best portions of the firstborn lambs from his flock. The Lord accepted Abel and his gift,

Adam and Eve and Cain and Abel were now God's enemies because they had chosen to disobey him. But God had made a way for them to return to him. God loved them and wanted them to have a way to come back to him. God had shown them that to do so, they must kill an animal and let its blood flow out. Earlier, God had made clothes for Adam and Eve from animal skins. He had killed the animals to make those clothes. That was how God showed them how to return to him. There had to be death and there had to be blood. This was because they had made themselves God's enemies. God wanted to remind them that they had chosen the way of death. So now they must kill an animal and let its blood flow out. This is the only way that they could come back to God.

God's story says that Cain and Abel both brought an *gift* to God. Cain was a man who grew food in the form of plants, like vegetables⁴⁴ and grains.⁴⁵ So he brought some of the food he had grown to give to the Lord as a gift. Abel was a shepherd.⁴⁶ So he brought the best lambs⁴⁷ from his flock of sheep as a gift for the Lord. Abel would have cut the throats of the lambs to kill them. Their blood would have flowed out. God's story says that the Lord accepted⁴⁸ Abel and his gift.

GENESIS 4:5-7

⁵ but he did not accept Cain and his gift. This made Cain very angry, and he looked dejected.

⁶ "Why are you so angry?" the Lord asked Cain. "Why do you look so dejected? ⁷ You will be accepted if you do what is right. But if you refuse to do what is right, then watch out! Sin is crouching at the door, eager to control you. But you must subdue it and be its master."

God did not accept Cain's gift. Why? Because Cain did not come to God in the way that God had shown that he should – Cain did not kill an animal, and there

---
44. **vegetables** - food that comes from plants like carrots, potatoes and onions
45. **grains** - food that people get from plants like wheat and rice
46. **shepherd** - someone who takes care of sheep
47. **lambs** - young sheep
48. **accepted** - he took it

HIS STORY: THE RESCUE

was no death and no blood. There had to be death and blood because Cain and Abel were God's enemies. They were born outside of the garden. They were born into the world that had changed. There was now pain and death because people had disobeyed God. God wanted them to remember that they had chosen the way of death. But he also wanted them to know that he had made a way for them to return to him. When they came to him there must be death and blood. There was no other way to come to God.

God always does what is good and right. He always speaks the truth and he always does things that are true and real. People were now God's enemies so they could no longer freely come to him. If they did, it would have been false.[49] It would not have been a real or true relationship[50] with God. God is always real and true with people and in everything he does. So God said that for them to come to him, there had to be death and blood must flow. But Cain did not listen to God. He did not do what God said. Cain did not listen to God or think that what God said was true.

The lambs that Abel killed had not done anything wrong. Abel was the one who should have died. He was God's enemy, not the lambs. Abel killed them because he knew that he should have been the one to die. But God had made this the way to save him. Abel was God's enemy but he could come to God in this way, by killing the lambs. Abel listened to what God said and he did what God said. Abel thought that what God said was true so he did what God said.

God accepted Abel's gift but he did not accept Cain's gift. Cain was very angry. God talked to Cain to try to help him. God told Cain that he must do what is right. God said that if Cain did what was right, he would be accepted. God wanted Cain to listen to him and to come to him in the way that he had said to come. That was the best thing for Cain. God went to Cain and talked to him because God loves people and wants the best for them. Cain had disobeyed God, but God still came to him to help him. God told Cain to be stronger than the sin that was trying to control him.

GENESIS 4:8

⁸ One day Cain suggested to his brother, "Let's go out into the fields." And while they were in the field, Cain attacked his brother, Abel, and killed him.

---

49. **false** - not real or true
50. **relationship** - the way in which two or more people are connected or linked together, a friendship

SESSION 5: CAIN AND ABEL WERE BORN OUTSIDE OF THE GARDEN

Cain did not listen to God. He asked his brother Abel to go with him out to the fields. Then Cain killed Abel. Cain made the decision to kill Abel. Satan would have been very happy that Cain did that because Satan hates God and he hates people. Satan loves to destroy life.

GENESIS 4:9

⁹ Afterward the Lord asked Cain, "Where is your brother? Where is Abel?"

"I don't know," Cain responded. "Am I my brother's guardian?"

God came to Cain again to speak to him. God asked Cain where Abel was. God knew where Abel was, but God wanted Cain to tell him the truth. God wanted Cain to tell him what he had done. Cain answered God, *"I don't know... Am I my brother's guardian?"* Cain lied to God. He showed that he was not sorry for killing his brother.

GENESIS 4:10-15

¹⁰ But the Lord said, "What have you done? Listen! Your brother's blood cries out to me from the ground! 11 Now you are cursed and banished from the ground, which has swallowed your brother's blood. ¹² No longer will the ground yield good crops for you, no matter how hard you work! From now on you will be a homeless wanderer on the earth."
¹³ Cain replied to the Lord, "My punishment is too great for me to bear! ¹⁴ You have banished me from the land and from your presence; you have made me a homeless wanderer. Anyone who finds me will kill me!"
¹⁵ The Lord replied, "No, for I will give a sevenfold punishment to anyone who kills you." Then the Lord put a mark on Cain to warn anyone who might try to kill him.

God tells us that he thought that Cain had done a terrible thing. This was the first time that a person had ever killed another person. God gave life to people and he would punish Cain for taking life from Abel. God told Cain that he would not have a home. He would have to move around and could not stay in one place.

Cain did not say he was sorry for what he had done. He only said that his punishment was too great. He was not thinking of God or of his brother. He was thinking only of himself.

HIS STORY: THE RESCUE

God's story tells us about the rest of Cain's life. It tells us about his family who came after him. They didn't listen to God or think about God either. They did not do what God said. They only thought about themselves and their lives on earth. You can read about Cain's life in Genesis 4:16-24.

Then God's story tells us more about Adam and Eve.

GENESIS 4:25,26

> 25 Adam had sexual relations with his wife again, and she gave birth to another son. She named him Seth, for she said, "God has granted me another son in place of Abel, whom Cain killed." 26 When Seth grew up, he had a son and named him Enosh. At that time people first began to worship the Lord by name.

God gave Adam and Eve another son because Abel was dead. Their new son's name was Seth. Seth grew up and started a family that knew about God. They started to worship[51] the Lord by name. Seth and his family were able to come to God because they did it in the way that he had asked. They were born as God's enemies but they could still go to him and worship him. God had made a way for them to come to him because he loved them and he wanted to have a close relationship with them.

1. Where were Cain and Abel born? What was it like there?
2. What different gifts did Cain and Abel bring to God?
3. Because people were God's enemies, what did they have to do to come to him?
4. Why didn't Cain come to God in the way God had said he should?

---

51. **worship** - to show love for God, to enjoy God, to talk about how good God is and to thank him for all he has done

SESSION 6

GOD DESTROYED THE EARTH WITH A FLOOD

In Genesis Chapter 5, God's story tells us about each generation[52] of Seth's family. You can read the names of the men who were the heads of each generation, the number of years each one lived and the names of their sons. God wanted us to know the names of the people in Seth's family so he made sure they were written down in the Bible. Seth's family listened to God and came to him in the way that he had said they should come.

For each man in Seth's family it says *and then he died*. Death was now part of life on the earth. The people who were born on the earth were born with death and sin in them. Sin means to disobey what God has said. They were born separated from God, outside of the garden God had made for them. So they grew old and they died.

The list of generations begins with Seth and goes to a man named Noah. There were ten generations from the time that Adam and Eve had disobeyed God to when Noah lived. God's story tells us that by that time people had become very evil. People did not listen to God. The way that they lived was very, very bad.

---

52. **generation** - a set of members of a family that are alive at the same time; the time in a family when children are born, grow up and have children of their own

HIS STORY: THE RESCUE

GENESIS 6:5

⁵ The Lord observed the extent of human wickedness on the earth, and he saw that everything they thought or imagined was consistently and totally evil.

God's story says that *the Lord observed the extent of human wickedness*[53] *on the earth*. People were not listening to God at all. They were just doing what they wanted to do. God's story says that everything they did and everything they thought was evil. People were so evil that they planned and thought about evil things all the time. God knew what they were thinking. God knows everything and so he knew all about them.

GENESIS 6:6,7

⁶ So the Lord was sorry he had ever made them and put them on the earth. It broke his heart. ⁷ And the Lord said, "I will wipe this human race I have created from the face of the earth. Yes, and I will destroy every living thing—all the people, the large animals, the small animals that scurry along the ground, and even the birds of the sky. I am sorry I ever made them."

God said that he was very sorry he had made people and put them on the earth. God had made people and he loved them. God wanted to have a real and close relationship with people. He wanted what was best for people. But they had turned away from him. They did not listen to him. God knew that this would be very bad for people. They would just think of themselves first. They would hurt and kill other people. They would not take care of the earth or the animals like God wanted them to. Then, after people died, they would go to the place of death. So God decided to stop all of this. He decided to destroy all the people and all the living things on the earth.

GENESIS 6:8-10

⁸ But Noah found favor with the Lord.

⁹ This is the account of Noah and his family. Noah was a righteous man, the only blameless person living on earth at the time, and he walked in close fellowship with God. ¹⁰ Noah was the father of three sons: Shem, Ham, and Japheth.

---

53. **wickedness** - to do very bad or evil things

SESSION 6: GOD DESTROYED THE EARTH WITH A FLOOD

The people on the earth were evil and did not listen to God. But there was one man who did listen to God. That man's name was Noah. God's story says that Noah was a *righteous man*. God says Noah was righteous because Noah had come to God in the way that God said he should come. Noah was born outside of the garden, like all the other people, but Noah had listened to God. He had believed[54] that what God said was true. So God was happy with Noah and he was close to him. Noah had three sons called Shem, Ham and Japheth.

GENESIS 6:11-17

> [11] Now God saw that the earth had become corrupt and was filled with violence. [12] God observed all this corruption in the world, for everyone on earth was corrupt. [13] So God said to Noah, "I have decided to destroy all living creatures, for they have filled the earth with violence. Yes, I will wipe them all out along with the earth!
>
> [14] "Build a large boat from cypress wood and waterproof it with tar, inside and out. Then construct decks and stalls throughout its interior. [15] Make the boat 450 feet long, 75 feet wide, and 45 feet high. [16] Leave an 18-inch opening below the roof all the way around the boat. Put the door on the side, and build three decks inside the boat—lower, middle, and upper.
>
> [17] "Look! I am about to cover the earth with a flood that will destroy every living thing that breathes. Everything on earth will die.

God saw that the earth was *corrupt*. Corrupt means that it was evil, rotten and ruined. God had decided to destroy all people and all living things on the earth. But God wanted to save Noah and his family. Noah and his family were born outside the garden into the world of sin and death. But Noah had listened to God, and he had come to God in the way God said to come. He had a close relationship with God. Noah knew that he and his family were born into the world of sin and death. He knew that without God's help they were going to die and go to the place of death. He knew that only God could save them. Noah agreed with God that everything God said was true. So God planned to rescue Noah – to save him from death.

God told Noah to build a large boat. He told Noah how to build it, what wood to use, how long it should be, how high and how wide it should be. He told Noah it

---

54. **believed** - to believe is to think that something is true

HIS STORY: THE RESCUE

should have one door on the side. God told Noah that a great flood was coming to the earth. He said the flood would cover the earth and that every living thing would die.

God told Noah everything very clearly. He gave Noah and his sons this important work to do. They would need to work very hard. It would take a very long time. Only God could plan how the boat should be. Only God knew how bad the flood would be. So Noah needed to listen to God and do what he said. This boat would have to be built just like God said. It must have just one door. God wanted to save Noah and his sons, but they must do everything as God said.

GENESIS 6:22

²² So Noah did everything exactly as God had commanded him.

Noah listened to God. He did everything just like God said he should do it. Noah knew that what God said was true. He knew that only God could rescue them.

GENESIS 7:1-15

¹ When everything was ready, the Lord said to Noah, "Go into the boat with all your family, for among all the people of the earth, I can see that you alone are righteous. ² Take with

SESSION 6: GOD DESTROYED THE EARTH WITH A FLOOD

you seven pairs—male and female—of each animal I have approved for eating and for sacrifice, and take one pair of each of the others. ³ Also take seven pairs of every kind of bird. There must be a male and a female in each pair to ensure that all life will survive on the earth after the flood. ⁴ Seven days from now I will make the rains pour down on the earth. And it will rain for forty days and forty nights, until I have wiped from the earth all the living things I have created."

⁵ So Noah did everything as the Lord commanded him.

⁶ Noah was 600 years old when the flood covered the earth. ⁷ He went on board the boat to escape the flood—he and his wife and his sons and their wives. ⁸ With them were all the various kinds of animals—those approved for eating and for sacrifice and those that were not—along with all the birds and the small animals that scurry along the ground. ⁹ They entered the boat in pairs, male and female, just as God had commanded Noah. ¹⁰ After seven days, the waters of the flood came and covered the earth.

¹¹ When Noah was 600 years old, on the seventeenth day of the second month, all the underground waters erupted from the earth, and the rain fell in mighty torrents from the sky. ¹² The rain continued to fall for forty days and forty nights.

¹³ That very day Noah had gone into the boat with his wife and his sons—Shem, Ham, and Japheth—and their wives. ¹⁴ With them in the boat were pairs of every kind of animal—domestic and wild, large and small—along with birds of every kind. ¹⁵ Two by two they came into the boat, representing every living thing that breathes.

One week before it started to rain, God told them it was time to get into the boat. Noah and his three sons and their wives went into the boat. They went in through the only door. They took the animals in just like God said.

GENESIS 7:16

¹⁶ A male and female of each kind entered, just as God had commanded Noah. Then the Lord closed the door behind them.

God says that he, the Lord, *closed the door behind them*. God was taking care of them. He was making sure that they were safe. He would rescue them. He shut

HIS STORY: THE RESCUE

the door so they would be safe from the flood that was going to destroy all other living things.

GENESIS 7:17-24

¹⁷ For forty days the floodwaters grew deeper, covering the ground and lifting the boat high above the earth. ¹⁸ As the waters rose higher and higher above the ground, the boat floated safely on the surface. ¹⁹ Finally, the water covered even the highest mountains on the earth, ²⁰ rising more than twenty-two feet above the highest peaks. ²¹ All the living things on earth died—birds, domestic animals, wild animals, small animals that scurry along the ground, and all the people. ²² Everything that breathed and lived on dry land died. ²³ God wiped out every living thing on the earth—people, livestock, small animals that scurry along the ground, and the birds of the sky. All were destroyed. The only people who survived were Noah and those with him in the boat. ²⁴ And the floodwaters covered the earth for 150 days.

The flood came just like God said it would. The people outside the boat could not get inside. The door was shut so they could not escape the water. God always does what he says he will do. He saw the evil on the earth and he decided to destroy the people and all the living things. He said he would do it and then he did it.

Everything on the earth was covered with water. Even the high mountains were covered. The boat that Noah had made floated safely on the top of the deep water. Noah and his sons and their wives were safe. The animals inside the boat were safe. All the people and all the living things outside the boat were killed. Like everything in God's story, this is all true. It really happened to real people and animals at a real time and in a real place.

GENESIS 8:1-4

¹ But God remembered Noah and all the wild animals and livestock with him in the boat. He sent a wind to blow across the earth, and the floodwaters began to recede. ² The underground waters stopped flowing, and the torrential rains from the sky were stopped. ³ So the floodwaters gradually receded from the earth. After 150 days, ⁴ exactly five months from the time the flood began, the boat came to rest on the mountains of Ararat.

SESSION 6: GOD DESTROYED THE EARTH WITH A FLOOD

God did not forget the boat floating along with Noah and his family inside. God had planned to rescue them and he did. God made a wind to blow until the waters went down. The mountain tops appeared out of the water. Five months after the flood began, the boat came to rest on the mountains of Ararat. Ararat is in the country we call Turkey today. It took a long time for the earth to dry out. You can read about that in Genesis 8:5-14. After the earth was dry, God told them to leave the boat. He said they should let all the animals out, too. So Noah and his family and all the animals left the boat.

GENESIS 8:15-19

¹⁵ Then God said to Noah, ¹⁶ "Leave the boat, all of you—you and your wife, and your sons and their wives. ¹⁷ Release all the animals—the birds, the livestock, and the small animals that scurry along the ground—so they can be fruitful and multiply throughout the earth."

¹⁸ So Noah, his wife, and his sons and their wives left the boat. ¹⁹ And all of the large and small animals and birds came out of the boat, pair by pair.

Noah wanted to thank God for saving them from death. He wanted to come to God in the way that God had told people to come to him. Because people had disobeyed God, and were born with death and sin in them, they had to come to God by killing an animal.

GENESIS 8:20-22

²⁰ Then Noah built an altar to the Lord, and there he sacrificed as burnt offerings the animals and birds that had been approved for that purpose. ²¹ And the Lord was pleased with the aroma of the sacrifice and said to himself, "I will never again curse the ground because of the human race, even though everything they think or imagine is bent toward evil from childhood. I will never again destroy all living things. ²² As long as the earth remains, there will be planting and harvest, cold and heat, summer and winter, day and night."

Noah built an *altar*. An altar is a pile of stones with a flat top. Noah killed some animals and birds and burnt them there on the altar. These animals were special ones that God had told Noah to bring in the boat. They were meant for Noah to kill and burn for God.

HIS STORY: THE RESCUE

The animals and birds that Noah killed on the altar had not done anything wrong. They had been in the boat with Noah and his family. Now, these animals and birds were killed. God had created these animals. He did not want them to die. But he wanted Noah and his family to have a way to come to him. Noah and his family were born with death and sin in them. The only way that they could come to God was for them to kill these animals and birds that had not done anything wrong. The animals had to die so that Noah and his family would not be separated from God. The animals had to die so that Noah and his family would not. Noah was showing that he agreed with God and that only God could save them. God was pleased with what Noah had done.

GENESIS 9:11-13

> ¹¹ Yes, I am confirming my covenant with you. Never again will floodwaters kill all living creatures; never again will a flood destroy the earth."
>
> ¹² Then God said, "I am giving you a sign of my covenant with you and with all living creatures, for all generations to come. ¹³ I have placed my rainbow in the clouds. It is the sign of my covenant with you and with all the earth.

God said that he would not destroy the earth with a flood ever again. He made a rainbow[55] in the sky so people would remember what he had said. Now the flood had finished and the rain had stopped. God put a rainbow in the sky as a sign to Noah and his family. We can still see this sign today.

GENESIS 9:18,19

> ¹⁸ The sons of Noah who came out of the boat with their father were Shem, Ham, and Japheth. (Ham is the father of Canaan.) ¹⁹ From these three sons of Noah came all the people who now populate the earth.

God's story says that Noah's three sons, Ham, Shem and Japheth, are the ancestors of all the people who are now on the earth. In Genesis Chapter 10, you can read about the families of each of Noah's sons. It tells us about their children and their children's children. It talks about some of the nations[56] that came from each of Noah's three sons.

Now God's story moves forward to a time more than three generations after the flood. A large group of people had settled in a place called Shinar.

---

55. **rainbow** - an arch of many colors that can be seen in the sky
56. **nation** - a large group of people who all share one ancestor

SESSION 6: GOD DESTROYED THE EARTH WITH A FLOOD

GENESIS 11:1-4

¹At one time all the people of the world spoke the same language and used the same words. ² As the people migrated to the east, they found a plain in the land of Babylonia and settled there.
³ They began saying to each other, "Let's make bricks and harden them with fire." (In this region bricks were used instead of stone, and tar was used for mortar.) ⁴ Then they said, "Come, let's build a great city for ourselves with a tower that reaches into the sky. This will make us famous and keep us from being scattered all over the world."

These people wanted to build a large city with a high tower. They wanted to show everyone how great they were. They wanted the tower to be so high that it would reach the sky. They were following God's enemy, Satan, who had wanted to take the place of God. They thought that if they built a high tower it would make them great. God had given people the work of spreading out over the earth. But these people decided to stay where they were and to build a great city instead.

These people had forgotten what God had done only three generations before. They had forgotten the story of the great flood, and how God had saved Noah and his three sons. They had stopped coming to God in the way he said, by killing animals. They did not listen to God or believe that what God said was true. They did not want a relationship with God and did not care about what God said.

GENESIS 11:5-9

⁵ But the Lord came down to look at the city and the tower the people were building. ⁶ "Look!" he said. "The people are united, and they all speak the same language. After this, nothing they set out to do will be impossible for them! ⁷ Come, let's go down and confuse the people with different languages. Then they won't be able to understand each other."

⁸ In that way, the Lord scattered them all over the world, and they stopped building the city. ⁹ That is why the city was called Babel, because that is where the Lord confused the people with different languages. In this way he scattered them all over the world.

HIS STORY: THE RESCUE

God knew what these people were planning to do. He did not want them to stay where they were. He did not want them to keep showing everyone that they thought they were great and that they didn't need God.

God *confused* the people by making them speak different languages. Because they could not understand each other, they could not keep building the city or the tower. They had to spread to other places all over the earth, just like God wanted them to. The name of the place was called Babel. Babel comes from the Hebrew word *balal* which means 'confuse'.

1. What do you think about God destroying all living things in the flood?
2. Why do you think God saved Noah and his family?
3. Why did God make the rainbow?
4. Why did the people want to build the tall tower?
5. Do people today still think that they don't need God?
6. Why did God confuse the languages of the people who were building the tower?

SESSION 7

GOD TOOK ABRAM TO CANAAN

God's story now tells us about a man called Abram. He lived about ten generations after the people built the tower at Babylon. Ten generations is about 350 years. Abram was part of Shem's family. Shem was one of Noah's sons. You can read the names of all the generations between Shem and Abram in Genesis 11:10-26.

Abram had grown up in the southern part of Mesopotamia. Today, we call that area Iraq. Back when God confused all the languages at Babylon, a group of people began to speak a language that we now know as Aramaic. They stayed close to the Babylon area and lived there. The city they started was called Ur. At the time that Abram was born, these people did not worship God. They worshiped other things that they had made themselves out of wood, stone or metal. They said that these things had the power of God. They also worshiped things that God had created, like trees or animals. They asked these things for help that only God could give them. Instead of listening to God and asking him to help them, they asked these other things to help them.

God's story tells us about Abram's family and also about his wife. Abram's wife, Sarai, could not have children. She was not able to get pregnant.

HIS STORY: THE RESCUE

GENESIS 11:27-30

²⁷ This is the account of Terah's family. Terah was the father of Abram, Nahor, and Haran; and Haran was the father of Lot. ²⁸ But Haran died in Ur of the Chaldeans, the land of his birth, while his father, Terah, was still living. ²⁹ Meanwhile, Abram and Nahor both married. The name of Abram's wife was Sarai, and the name of Nahor's wife was Milcah. (Milcah and her sister Iscah were daughters of Nahor's brother Haran.) ³⁰ But Sarai was unable to become pregnant and had no children.

One day, Abram's father, Terah, wanted to move away from Ur.

GENESIS 11:31,32

³¹ One day Terah took his son Abram, his daughter-in-law Sarai (his son Abram's wife), and his grandson Lot (his son Haran's child) and moved away from Ur of the Chaldeans. He was headed for the land of Canaan, but they stopped at Haran and settled there. ³² Terah lived for 205 years and died while still in Haran.

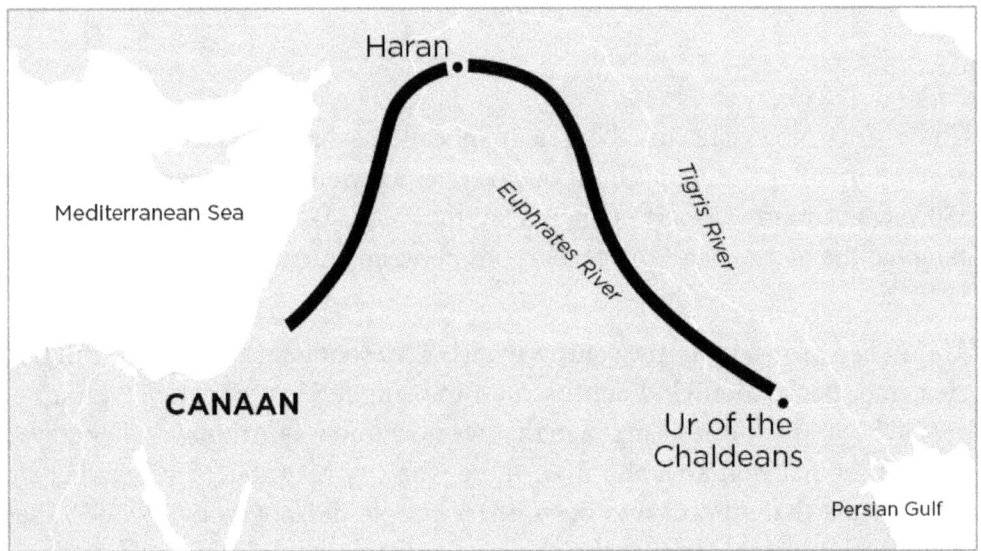

Terah wanted to move his family to Canaan. Canaan was west of Ur near the Mediterranean Sea. Abram left the city of Ur with his wife and his father. His brother's son, Lot, also went with them. First, they had to go north, because there was a desert⁵⁷ between Ur and Canaan. They couldn't go through the desert, so they went north and arrived in a city called Haran. Haran is in the

---

57. **desert** - a very dry place with no water

SESSION 7: GOD TOOK ABRAM TO CANAAN

area we call Turkey today. While they were staying in Haran, Terah died. God's story says that God spoke to Abram.

GENESIS 12:1

¹ The Lord had said to Abram, "Leave your native country, your relatives, and your father's family, and go to the land that I will show you.

Abram was different from most of the other people who were alive then. Most people worshiped false gods.⁵⁸ God's story tells us that Abram knew the true Creator⁵⁹ God, because God spoke to him. God told Abram to start out again and go to a land that God would show him. God also said some other things to Abram.

GENESIS 12:2,3

² I will make you into a great nation. I will bless you and make you famous, and you will be a blessing to others. ³ I will bless those who bless you and curse those who treat you with contempt. All the families on earth will be blessed through you."

God told Abram that he would use Abram to start *a great nation*. God meant that Abram's family would grow very large and that many other people would know about it. God also told Abram that he would be a *famous*⁶⁰ and important man.

God said that he would take care of Abram. God said he would help people who helped Abram and *curse*⁶¹ people who went against Abram. The last thing God said to Abram was that *all the families on earth will be blessed* through him. Blessed means that good things would come to all the people of the earth through Abram.

Remember when Adam and Eve were sent away from the garden that God had made for them? God spoke to the snake and said that a man would come who would hurt Satan's head. This man would defeat⁶² Satan. He would come because God said he would come. When God says something, it always happens. The man that God talked about who would defeat Satan would be a member of

---

58. **gods** - we write the name of the true God with a capital "G" but false gods with a small "g"
59. **Creator** - the one who created, or made, everything
60. **famous** - known about by many people
61. **curse** - to want hurt or harm to happen to someone
62. **defeat** - to win over someone else in a fight or competition; to overcome or beat

HIS STORY: THE RESCUE

Abram's family. We will hear all about that as we follow God's story. That is why God said to Abram that all the families of the earth would be blessed through him.

GENESIS 12:4,5

⁴ So Abram departed as the Lord had instructed, and Lot went with him. Abram was seventy-five years old when he left Haran. ⁵ He took his wife, Sarai, his nephew Lot, and all his wealth—his livestock and all the people he had taken into his household at Haran—and headed for the land of Canaan.

Abram listened to God and he believed that what God said was true. He had no children because his wife could not get pregnant. But Abram believed that what God said was true. He believed that he would be the father of a great nation because God said that he would. When someone believes that what God says is true, we call it 'faith.'

Abram listened to God and left the city of Haran. He took his nephew[63] Lot and their families, servants, and all of their animals. They started to move west and then south. They went down the coast of the Mediterranean Sea to Canaan.

GENESIS 13:5-13

⁵ Lot, who was traveling with Abram, had also become very wealthy with flocks of sheep and goats, herds of cattle, and many tents. ⁶ But the land could not support both Abram and Lot with all their flocks and herds living so close together. ⁷ So disputes broke out between the herdsmen of Abram and Lot. (At that time Canaanites and Perizzites were also living in the land.)

⁸ Finally Abram said to Lot, "Let's not allow this conflict to come between us or our herdsmen. After all, we are close relatives! ⁹ The whole countryside is open to you. Take your choice of any section of the land you want, and we will separate. If you want the land to the left, then I'll take the land on the right. If you prefer the land on the right, then I'll go to the left."

¹⁰ Lot took a long look at the fertile plains of the Jordan Valley in the direction of Zoar. The whole area was well watered everywhere, like the garden of the Lord or the beautiful land of Egypt. (This was before the Lord destroyed Sodom and Gomorrah.) ¹¹ Lot chose for himself the whole Jordan Valley to

---

63. **nephew** - the son of your brother or sister

the east of them. He went there with his flocks and servants and parted company with his uncle Abram. ¹² So Abram settled in the land of Canaan, and Lot moved his tents to a place near Sodom and settled among the cities of the plain. ¹³ But the people of this area were extremely wicked and constantly sinned against the Lord.

God said that he would take care of Abram and Abram was a rich man because God had helped him. He had many animals and a big group of people with him. They settled in the land of Canaan and had a big area of land for their animals to graze.⁶⁴ Abram's nephew, Lot, was also a rich man with many animals. They needed a big area of land for all their animals. Abram and Lot moved away from each other to get more land for their animals. Lot found good land with a lot of grass beside the Jordan River. This land was near a city called Sodom. Abraham went to a place further west, where the land was dry. It was near the city of Hebron.

GENESIS 13:14,15

¹⁴ After Lot had gone, the Lord said to Abram, "Look as far as you can see in every direction—north and south, east and west. ¹⁵ I am giving all this land, as far as you can see, to you and your descendants as a permanent possession.

After Lot had gone, God spoke to Abram again. He gave Abram all the land that Abram could see. God gave that land to Abram and his descendants.⁶⁵

GENESIS 13:16

¹⁶ And I will give you so many descendants that, like the dust of the earth, they cannot be counted!

God also said that he would give Abram *so many descendants that, like the dust of the earth, they cannot be counted!* God meant that Abram would have many, many descendants. Abram's wife, Sarai, could not have children. And Abram and Sarai were now old. So, Abram needed to believe that what God said was true. He needed to have faith⁶⁶ in God. A bit later, God again said to Abram that he would have a son and that he would have many descendants.

---

64. **graze** - eat the grass
65. **descendants** - any people in your family who are born and live after you
66. **faith** - when someone believes that the things that God says are true

HIS STORY: THE RESCUE

GENESIS 15:1-6

¹ Some time later, the Lord spoke to Abram in a vision and said to him, "Do not be afraid, Abram, for I will protect you, and your reward will be great."

² But Abram replied, "O Sovereign Lord, what good are all your blessings when I don't even have a son? Since you've given me no children, Eliezer of Damascus, a servant in my household, will inherit all my wealth. ³ You have given me no descendants of my own, so one of my servants will be my heir."

⁴ Then the Lord said to him, "No, your servant will not be your heir, for you will have a son of your own who will be your heir." ⁵ Then the Lord took Abram outside and said to him, "Look up into the sky and count the stars if you can. That's how many descendants you will have!"

⁶ And Abram believed the Lord, and the Lord counted him as righteous because of his faith.

It says that Abram believed the Lord and that *the Lord counted him as righteous*. What does that mean? Abram, like every other person, was born into the world of sin and death. Like all other people, he did not always do everything right. God is perfect and everything God does is perfect. But people are not perfect. They are born as people who sin. Sin means that they disobey God. Abram was born that way, too. In Genesis 20:1-18, you can read about a time that Abram did not trust in God. He was not perfect. If God didn't rescue Abram, he would go to the place of death after he died. He would be separated from God forever.

But God had made a way for people to come to him. Abram came to God that way. He came to God in the way that God said he should, by killing animals and letting their blood run out. Abram believed that what God said was true. He showed that he believed God by coming to God in the way that God said. Abram believed the things that God said. He wanted a relationship with God and he did not want to be separated from God. He believed that God would give him a son and many descendants. So, because Abram believed what God said, God said that Abram was 'righteous'. That meant that Abram did not have to pay for his sin with his own death.

Like all people, Abram had a debt[67] to God that he could not pay back. He was born into the world of sin and death and he could not save himself. Only

---

67. **debt** - something that you owe to someone else and have to pay back

SESSION 7: GOD TOOK ABRAM TO CANAAN

God could save him. Abram knew that, so he killed animals and let their blood run out. He did that to show that he believed that only God could save him. Abram knew that he should be the one to die, not the animals who had not done anything wrong. God had made a way for Abram to come to him so that he didn't have to die and so that he could be close to God and not be separated from him. Abram came to God in the way God said because he believed what God said.

God saw that Abram believed him. God did not have to save Abram, but he did because he wanted to. God gave Abram a free gift and saved him from going to the place of death. God said that Abram did not have to pay back the debt that he owed God. Abram did not have to die for his sin. That is what it means when the Bible says that the Lord counted Abram as righteous.

God says some more things about Abram's descendants.

GENESIS 15:12-16

¹² As the sun was going down, Abram fell into a deep sleep, and a terrifying darkness came down over him. ¹³ Then the Lord said to Abram, "You can be sure that your descendants will be strangers in a foreign land, where they will be oppressed as slaves for 400 years. ¹⁴ But I will punish the nation that enslaves them, and in the end they will come away with great wealth. ¹⁵ (As for you, you will die in peace and be buried at a ripe old age.) ¹⁶ After four generations your descendants will return here to this land, for the sins of the Amorites do not yet warrant their destruction."

God said that Abram's descendants would be *strangers in a foreign*[68] *land*. He said that they would be slaves[69] for 400 years. God said that he would punish the nation that made them slaves. He said he would bring Abram's descendants back to the land he had given to Abram.

Sometime later, God said again to Abram that his family would grow to become many nations. He told Abram that he was making a contract or a *covenant* with him. A covenant is a very strong promise[70] to do something that you say you will do. God wanted Abram to know that he always does what he says he will do. Then God changed Abram's name to Abraham. The name Abraham means 'father of many.'

---

68. **foreign** - a land that was not their own land
69. **slaves** - people who have to work for other people without being paid
70. **promise** - to say that you will do something

HIS STORY: THE RESCUE

GENESIS 17:4,6

⁴ "This is my covenant with you: I will make you the father of a multitude of nations! ⁵ What's more, I am changing your name. It will no longer be Abram. Instead, you will be called Abraham, for you will be the father of many nations. ⁶ I will make you extremely fruitful. Your descendants will become many nations, and kings will be among them!

Then God changed the name of Abraham's wife from Sarai to Sarah. The name Sarah means 'mother of many.'

GENESIS 17:15-17

¹⁵ Then God said to Abraham, "Regarding Sarai, your wife—her name will no longer be Sarai. From now on her name will be Sarah. ¹⁶ And I will bless her and give you a son from her! Yes, I will bless her richly, and she will become the mother of many nations. Kings of nations will be among her descendants."

¹⁷ Then Abraham bowed down to the ground, but he laughed to himself in disbelief. "How could I become a father at the age of 100?" he thought. "And how can Sarah have a baby when she is ninety years old?"

God told Abraham that Sarah would have a son. This did not seem possible to Abraham. He was already 100 years old and Sarah was 90 years old. Sarah had never had any children before. So Abraham did not think that they could have a son. But God can do anything that he wants to do. He is the only one who can create life. And God always does what he says he will do.

SESSION 7: GOD TOOK ABRAM TO CANAAN

1. God spoke to Abram. Think back over God's story so far and try to remember all the times that God spoke to people.

2. Today, God speaks to us through his words written in the Bible. Why do you think that God tries so hard to speak to people?

3. Where Abram grew up, most people did not listen to God. But Abram believed in the Creator God. Do you think it would have been hard for Abram to grow up there? Why?

4. What does it mean when it says that 'God counted Abram as righteous'? Was it because Abram always did the right thing?

5. God told Abraham and Sarah that they would have a son, and many descendants. How could God know about something that had not yet happened?

SESSION 8

GOD RESCUED LOT. GOD SAVED ABRAHAM'S SON, ISAAC

God's story also tells us about Lot, Abraham's nephew. Lot and his family had gone to live on good land with a lot of grass beside the Jordan River. This land was near a city called Sodom. Lot and his family had moved into the city of Sodom. There was another city near Sodom called Gomorrah.

GENESIS 18:20,21

[20] So the Lord told Abraham, "I have heard a great outcry from Sodom and Gomorrah, because their sin is so flagrant. [21] I am going down to see if their actions are as wicked as I have heard. If not, I want to know."

The people in Sodom and Gomorrah had become very evil in the way that they lived. They had turned against God and did not listen to him. They did not want to be close to God or have any relationship with him. God said that their sin was *flagrant*. That means that they did not care about their sin against God. God decided that the things they were doing were so bad that they could not be allowed to keep doing them. When people don't listen to God, it is very bad for them. God wants people to listen to him because that is the best thing for them.

HIS STORY: THE RESCUE

Because the people in Sodom and Gomorrah had decided not to listen to him, and because they way that they lived was so bad, he decided to destroy them.

Abraham talked to God about his plan to destroy the cities.

GENESIS 18:23-26

²³ Abraham approached him and said, "Will you sweep away both the righteous and the wicked? ²⁴ Suppose you find fifty righteous people living there in the city—will you still sweep it away and not spare it for their sakes? ²⁵ Surely you wouldn't do such a thing, destroying the righteous along with the wicked. Why, you would be treating the righteous and the wicked exactly the same! Surely you wouldn't do that! Should not the Judge of all the earth do what is right?"

²⁶ And the Lord replied, "If I find fifty righteous people in Sodom, I will spare the entire city for their sake."

Abraham asked God not to destroy the city of Sodom if there were even 50 people living there who still listened to God. But Abraham knew that there may not have been 50 people in Sodom who listened to God, so then he asked God not to destroy Sodom if there were 45 people there who listened to God. Then Abraham kept asking God not to destroy Sodom if there were even 40, or 30, or 20 people in the city who listened to God.

GENESIS 18:32,33

³² Finally, Abraham said, "Lord, please don't be angry with me if I speak one more time. Suppose only ten are found there?"

And the Lord replied, "Then I will not destroy it for the sake of the ten."

³³ When the Lord had finished his conversation with Abraham, he went on his way, and Abraham returned to his tent.

The Lord said he would not destroy Sodom if there were only ten people there who listened to him. God sent two of his angel servants to Sodom to see if there were even ten people there who listened to him. These angels took the form of young men.

GENESIS 19:1-9

¹ That evening the two angels came to the entrance of the city of Sodom. Lot was sitting there, and when he saw them, he stood up to meet them. Then he welcomed them and bowed with his face to the ground. ² "My lords," he said, "come to

SESSION 8: GOD RESCUED LOT. GOD SAVED ABRAHAM'S SON, ISAAC

> my home to wash your feet, and be my guests for the night. You may then get up early in the morning and be on your way again."
>
> "Oh no," they replied. "We'll just spend the night out here in the city square."
>
> ³ But Lot insisted, so at last they went home with him. Lot prepared a feast for them, complete with fresh bread made without yeast, and they ate. ⁴ But before they retired for the night, all the men of Sodom, young and old, came from all over the city and surrounded the house. ⁵ They shouted to Lot, "Where are the men who came to spend the night with you? Bring them out to us so we can have sex with them!"
>
> ⁶ So Lot stepped outside to talk to them, shutting the door behind him. ⁷ "Please, my brothers," he begged, "don't do such a wicked thing. ⁸ Look, I have two virgin daughters. Let me bring them out to you, and you can do with them as you wish. But please, leave these men alone, for they are my guests and are under my protection."
>
> ⁹ "Stand back!" they shouted. "This fellow came to town as an outsider, and now he's acting like our judge! We'll treat you far worse than those other men!" And they lunged toward Lot to break down the door.

Lot did not know that these two young men were angels of God. But he did not want them to stay out in the city. He knew that the men of Sodom would want to have sex with them. So Lot asked them to stay at his home. That night, men from all over Sodom came to Lot's house. They wanted Lot to send out the two men. Lot went outside and told them he could send out his two virgin[71] daughters instead. But the men of Sodom only wanted the two young men to come out. These men from Sodom had stopped listening to God. The way that they lived showed that they did not care about God.

God made men and women to be together so that they could have children. Remember that God made Eve for Adam to be his helper and companion. God wanted Adam and Eve to take care of the earth and to have children. He wanted them to be together and help one another, and take care of their children. This was how God intended people to live with one another. He wanted a man to have a wife so that they could help each other and so that they could have children.

---

71. **virgin** - someone who has never had sex

HIS STORY: THE RESCUE

The men from Sodom did not care about the way that God wanted things to be. They did not think about what God wanted. They only thought about what they wanted.

GENESIS 19:10,11

¹⁰ But the two angels reached out, pulled Lot into the house, and bolted the door. ¹¹ Then they blinded all the men, young and old, who were at the door of the house, so they gave up trying to get inside.

The angels blinded the eyes of the men of Sodom so that they would go away.

GENESIS 19:12-25

¹² Meanwhile, the angels questioned Lot. "Do you have any other relatives here in the city?" they asked. "Get them out of this place—your sons-in-law, sons, daughters, or anyone else. ¹³ For we are about to destroy this city completely. The outcry against this place is so great it has reached the Lord, and he has sent us to destroy it."

¹⁴ So Lot rushed out to tell his daughters' fiancés, "Quick, get out of the city! The Lord is about to destroy it." But the young men thought he was only joking.

¹⁵ At dawn the next morning the angels became insistent. "Hurry," they said to Lot. "Take your wife and your two daughters who are here. Get out right now, or you will be swept away in the destruction of the city!"

¹⁶ When Lot still hesitated, the angels seized his hand and the hands of his wife and two daughters and rushed them to safety outside the city, for the Lord was merciful. ¹⁷ When they were safely out of the city, one of the angels ordered, "Run for your lives! And don't look back or stop anywhere in the valley! Escape to the mountains, or you will be swept away!"

¹⁸ "Oh no, my lord!" Lot begged. ¹⁹ "You have been so gracious to me and saved my life, and you have shown such great kindness. But I cannot go to the mountains. Disaster would catch up to me there, and I would soon die. ²⁰ See, there is a small village nearby. Please let me go there instead; don't you see how small it is? Then my life will be saved."

²¹ "All right," the angel said, "I will grant your request. I will not destroy the little village. ²² But hurry! Escape to it, for I can do nothing until you arrive there." (This explains why that village was known as Zoar, which means "little place.")

SESSION 8: GOD RESCUED LOT. GOD SAVED ABRAHAM'S SON, ISAAC

> ²³ Lot reached the village just as the sun was rising over the horizon. ²⁴ Then the Lord rained down fire and burning sulfur from the sky on Sodom and Gomorrah. ²⁵ He utterly destroyed them, along with the other cities and villages of the plain, wiping out all the people and every bit of vegetation.

God decided to rescue Lot so the angels helped Lot and his family to get out of the city. Then fire and burning sulfur⁷² came raining down. The cities and all the people and all the trees and growing things were destroyed.

After this time, God's story tells us that Abraham and Sarah had a son. Abraham was 100 years old and Sarah was 90 years old when their son was born.

GENESIS 21:1-5

> ¹ The Lord kept his word and did for Sarah exactly what he had promised. ² She became pregnant, and she gave birth to a son for Abraham in his old age. This happened at just the time God had said it would. ³ And Abraham named their son Isaac. ⁴ Eight days after Isaac was born, Abraham circumcised him as God had commanded. ⁵ Abraham was 100 years old when Isaac was born.

God's story tells us that God did what he said he would do. He gave Abraham and Sarah a son at the time he said he would. God always does what he says he will do. Abraham and Sarah's son was named Isaac.

God's story tells us about something that happened a bit later, once Isaac had grown up and become a young man.

GENESIS 22:1,2

> ¹ Some time later, God tested Abraham's faith. "Abraham!" God called.
>
> "Yes," he replied. "Here I am."
>
> ² "Take your son, your only son—yes, Isaac, whom you love so much—and go to the land of Moriah. Go and sacrifice him as a burnt offering on one of the mountains, which I will show you."

It says that God *tested*⁷³ *Abraham's faith*. That means that God wanted to see what Abraham would do. One day, God told Abraham to go with Isaac to a

---

72. **sulfur** - a yellow powder found in rocks and in dirt. It can burn.
73. **tested** - tried it to see if it was real or not

HIS STORY: THE RESCUE

mountain that God would show him. God said that Abraham should kill Isaac there. He said that Abraham should then burn Isaac's body as an offering.

Abraham had known the Lord for many years. He had listened to God. He knew that the things that God said were true. Abraham knew that God always does what he says he will do. God had said that one day the whole land of Canaan would belong to Abraham's descendants. These descendants would start with Abraham and Sarah's son, Isaac. God had said that through Abraham, all the families of the earth would be blessed.

God kept his word and gave Abraham and Sarah a son. God did what he said he would do and their son Isaac was born. Abraham and Sarah had taken care of Isaac. They had watched him grow up. They knew that God said he was going to have many descendants and that many nations would come from this one boy. God said he would do that, so Abraham knew God would do it.

But now God had asked Abraham to build a platform of stones on a mountain. God asked Abraham to kill Isaac there. Abraham would have to cut Isaac's throat until his blood ran out. And then he would have to burn Isaac's body. God asked Abraham to kill Isaac as an offering.

Abraham would have done this many times with lambs. He would have killed them as an offering[74] to God. But this time God was asking him to offer his son. This was the boy that God had given him when he was old. This was the one that God said would be the start of a long line of people. Through him, all the families of the earth would be blessed. How would all of those things happen if Isaac were dead?

GENESIS 22:3-8

> ³ The next morning Abraham got up early. He saddled his donkey and took two of his servants with him, along with his son, Isaac. Then he chopped wood for a fire for a burnt offering and set out for the place God had told him about. ⁴ On the third day of their journey, Abraham looked up and saw the place in the distance. ⁵ "Stay here with the donkey," Abraham told the servants. "The boy and I will travel a little farther. We will worship there, and then we will come right back."
>
> ⁶ So Abraham placed the wood for the burnt offering on Isaac's shoulders, while he himself carried the fire and the knife. As the two of them walked on together, ⁷ Isaac turned

---

74. offering - a gift that is given to God

SESSION 8: GOD RESCUED LOT. GOD SAVED ABRAHAM'S SON, ISAAC

to Abraham and said, "Father?"

"Yes, my son?" Abraham replied.

"We have the fire and the wood," the boy said, "but where is the sheep for the burnt offering?"

⁸ "God will provide a sheep for the burnt offering, my son," Abraham answered. And they both walked on together.

Abraham listened to God and did what he said. He got everything ready and went to the mountain that God showed him. He took firewood and fire so that the offering could be burned. He went with two servants and with his son, Isaac. They walked for three days until they could see the mountain. Then Abraham and Isaac left the servants and the donkey. Abraham and Isaac went on alone to the mountain. Isaac carried the firewood on his shoulders.

As they climbed up the mountain, Isaac asked his father, *"where is the sheep for the burnt offering?"* Isaac had seen lambs being killed for offerings many times before. So he wanted to know why they didn't have a lamb with them this time. Abraham told him, *"God will provide⁷⁵ a sheep for the burnt offering, my son."* Abraham knew that God was the only one who could save his son.

GENESIS 22:9-11

⁹ When they arrived at the place where God had told him to go, Abraham built an altar and arranged the wood on it. Then he tied his son, Isaac, and laid him on the altar on top of the wood. ¹⁰ And Abraham picked up the knife to kill his son as a sacrifice. ¹¹ At that moment the angel of the Lord called to him from heaven, "Abraham! Abraham!"

"Yes," Abraham replied. "Here I am!"

Abraham tied Isaac up and laid him on the firewood on top of the pile of stones. Then, he picked up the knife to kill his son. God saw that Abraham was going to obey him. Abraham was going to do what God had told him to do. Before he could kill Isaac, an angel of God called out to Abraham.

---

75. **provide** - to give something

HIS STORY: THE RESCUE

GENESIS 22:12,13

¹² "Don't lay a hand on the boy!" the angel said. "Do not hurt him in any way, for now I know that you truly fear God. You have not withheld from me even your son, your only son."

¹³ Then Abraham looked up and saw a ram caught by its horns in a thicket. So he took the ram and sacrificed it as a burnt offering in place of his son.

The angel of God called out to Abraham and told him to stop. He said that Abraham should not hurt Isaac in any way. God saw that Abraham had wanted to obey him, and was even willing to kill his own son. Abraham had showed that he loved and trusted[76] God and that he would do what God said.

But an offering still had to be made. The only way to come to God is with death. So God provided a sheep for the burnt offering, just like Abraham said he would. A ram[77] was caught in the bushes nearby. So Abraham killed the ram in Isaac's place. God had saved Isaac from death. God allowed a sheep to die so that Isaac would not have to die. God was the only one who could save Isaac from death.

GENESIS 22:14-18

¹⁴ Abraham named the place Yahweh-Yireh (which means "the Lord will provide"). To this day, people still use that name as a proverb: "On the mountain of the Lord it will be provided."

¹⁵ Then the angel of the Lord called again to Abraham from heaven. ¹⁶ "This is what the Lord says: Because you have obeyed me and have not withheld even your son, your only son, I swear by my own name that ¹⁷ I will certainly bless you. I will multiply your descendants beyond number, like the stars in the sky and the sand on the seashore. Your descendants will conquer the cities of their enemies. ¹⁸ And through your descendants all the nations of the earth will be blessed—all because you have obeyed me."

Abraham listened to God and knew that what God said was true. He had faith in God. He knew that God had a plan for his family. Isaac was Abraham and Sarah's eldest son, so Abraham knew that Isaac had to live. God said that through Abraham's family all the families of the earth would be blessed. A nation would start with Isaac and through his family all the nations of the earth

---

76. **trusted** - he believed what God said was true and that God would always do the best thing
77. **ram** - a male sheep

SESSION 8: GOD RESCUED LOT. GOD SAVED ABRAHAM'S SON, ISAAC

would be blessed. The man that God said would come and defeat Satan would be a member of Isaac's family. God had made a promise that this man would come. God said in the garden that this man would defeat Satan. Then he said to Abraham that this man would come through his family. He would come through the family of Abraham and Isaac.

1. Why did God decide to destroy Sodom and Gomorrah?
2. Why did God tell Abraham to kill Isaac?
3. What were all the things that God said would happen through Abraham's family?
4. What is the only way that people can come to God?
5. How did Abraham show that he had faith in God?
6. What did it mean when God said to Abraham: "through your descendants all the nations of the earth will be blessed"?

SESSION 9

GOD CHOSE JACOB. GOD SENT JACOB'S SON, JOSEPH, TO EGYPT

God's story tells us about when Abraham died.

GENESIS 25:7-11

⁷ Abraham lived for 175 years, ⁸ and he died at a ripe old age, having lived a long and satisfying life. He breathed his last and joined his ancestors in death. ⁹ His sons Isaac and Ishmael buried him in the cave of Machpelah, near Mamre, in the field of Ephron son of Zohar the Hittite. ¹⁰ This was the field Abraham had purchased from the Hittites and where he had buried his wife Sarah. ¹¹ After Abraham's death, God blessed his son Isaac, who settled near Beer-lahai-roi in the Negev.

Isaac was Abraham and Sarah's first son. He was the son that God had promised to them. So when Abraham died, he gave everything that he owned to Isaac. After Abraham died, God took care of Isaac. God said that Isaac was the ancestor of the Promised One who would come later and defeat Satan.

God's story tells us about Isaac's life. Abraham did not want Isaac to marry a woman from Canaan. So Abraham sent Isaac back to his home territory so he could find a wife from among his own people. When Isaac was 40 years old, he married a woman named Rebekah.

HIS STORY: THE RESCUE

GENESIS 25:19,20

¹⁹ This is the account of the family of Isaac, the son of Abraham. ²⁰ When Isaac was forty years old, he married Rebekah, the daughter of Bethuel the Aramean from Paddan-aram and the sister of Laban the Aramean.

Isaac's wife Rebekah could not have children. So Isaac prayed⁷⁸ to ask the Lord to help her to have children.

GENESIS 25:21-23

²¹ Isaac pleaded with the Lord on behalf of his wife, because she was unable to have children. The Lord answered Isaac's prayer, and Rebekah became pregnant with twins. ²² But the two children struggled with each other in her womb. So she went to ask the Lord about it. "Why is this happening to me?" she asked.

²³ And the Lord told her, "The sons in your womb will become two nations. From the very beginning, the two nations will be rivals. One nation will be stronger than the other; and your older son will serve your younger son."

Rebekah was worried⁷⁹ about what was happening to her. So she asked the Lord what was happening. The Lord said *"The sons in your womb⁸⁰ will become two nations."* He told her that she had two babies inside her. Each child would grow up and have a family that would become a nation. And these two nations would fight against each other. God said that the nation that came from the older child would serve the nation that came from the younger one.

God knew all about the two babies. Only God could know all about them. He knew that they would grow up and have families. He knew that those families would become nations. And he knew that those nations would fight against one another. God knows everything, so he knew all about these two children even before they were born. God can be everywhere at one time. He made everything and he knows everything.

God's story says that Rebekah asked God a question. Rebekah was a woman, but she could go to the Lord and ask him a question. She could go to the Lord because she came in the way that God said to come. She and her husband would

---

78. **prayed** - to pray means to talk to God about something
79. **worried** - thought something bad would happen
80. **womb** - the place in a woman's body where a baby grows before it is born

SESSION 9: GOD CHOSE JACOB. GOD SENT JACOB'S SON, JOSEPH, TO EGYPT

have killed animals and let their blood run out. They would have done that to show that they agreed with God. They did it to show that they knew that they deserved death. They knew that only God could save them. God accepted their offerings and so Rebekah had a relationship with God and she could go to God to ask a question.

GENESIS 25:24-28

²⁴ And when the time came to give birth, Rebekah discovered that she did indeed have twins! ²⁵ The first one was very red at birth and covered with thick hair like a fur coat. So they named him Esau. ²⁶ Then the other twin was born with his hand grasping Esau's heel. So they named him Jacob. Isaac was sixty years old when the twins were born.
²⁷ As the boys grew up, Esau became a skillful hunter. He was an outdoorsman, but Jacob had a quiet temperament, preferring to stay at home. ²⁸ Isaac loved Esau because he enjoyed eating the wild game Esau brought home, but Rebekah loved Jacob.

Rebekah had twin⁸¹ sons, just like God said she would. The boys were different from each other. The first one that was born was named Esau. He was hairy. Esau means 'hairy' in the Hebrew language. Esau grew up to be a very good hunter.⁸² He was Isaac's favorite⁸³ son because Isaac liked to eat meat. The second son who was born was named Jacob. Jacob grew up to become a quiet man who liked to stay at home. Rebekah loved Jacob more than she loved Esau.

Esau was born first. So when Isaac died, Esau should have been given everything that Isaac owned. He should have received all of Isaac's things and he should have taken Isaac's place as the head⁸⁴ of the family. That was normal at that time. Esau was the oldest son, but God's story tells us that something else happened.

GENESIS 25:29-34

²⁹ One day when Jacob was cooking some stew, Esau arrived home from the wilderness exhausted and hungry. ³⁰ Esau said to Jacob, "I'm starved! Give me some of that red stew!" (This is how Esau got his other name, Edom, which means "red.")
³¹ "All right," Jacob replied, "but trade me your rights as the firstborn son."
³² "Look, I'm dying of starvation!" said Esau. "What good is my birthright to me now?"

---

81. **twins** - two children born at the same birth
82. **hunter** - someone who goes out to find and kill animals to eat
83. **favorite** - the one that he likes the most
84. **head** - the leader

HIS STORY: THE RESCUE

> ³³ But Jacob said, "First you must swear that your birthright is mine." So Esau swore an oath, thereby selling all his rights as the firstborn to his brother, Jacob.
> ³⁴ Then Jacob gave Esau some bread and lentil stew. Esau ate the meal, then got up and left. He showed contempt for his rights as the firstborn.

Esau *arrived home from the wilderness exhausted and hungry.* Exhausted means very, very tired. Esau told Jacob to give him some of the food that Jacob was cooking. It was a red-colored food, probably made of red lentils.[85] Esau was also called 'Edom' which means 'red' in the Hebrew language. Jacob said that Esau could have some of the food if he did something for him first. Jacob asked Esau to give him his *birthright.*[86] Esau *swore an oath, thereby selling all his rights as the firstborn to his brother, Jacob.* That means that Esau made a very strong promise to give his birthright to Jacob if Jacob gave him some food. Then he ate the food Jacob gave to him.

Esau did a very foolish thing. God's story says that Esau *showed contempt for his rights as the firstborn.* To show contempt means to hate something or to think that is not worth anything to you. Esau gave away everything he was going to receive after Isaac died. He did that because he did not believe the things that God had said about his family. He did not believe that all the nations of the earth would be blessed through Isaac's family. He did not think that the Promised One would come through this family. So Esau gave away his birthright for a bowl of food. Later, God's story refers to Esau as "godless."

---

85. **lentils** - small beans that come from a plant and can be dried and then eaten
86. **birthright** - all the things that would belong to the firstborn son after his father's death; also the blessing that the father would give to the oldest son to say that he would become the head of the family

SESSION 9: GOD CHOSE JACOB. GOD SENT JACOB'S SON, JOSEPH, TO EGYPT

Jacob was different from Esau. He did believe what God had said. So he knew that his brother's birthright was a very important thing. God chose Jacob to lead the family. Being the head of the family was a special position. This family was the one that the Promised One would be born into. This Promised One was going to be the one who would defeat Satan. All the nations of the earth would be blessed because of this man who would come. God had a plan for Jacob's family. So God created a way for Jacob to become the head of the family.

GENESIS 27:41-44

> ⁴¹ From that time on, Esau hated Jacob because their father had given Jacob the blessing. And Esau began to scheme: "I will soon be mourning my father's death. Then I will kill my brother, Jacob."
> ⁴² But Rebekah heard about Esau's plans. So she sent for Jacob and told him, "Listen, Esau is consoling himself by plotting to kill you. ⁴³ So listen carefully, my son. Get ready and flee to my brother, Laban, in Haran. ⁴⁴ Stay there with him until your brother cools off.

It says that *Esau hated Jacob*. Esau had given away his birthright to Jacob. When Isaac died, he gave Jacob the *blessing* of the firstborn son. Esau wanted to kill Jacob as soon as their father Isaac died. Rebekah heard about Esau's plan to kill Jacob, so she helped Jacob to go away. She told Jacob to go to Haran. Haran is the city where Abraham had lived on his way to Canaan.

Jacob had a dream while he was sleeping outside one night on his way to Haran.

GENESIS 28:10-16

> ¹⁰ Meanwhile, Jacob left Beersheba and traveled toward Haran. ¹¹ At sundown he arrived at a good place to set up camp and stopped there for the night. Jacob found a stone to rest his head against and lay down to sleep. ¹² As he slept, he dreamed of a stairway that reached from the earth up to heaven. And he saw the angels of God going up and down the stairway.
>
> ¹³ At the top of the stairway stood the Lord, and he said, "I am the Lord, the God of your grandfather Abraham, and the God of your father, Isaac. The ground you are lying on belongs to you. I am giving it to you and your descendants. ¹⁴ Your descendants will be as numerous as the dust of the earth! They will spread out in all directions—to the west and the east, to the north and the south. And all the families of

> the earth will be blessed through you and your descendants. ¹⁵ What's more, I am with you, and I will protect you wherever you go. One day I will bring you back to this land. I will not leave you until I have finished giving you everything I have promised you."
>
> ¹⁶ Then Jacob awoke from his sleep and said, "Surely the Lord is in this place, and I wasn't even aware of it!"

God was speaking to Jacob in the dream. He showed Jacob a set of stairs. The stairs went from earth up to heaven.[87] Angels of God were going up and down them. In his dream, Jacob saw the stairs and he heard the Lord saying things about his family. The Lord said that Jacob's family would be huge, and that it would spread out over a large area. The Lord said that all the families of the earth would be blessed through Jacob's family. God was talking about his plan to bring the Promised One who would defeat Satan. This man, who would be sent by God, would be a part of Jacob's family. God was saying the same thing to Jacob that he had said before to Abraham and then to Isaac. God does not ever forget what he plans to do. If God plans to do something, he always does it.

God showed Jacob the stairs that went up to heaven in a dream. God wanted to tell Jacob something about the Promised One who would come through his family. The stairs from earth up to heaven showed that God was going to make a way for people to get to him and to be with him.

When Adam and Eve disobeyed God, they were taken out of the garden of Eden. Every person who has been born since then was born outside of the garden. People then were born into a world of sin and death. People now are born into a world of sin and death. Satan, sin and death are in control.

The people in Jacob's time could only come to God in the way that God had said, which was by killing animals. This was something that they had to keep doing, over and over again. They were separated from God by Satan, sin and death, so they had to keep killing animals. But God wanted to make a way for people to be able to come to him freely. He wanted people to be with him forever. God loves people and he doesn't want them to be separated from him by their sin.

So God told Jacob in the dream that he would make a way for people to come to him that would last forever. They would be able to come freely to be with him. God was showing Jacob that the man who would come through Jacob's family

---

87. **heaven** - a real place where God's story says that God is

SESSION 9: GOD CHOSE JACOB. GOD SENT JACOB'S SON, JOSEPH, TO EGYPT

would defeat Satan. This man would make a way for people to freely come to God.

In Genesis Chapters 29 to 35, God's story tells us that Jacob went to northern Mesopotamia. He lived there in the land of his family for 20 years. While he was there, he married two sisters called Leah and Rachel. Jacob and his family went back to Canaan. On the way back, God gave Jacob a new name, Israel.

GENESIS 35:9-12

⁹ Now that Jacob had returned from Paddan-aram, God appeared to him again at Bethel. God blessed him, ¹⁰ saying, "Your name is Jacob, but you will not be called Jacob any longer. From now on your name will be Israel." So God renamed him Israel.

¹¹ Then God said, "I am El-Shaddai—'God Almighty.' Be fruitful and multiply. You will become a great nation, even many nations. Kings will be among your descendants! ¹² And I will give you the land I once gave to Abraham and Isaac. Yes, I will give it to you and your descendants after you."

Sometimes God's story uses the name Jacob and sometimes it uses the name Israel. Sometimes it uses the name to talk about the individual man, and sometimes it uses the name to refer to his whole family. Israel had 12 sons. Israel lived in Canaan with his sons and family. Israel's family grew larger and larger, just like God said it would. One of Israel's sons was called Joseph.

GENESIS 37:3,4

³ Jacob loved Joseph more than any of his other children because Joseph had been born to him in his old age. So one day Jacob had a special gift made for Joseph—a beautiful robe. ⁴ But his brothers hated Joseph because their father loved him more than the rest of them. They couldn't say a kind word to him.

God's story tells us a lot about Joseph. He was Jacob's favorite son. Joseph's brothers hated him. Joseph listened to God and was very close to him. Later, God's story says that Joseph had great faith in God. God's story tells us all about Joseph's life. You can read the story of his life in Genesis, from Chapter 37 to Chapter 47. For now, we will just go through the main points of the story. You can read the whole story in your Bible later.

HIS STORY: THE RESCUE

Genesis 37:5-11

Joseph was a shepherd. He had some dreams that his brothers would bow down to him. His brothers hated him because of those dreams. In the dreams, God was showing Joseph that he would become the most powerful person in his family.

Genesis 37:12-36

Joseph's brothers hated him and wanted to kill him. One day they saw some men from another country passing by and so they sold Joseph to these men to be a slave. These men were on their way to sell things in Egypt. They took Joseph with them to Egypt. When they got there, they sold Joseph to a man called Potiphar. Potiphar worked for the king of Egypt. In Egypt, all the kings were called 'Pharaoh.' Joseph's brothers showed their father his coat covered with goat's blood. They made Jacob think that Joseph had been killed by a wild animal.

Genesis 39:1-6

Joseph worked for Potiphar. Potiphar was the head of Pharaoh's guards. God said that he was with Joseph and was helping him. God helped Joseph and he was put in charge of Potiphar's house and everything he had.

Genesis 39:7-20

Potiphar's wife wanted to have sex with Joseph. But Joseph did not listen to her. He did not want to sin against God in that way. Potiphar's wife told her husband that Joseph tried to rape[88] her. Potiphar believed his wife and so Joseph was sent to prison.

Genesis 39:21-23

The Lord was with Joseph in prison. He was helping Joseph. He showed Joseph that he loved him and would take care of him. Joseph was put in charge of the prison and all of the prisoners.

---

88. **rape** - to force someone to have sex when they don't want to

SESSION 9: GOD CHOSE JACOB. GOD SENT JACOB'S SON, JOSEPH, TO EGYPT

Genesis 40:1-23

God helped Joseph to tell people the meaning of their dreams. He helped Joseph to tell two men in the prison about their dreams. Both of these men had worked for Pharaoh. Joseph told them what their dreams meant. One of the men was freed from prison and one of the men was killed. This is what Joseph said would happen.

Genesis 41:1-13

Two years later, Pharaoh had two dreams. He was very worried about these dreams and wanted to know what they meant. He asked other men what the dreams meant, but they could not tell him. The man who had been freed from prison told Pharaoh about Joseph. He said that Joseph could tell Pharaoh what his dreams meant.

Genesis 41:14-32

Pharaoh called Joseph to come and help him. Joseph was freed from prison and taken to Pharaoh. Joseph said that it was God who could help Pharaoh to know what his dreams meant. Pharaoh told Joseph his dream. The first dream was of seven very thin cows that ate seven fat cows. The second dream was of seven sick stalks of grain eating seven healthy stalks of grain.

Joseph told Pharaoh that God had helped him to know what the dreams meant. There would be seven good years in Egypt. A lot of food would grow in those years. Then there would be seven bad years. There would be no food growing in those years.

Genesis 41:33-36

Joseph said someone should be put in charge of the food in Egypt. Joseph said that that person could help to save food in the good years and store it. Then that food could be eaten during the bad years.

Genesis 41:37-46

Pharaoh saw that Joseph was very wise and that God was with him. So Pharaoh put Joseph in charge of all the food in Egypt. Pharaoh was the only one higher than Joseph. Joseph was in charge of everyone else in Egypt.

HIS STORY: THE RESCUE

Genesis 41:47-57

There were seven good years and seven bad years, just like God had said. Joseph saved the food from the good years. He had a huge amount of food saved. Then, in the bad years, he gave that food away. The countries around Egypt needed food, too. So people from those countries came to Egypt to buy food. People from the land of Canaan needed food as well.

Genesis 42:1-38

Joseph's father, Jacob, and his brothers lived in Canaan, so they were hungry. Jacob sent ten of his sons to Egypt to buy food. Joseph's brothers came to buy food from Joseph in Egypt. They did not know that he was their brother Joseph. They thought he was just a man from Egypt. But Joseph knew that they were his brothers. Joseph's brothers came and bowed down to him. They bowed down to him just like God said they would in Joseph's dream many years before.

Joseph told his brothers to go back to Canaan to get the other brother they had left there. He also wanted them to get their father and the whole family. Joseph wanted them to be safe in Egypt and to have food.

Genesis 43-45

So Joseph's brothers went back to Canaan. Then they came back to Egypt again with their other brother. After a while, Joseph told them who he was. He told them that he was the brother that they had sold as a slave many years before. They thought he would be angry with them. But Joseph told them that God had planned it all. God was taking care of their family. Pharaoh was happy that Joseph's family had come. He told Joseph to ask his father to come to Egypt. Pharaoh helped them to bring all their people, animals and belongings to Egypt.

Genesis 46:1-33

God spoke to Jacob in a dream. He told Jacob to go to Egypt. God said that he would make Jacob's family into a great nation. So Jacob (also known as Israel) and his large family went to Egypt. They settled there and lived there. They were known as "The Children of Israel." Each one of Jacob's twelve sons was the head of a family that would grow into a tribe.[89] So there were twelve tribes that made up the Children of Israel. Their names are written in Genesis Chapter 46:8-26.

---

89. **tribe** - a group of people who share the same language and culture and come from the same ancestors

SESSION 9: GOD CHOSE JACOB. GOD SENT JACOB'S SON, JOSEPH, TO EGYPT

We can see that God was taking care of Jacob's family. God had planned things in Joseph's life in order to take care of his family. Do you remember that God had made a promise to Abraham, Jacob's grandfather? God said that his descendants would go to a foreign land where they would be strangers. This is how God described it earlier in Genesis 15.

GENESIS 15:12-16

¹² As the sun was going down, Abram fell into a deep sleep, and a terrifying darkness came down over him. ¹³ Then the Lord said to Abram, "You can be sure that your descendants will be strangers in a foreign land, where they will be oppressed as slaves for 400 years. ¹⁴ But I will punish the nation that enslaves them, and in the end they will come away with great wealth. ¹⁵ (As for you, you will die in peace and be buried at a ripe old age.) ¹⁶ After four generations your descendants will return here to this land, for the sins of the Amorites do not yet warrant their destruction."

God's plan was happening just like he said it would. Jacob's family was now living in the foreign land of Egypt. God was making his plan happen through the lives of real people. God's plan was to bring a man to the world who would defeat Satan. He wanted this man to defeat Satan and create an everlasting[90] way for people to come to God. He said that this man would come through Jacob's family. God made this plan because he loves people and wants them to know him and love him. He was making sure his plan would happen.

You can read the whole story of Joseph's life for yourself in Genesis, from Chapter 37 to Chapter 46. As you read it, think about God's plan. The people then were just ordinary people like you and me. But God was doing things through their lives to make his rescue plan happen.

---

90. **everlasting** - something that lasts forever

HIS STORY: THE RESCUE

1. Esau and Jacob were very different kinds of people. How were they different?

2. What was God telling Jacob in the dream about the stairs that he had on his way to Haran?

3. Think about all that happened to Abraham, Isaac, Jacob and Joseph. What does that tell us about God and how he works in the lives of people?

SESSION 10

GOD SENT TEN DISASTERS TO EGYPT

We will start reading God's story again in the Book of Exodus. Jacob's family had been living in the foreign land of Egypt for a few generations. By this time, the family had grown very large. There were hundreds of thousands of Jacob's descendants. As a group, they were rich and powerful. They all spoke the same Hebrew language. They worshiped the one true Creator God.

EXODUS 1:6-22

⁶ In time, Joseph and all of his brothers died, ending that entire generation. ⁷ But their descendants, the Israelites, had many children and grandchildren. In fact, they multiplied so greatly that they became extremely powerful and filled the land.

⁸ Eventually, a new king came to power in Egypt who knew nothing about Joseph or what he had done. ⁹ He said to his people, "Look, the people of Israel now outnumber us and are stronger than we are. ¹⁰ We must make a plan to keep them from growing even more. If we don't, and if war breaks out, they will join our enemies and fight against us. Then they will escape from the country."

¹¹ So the Egyptians made the Israelites their slaves. They

appointed brutal slave drivers over them, hoping to wear them down with crushing labor. They forced them to build the cities of Pithom and Rameses as supply centers for the king. ¹² But the more the Egyptians oppressed them, the more the Israelites multiplied and spread, and the more alarmed the Egyptians became. ¹³ So the Egyptians worked the people of Israel without mercy. ¹⁴ They made their lives bitter, forcing them to mix mortar and make bricks and do all the work in the fields. They were ruthless in all their demands.

¹⁵ Then Pharaoh, the king of Egypt, gave this order to the Hebrew midwives, Shiphrah and Puah: ¹⁶ "When you help the Hebrew women as they give birth, watch as they deliver. If the baby is a boy, kill him; if it is a girl, let her live." ¹⁷ But because the midwives feared God, they refused to obey the king's orders. They allowed the boys to live, too.

¹⁸ So the king of Egypt called for the midwives. "Why have you done this?" he demanded. "Why have you allowed the boys to live?"

¹⁹ "The Hebrew women are not like the Egyptian women," the midwives replied. "They are more vigorous and have their babies so quickly that we cannot get there in time."

²⁰ So God was good to the midwives, and the Israelites continued to multiply, growing more and more powerful. ²¹ And because the midwives feared God, he gave them families of their own.

²² Then Pharaoh gave this order to all his people: "Throw every newborn Hebrew boy into the Nile River. But you may let the girls live."

The Pharaoh, or King, of Egypt at this time was afraid of the Israelites. He thought that they could help an enemy nation to fight against Egypt. But he also needed them to do building and farming work in Egypt. So Pharaoh decided to make the Israelites slaves and to treat them very badly. He did not want them to turn against Egypt so he tried to make them weak. God's story says that their lives were *made bitter*.[91] But God was taking care of the Israelites. More babies were born and the number of Israelites grew. So Pharaoh decided that all newborn Hebrew boys must be drowned in the Nile River.

---

91. **bitter** - very difficult and unhappy

SESSION 10: GOD SENT TEN DISASTERS TO EGYPT

God's enemy, Satan, was guiding Pharaoh. He was trying to destroy God's people. Satan did not want Jacob's family - the nation of Israel - to live. God had said that a man would come from this nation to destroy Satan and to take away his power over the earth and over people. We can be sure that Satan wanted to stop God's plan.

God knew what Satan was trying to do and he knew everything that would happen to the Children of Israel. Many years before, God had told Abraham that his descendants would be slaves in a foreign land. God loves people and does not want them to suffer[92]. He loves to show mercy and to be kind. He reaches out and rescues people who accept that they need him. God would not let Satan stop his plan to rescue people. So God had a plan to save the Israelites.

EXODUS 2:1-10

¹ About this time, a man and woman from the tribe of Levi got married. ² The woman became pregnant and gave birth to a son. She saw that he was a special baby and kept him hidden for three months. ³ But when she could no longer hide him, she got a basket made of papyrus reeds and waterproofed it with tar and pitch. She put the baby in the basket and laid it among the reeds along the bank of the Nile River. ⁴ The baby's sister then stood at a distance, watching to see what would happen to him.

⁵ Soon Pharaoh's daughter came down to bathe in the river, and her attendants walked along the riverbank. When the princess saw the basket among the reeds, she sent her maid to get it for her. ⁶ When the princess opened it, she saw the baby. The little boy was crying, and she felt sorry for him. "This must be one of the Hebrew children," she said.

⁷ Then the baby's sister approached the princess. "Should I go and find one of the Hebrew women to nurse the baby for you?" she asked.

⁸ "Yes, do!" the princess replied. So the girl went and called the baby's mother.

⁹ "Take this baby and nurse him for me," the princess told the baby's mother. "I will pay you for your help." So the woman took her baby home and nursed him.

¹⁰ Later, when the boy was older, his mother brought him back to Pharaoh's daughter, who adopted him as her own son. The princess named him Moses, for she explained, "I lifted him out of the water."

---
92. **suffer** - to have something bad or painful or harmful happen to you

HIS STORY: THE RESCUE

A man and his wife from the Israelite tribe of Levi had a son. If he were found, the Egyptians would have drowned him in the Nile River. So, for three months, his mother hid him. Then, she put him in a basket in the reeds at the edge of the river. She made the basket so that water could not get in.

Pharaoh's daughter went to the river to wash herself. She found the baby in the basket and decided that he should live. She named him "Moses" and later adopted[93] him as her own child. Moses grew up and had a very good education[94] in Egypt.

God was preparing[95] Moses. He wanted Moses to help carry out his plan to rescue the Israelites. God gives important work for people to do. He equips[96] them for the work he wants them to do. He wants people to be part of his plan to rescue other people. He had important work for Moses to do and he made sure that Moses was ready to do it.

EXODUS 2:11-14, 23

> [11] Many years later, when Moses had grown up, he went out to visit his own people, the Hebrews, and he saw how hard they were forced to work. During his visit, he saw an Egyptian beating one of his fellow Hebrews. [12] After looking in all directions to make sure no one was watching, Moses killed the Egyptian and hid the body in the sand.
>
> [13] The next day, when Moses went out to visit his people again, he saw two Hebrew men fighting. "Why are you beating up your friend?" Moses said to the one who had started the fight.
>
> [14] The man replied, "Who appointed you to be our prince and judge? Are you going to kill me as you killed that Egyptian yesterday?"...
>
> ... [23] Years passed, and the king of Egypt died. But the Israelites continued to groan under their burden of slavery. They cried out for help, and their cry rose up to God.

Moses wanted to help his people. He visited the places where they lived and worked. One day, he saw an Egyptian beating a Hebrew so he killed the Egyptian and buried his body. Pharaoh heard about what Moses had done and so Moses had to run away. Moses went to Midian, which was somewhere to the northeast

---

93. **adopted** - to take another person's child and bring it up as your own
94. **education** - going to school and learning
95. **preparing** - getting someone ready for something they have to do
96. **equips** - prepares someone for a task or for work they have to do

SESSION 10: GOD SENT TEN DISASTERS TO EGYPT

of Egypt. Moses married and settled in the area. He lived there for many years away from his own people and away from the Egyptians. Later, the Pharaoh of Egypt died and another Pharaoh took his place. But the Israelites still had terrible lives and they called out to God and asked him to help them.

EXODUS 2:24,25

²⁴ God heard their groaning, and he remembered his covenant promise to Abraham, Isaac, and Jacob. ²⁵ He looked down on the people of Israel and knew it was time to act.

God says that he *heard their groaning*. He heard them when they called out to him. He remembered his promise to Abraham, Isaac and Jacob. God is loving and merciful⁹⁷ and he wants to help people who know that they need his help. And God never forgets the things that he has said he will do; he always does them.

The Israelites were slaves in Egypt. They had no way to escape and they had no hope. God was the only one who could rescue them. God had a plan to use Moses to rescue the Israelites.

EXODUS 3:1-15, 4:1, 4:10-17

¹ One day Moses was tending the flock of his father-in-law, Jethro, the priest of Midian. He led the flock far into the wilderness and came to Sinai, the mountain of God. ² There the angel of the Lord appeared to him in a blazing fire from the middle of a bush. Moses stared in amazement. Though the bush was engulfed in flames, it didn't burn up. ³ "This is amazing," Moses said to himself. "Why isn't that bush burning up? I must go see it."

⁴ When the Lord saw Moses coming to take a closer look, God called to him from the middle of the bush, "Moses! Moses!"

"Here I am!" Moses replied.

⁵ "Do not come any closer," the Lord warned. "Take off your sandals, for you are standing on holy ground. ⁶ I am the God of your father—the God of Abraham, the God of Isaac, and the God of Jacob." When Moses heard this, he covered his face because he was afraid to look at God.

⁷ Then the Lord told him, "I have certainly seen the oppression of my people in Egypt. I have heard their cries of distress because of their harsh slave drivers. Yes, I am aware of their

---

97. **merciful** - showing forgiveness to someone who you have the power and the right to punish or harm

suffering. ⁸ So I have come down to rescue them from the power of the Egyptians and lead them out of Egypt into their own fertile and spacious land. It is a land flowing with milk and honey—the land where the Canaanites, Hittites, Amorites, Perizzites, Hivites, and Jebusites now live. ⁹ Look! The cry of the people of Israel has reached me, and I have seen how harshly the Egyptians abuse them. ¹⁰ Now go, for I am sending you to Pharaoh. You must lead my people Israel out of Egypt."

¹¹ But Moses protested to God, "Who am I to appear before Pharaoh? Who am I to lead the people of Israel out of Egypt?"

¹² God answered, "I will be with you. And this is your sign that I am the one who has sent you: When you have brought the people out of Egypt, you will worship God at this very mountain."

¹³ But Moses protested, "If I go to the people of Israel and tell them, 'The God of your ancestors has sent me to you,' they will ask me, 'What is his name?' Then what should I tell them?"

¹⁴ God replied to Moses, "I AM WHO I AM. Say this to the people of Israel: I AM has sent me to you." ¹⁵ God also said to Moses, "Say this to the people of Israel: Yahweh, the God of your ancestors—the God of Abraham, the God of Isaac, and the God of Jacob—has sent me to you.

This is my eternal name,
my name to remember for all generations...

... ⁴:¹ But Moses protested again, "What if they won't believe me or listen to me? What if they say, 'The Lord never appeared to you'?"...

... ¹⁰ But Moses pleaded with the Lord, "O Lord, I'm not very good with words. I never have been, and I'm not now, even though you have spoken to me. I get tongue-tied, and my words get tangled."

¹¹ Then the Lord asked Moses, "Who makes a person's mouth? Who decides whether people speak or do not speak, hear or do not hear, see or do not see? Is it not I, the Lord? ¹² Now go! I will be with you as you speak, and I will instruct you in what to say."

¹³ But Moses again pleaded, "Lord, please! Send anyone else."

¹⁴ Then the Lord became angry with Moses. "All right," he said. "What about your brother, Aaron the Levite? I know he

> speaks well. And look! He is on his way to meet you now. He will be delighted to see you. ¹⁵ Talk to him, and put the words in his mouth. I will be with both of you as you speak, and I will instruct you both in what to do. ¹⁶ Aaron will be your spokesman to the people. He will be your mouthpiece, and you will stand in the place of God for him, telling him what to say.
> ¹⁷ And take your shepherd's staff with you, and use it to perform the miraculous signs I have shown you."

God listened to his people when they called out to him. He moved ahead with his plan to rescue them. One day, Moses took his flock of sheep into the wilderness[98] on a mountain called Sinai. This mountain is sometimes called Horeb. There, Moses saw something amazing. He saw a bush that was on fire, but it was not being burned up. Moses moved closer to look at it. He heard his name being called from the burning bush. God was the one speaking. He said he was the God of Abraham, Isaac and Jacob. God told Moses that he saw the terrible lives of his people and that he had heard their cries for help. He said he would rescue them and lead them out of Egypt and back to the land of Canaan.

The Lord said that Moses would lead the people out of Egypt. But Moses did not think the Israelites would follow him or listen to him. He asked God who he should say had sent him. God said, *"I AM WHO I AM. Say this to the people of Israel: I AM has sent me to you."* God said this name was to be remembered for all generations. This name - I AM - that God gave to himself is a very, very important name. God was saying that he always was, always is, and always will be. He does not live in time like we do; he is able to live without help from anyone, and everything else gets life from him.

Moses still thought that the Israelites would not listen to him. He said that he was not able to do what God wanted him to do. God told Moses that he would be with him and would help him by showing signs of his power. Later, you can read about these signs in Exodus Chapters 3 and 4 in your Bible. And the Lord said that he would also give another sign that he was with Moses. God said that later, Moses would lead the Israelites back to the mountain at Sinai to worship God there.

Moses still did not think he would be able to do what God had asked him to do. He asked God to send someone else. After Moses said that, God was angry with

---

98. **wilderness** - an area where there are no people living and no farming

HIS STORY: THE RESCUE

him. Moses was part of God's plan but Moses did not trust God to help him. But God listened to Moses and said that Moses' brother Aaron could go with him. Aaron would be the one to speak.

EXODUS 4:29-31

²⁹ Then Moses and Aaron returned to Egypt and called all the elders of Israel together. ³⁰ Aaron told them everything the Lord had told Moses, and Moses performed the miraculous signs as they watched. ³¹ Then the people of Israel were convinced that the Lord had sent Moses and Aaron. When they heard that the Lord was concerned about them and had seen their misery, they bowed down and worshiped.

Moses and Aaron told the Israelites what God had said. They told the Israelites that God said he would rescue them. When the Israelites heard that the Lord cared about them and that he saw their terrible lives, they bowed down to worship him.

After they spoke to the Israelites, Moses and Aaron went to speak to Pharaoh.

EXODUS 5:1-9

¹ After this presentation to Israel's leaders, Moses and Aaron went and spoke to Pharaoh. They told him, "This is what the Lord, the God of Israel, says: Let my people go so they may hold a festival in my honor in the wilderness."

² "Is that so?" retorted Pharaoh. "And who is the Lord? Why should I listen to him and let Israel go? I don't know the Lord, and I will not let Israel go."

³ But Aaron and Moses persisted. "The God of the Hebrews has met with us," they declared. "So let us take a three-day journey into the wilderness so we can offer sacrifices to the Lord our God. If we don't, he will kill us with a plague or with the sword."

⁴ Pharaoh replied, "Moses and Aaron, why are you distracting the people from their tasks? Get back to work! ⁵ Look, there are many of your people in the land, and you are stopping them from their work."

⁶ That same day Pharaoh sent this order to the Egyptian slave drivers and the Israelite foremen: ⁷ "Do not supply any more straw for making bricks. Make the people get it themselves! ⁸ But still require them to make the same number of bricks as before. Don't reduce the quota. They are lazy. That's why they

SESSION 10: GOD SENT TEN DISASTERS TO EGYPT

are crying out, 'Let us go and offer sacrifices to our God.'
⁹ Load them down with more work. Make them sweat! That will teach them to listen to lies!"

Pharaoh did not listen to Moses and Aaron. He said that he did not know the Lord. Pharaoh decided to make life even harder for the Israelites. He said that now they would not only have the same amount of work to do, but they would also have to find their own straw to make bricks for building.

The Egyptian people thought that Pharaoh was a god. Pharaoh and the Egyptian people had turned away from God a long time ago. They had made up many stories that they believed about how the world began and about life and death. They had many false gods that they worshiped. Pharaoh did not believe in the God of the Hebrew people and he did not want to follow what he said. Because God knows everything, he knew that Pharaoh would not listen to Moses and Aaron.

EXODUS 6:1-8

¹ Then the Lord told Moses, "Now you will see what I will do to Pharaoh. When he feels the force of my strong hand, he will let the people go. In fact, he will force them to leave his land!"

² And God said to Moses, "I am Yahweh—'the Lord.'
³ I appeared to Abraham, to Isaac, and to Jacob as El-Shaddai—'God Almighty'—but I did not reveal my name, Yahweh, to them.
⁴ And I reaffirmed my covenant with them. Under its terms, I promised to give them the land of Canaan, where they were living as foreigners. ⁵ You can be sure that I have heard the groans of the people of Israel, who are now slaves to the Egyptians. And I am well aware of my covenant with them.

⁶ "Therefore, say to the people of Israel: 'I am the Lord. I will free you from your oppression and will rescue you from your slavery in Egypt. I will redeem you with a powerful arm and great acts of judgment. ⁷ I will claim you as my own people, and I will be your God. Then you will know that I am the Lord your God who has freed you from your oppression in Egypt.
⁸ I will bring you into the land I swore to give to Abraham, Isaac, and Jacob. I will give it to you as your very own possession. I am the Lord!'"

HIS STORY: THE RESCUE

God told Moses that he would show Pharaoh his great power. And after that, Pharaoh would let the people go. God said that when Pharaoh saw how strong he was, Pharaoh would *force them to leave his land*. Pharaoh would make the Israelites leave Egypt.

God said he would show his power to the Israelites. They would see that he was their God. He had chosen them as his own people. He wanted them to know him and to see him rescue them. He wanted to show them who he truly is by freeing them from slavery. He was their God and he would take care of them.

God's story now tells us about nine disasters or plagues[99] that God brought to the Egyptian people and their animals. It was a very terrible time for Egypt. You can read later in your Bible about the nine disasters in Exodus Chapters 7 to 10. The Nile River turned to blood, then a huge number of frogs came, then a huge number of gnats[100] and biting flies. Next, a sickness killed Egyptian animals in great numbers. After this, all the Egyptian animals and people got terrible boils,[101] then a huge hail[102] storm came, followed by a plague of locusts,[103] and finally three days of total darkness.

God was showing his great power. He wanted the Egyptians to know that he was the God of the Israelites, the One True Creator. The false gods that the Egyptians believed in could not save them. God clearly showed that it was he who had brought the disasters to Egypt. The Israelites and their animals did not

---

99. **plagues** - things that happen to cause damage or sickness to many people
100. **gnats** - small flies like mosquitoes
101. **boils** - inflamed pus-filled swellings on the skin
102. **hail** - pieces of ice that fall like rain
103. **locusts** - large flying grasshoppers that eat plants

SESSION 10: GOD SENT TEN DISASTERS TO EGYPT

suffer at all from the plagues. God showed his love and mercy[104] to them so that they knew that they were his chosen people.

As each new plague arrived, Pharaoh said he would let the Israelites go. But when each plague stopped, Pharaoh changed his mind and did not let them go. Finally, after the last plague of darkness, Pharaoh said he would kill Moses if he came again to ask him to let the Israelites go.

The Lord then told Moses that he would send one more disaster to Egypt. After that, Pharaoh would want the Israelites to leave Egypt. God said that the firstborn son of every Egyptian family would die. You can read later in your Bible exactly what God said to Moses in Exodus Chapter 11.

God told the Israelites that they must do something important before this last disaster came. He told them to carefully listen to what he said to do. If they did what he said, their firstborn sons would be saved.

EXODUS 12:3-7

> ³ Announce to the whole community of Israel that on the tenth day of this month each family must choose a lamb or a young goat for a sacrifice, one animal for each household. ⁴ If a family is too small to eat a whole animal, let them share with another family in the neighborhood. Divide the animal according to the size of each family and how much they can eat. ⁵ The animal you select must be a one-year-old male, either a sheep or a goat, with no defects.
>
> ⁶ "Take special care of this chosen animal until the evening of the fourteenth day of this first month. Then the whole assembly of the community of Israel must slaughter their lamb or young goat at twilight. ⁷ They are to take some of the blood and smear it on the sides and top of the doorframes of the houses where they eat the animal.

God said that the Children of Israel should choose a lamb or young goat. This animal must be perfect. It should not have even one thing wrong with it. Then, on the day that God told them, they should kill the lamb or goat. The blood of the animal should flow out. God wanted to them to do this to show that they believed certain things. If they did, it would show that they believed that what God said was true. It would show that they knew that they deserved to die just like the Egyptians. It would show that they understood that the only way to

---

104. **mercy** - love or forgiveness shown to someone when you could harm them

HIS STORY: THE RESCUE

escape death themselves was if a lamb or goat died in their place. They would be agreeing with God that they deserved death because of their sin, but that God had given them a way to escape that death. An animal would die in the place of their firstborn sons. God also said that the bones of the animal should not to be broken when they killed and ate it.

God said that the Israelite families should take some of the blood from the lamb or goat and smear it on the sides and top of the doorframes of the houses. This means they should put some blood above and also on both sides of the doors of their houses. Then, after they ate a meal of the meat of the lamb or goat, they should stay inside their houses with the blood on the wood at the sides and top of their doors.

EXODUS 12:12-14

> ¹² On that night I will pass through the land of Egypt and strike down every firstborn son and firstborn male animal in the land of Egypt. I will execute judgment against all the gods of Egypt, for I am the Lord! ¹³ But the blood on your doorposts will serve as a sign, marking the houses where you are staying. When I see the blood, I will pass over you. This plague of death will not touch you when I strike the land of Egypt.
>
> ¹⁴ "This is a day to remember. Each year, from generation to generation, you must celebrate it as a special festival to the Lord. This is a law for all time.

God said that he would go through the land of Egypt taking the life of the firstborn sons and animals. He would show that he is the One who is powerful, not the Egyptian false gods. He said that when he saw the blood on the houses where the Israelites were staying he would pass over those houses. The blood would show that death had already come to that house so God would not kill the firstborn there.

EXODUS 12:28-30

> ²⁸ So the people of Israel did just as the Lord had commanded through Moses and Aaron. ²⁹ And that night at midnight, the Lord struck down all the firstborn sons in the land of Egypt, from the firstborn son of Pharaoh, who sat on his throne, to the firstborn son of the prisoner in the dungeon. Even the firstborn of their livestock were killed. ³⁰ Pharaoh and all his officials and all the people of Egypt woke up during the night,

and loud wailing was heard throughout the land of Egypt. There was not a single house where someone had not died.

The Israelites believed God and did what he said to do. They put the blood on their doorposts and God saw it. He passed over the houses with the blood and did not kill their firstborn sons. God accepted the death of the animals in their place when he saw the blood.

But the Egyptians could not escape. There was no blood on the doors of their houses. There was nothing to show that death had already happened there. And so, at midnight, God killed all the firstborn sons of Egypt and all the firstborn animals as well. Pharaoh's own son was killed, too. That same night, Pharaoh called Moses and Aaron to him.

EXODUS 12:31-33

³¹ Pharaoh sent for Moses and Aaron during the night. "Get out!" he ordered. "Leave my people—and take the rest of the Israelites with you! Go and worship the Lord as you have requested. ³² Take your flocks and herds, as you said, and be gone. Go, but bless me as you leave." ³³ All the Egyptians urged the people of Israel to get out of the land as quickly as possible, for they thought, "We will all die!"

Pharaoh told Moses and Aaron to take the Israelites and leave his country. The Egyptians wanted them to leave so much that they gave them silver and gold and other valuable¹⁰⁵ things. God did what he said he would do for Moses and his people. And he did what he promised to Abraham hundreds of years before. He told Abraham that his people would come away with great wealth from the nation that had made them slaves. And that is what happened.

---

105. **valuable** - things that are worth a lot of money

HIS STORY: THE RESCUE

1. Why did Satan want to destroy the Children of Israel?
2. How did God take care of Moses and get him ready for the work he had for him to do?
3. God brought the disasters to Egypt. What about himself was he showing to the Egyptians? What about himself was he showing the Israelites?
4. Why did God pass over some of the houses in Egypt and not kill the firstborn in those houses?

SESSION 11

GOD RESCUED THE ISRAELITES AND MADE AN AGREEMENT WITH THEM

God did what he said he would do. He freed his chosen people from slavery in Egypt. He clearly showed his power and he kept his promises to Abraham, Isaac and Jacob. He also took care of Abraham's family, which had grown to be a large nation of people. This was the family from which the promised Rescuer[106] would come. He would be the man who would defeat Satan and rescue people. This was the person that God had promised would come.

Later in God's story we will see how the Israelites became his storytellers for the next 1500 years. Men called prophets[107] would speak his words to the people. Then those words would be written down in what we now call the Old Testament. And the Israelites would tell the other groups of people what it was like to have a relationship with God.

EXODUS 13:17-22

> [17] When Pharaoh finally let the people go, God did not lead them along the main road that runs through Philistine territory, even though that was the shortest route to the Promised Land. God said, "If the people are faced with a battle, they might change their minds and return to Egypt."

---

106. **Rescuer** - the One who saves people or rescues people
107. **prophets** - teachers or speakers of the words of God

HIS STORY: THE RESCUE

¹⁸ So God led them in a roundabout way through the wilderness toward the Red Sea. Thus the Israelites left Egypt like an army ready for battle.

¹⁹ Moses took the bones of Joseph with him, for Joseph had made the sons of Israel swear to do this. He said, "God will certainly come to help you. When he does, you must take my bones with you from this place."

²⁰ The Israelites left Succoth and camped at Etham on the edge of the wilderness. ²¹ The Lord went ahead of them. He guided them during the day with a pillar of cloud, and he provided light at night with a pillar of fire. This allowed them to travel by day or by night. ²² And the Lord did not remove the pillar of cloud or pillar of fire from its place in front of the people.

The Israelites were now a huge group of people. There were probably about two million adults and children. The easiest way to go from Egypt to Canaan was along the Mediterranean coast. But God led them out into the desert in a south-easterly direction. That way, they would not meet the Philistines. The Philistines were a very strong, warlike[108] people, who were very good sailors.[109] God said that if the Israelites met the Philistines and had to fight them, they might turn back to Egypt.

God led them by a pillar[110] of cloud in the daytime and a pillar of fire at night. This cloud and fire stayed with them throughout their whole trip. God was clearly showing them the way. Moses was the one he chose to speak his words aloud, but God was leading them.

EXODUS 14:1-4

¹ Then the Lord gave these instructions to Moses: ² "Order the Israelites to turn back and camp by Pi-hahiroth between Migdol and the sea. Camp there along the shore, across from Baal-zephon. ³ Then Pharaoh will think, 'The Israelites are confused. They are trapped in the wilderness!' ⁴ And once again I will harden Pharaoh's heart, and he will chase after you. I have planned this in order to display my glory through Pharaoh and his whole army. After this the Egyptians will know that I am the Lord!" So the Israelites camped there as they were told.

---

108. **warlike** - they often fought wars against other groups of people
109. **sailors** - people who travel on the water in boats
110. **pillar** - something that is tall and that stands up from the ground

SESSION 11: GOD RESCUED THE ISRAELITES AND MADE AN AGREEMENT WITH THEM

God led them to the shore[111] of the Red Sea and they camped[112] there.

EXODUS 14:5-9

⁵ When word reached the king of Egypt that the Israelites had fled, Pharaoh and his officials changed their minds. "What have we done, letting all those Israelite slaves get away?" they asked. ⁶ So Pharaoh harnessed his chariot and called up his troops.
⁷ He took with him 600 of Egypt's best chariots, along with the rest of the chariots of Egypt, each with its commander.
⁸ The Lord hardened the heart of Pharaoh, the king of Egypt, so he chased after the people of Israel, who had left with fists raised in defiance. ⁹ The Egyptians chased after them with all the forces in Pharaoh's army—all his horses and chariots, his charioteers, and his troops. The Egyptians caught up with the people of Israel as they were camped beside the shore near Pi-hahiroth, across from Baal-zephon.

Pharaoh heard that the Israelites were camped on the shores of the Red Sea. He decided to bring them back to Egypt to be his slaves and sent his army to get them.

EXODUS 14:10-14

¹⁰ As Pharaoh approached, the people of Israel looked up and panicked when they saw the Egyptians overtaking them. They cried out to the Lord, ¹¹ and they said to Moses, "Why did you bring us out here to die in the wilderness? Weren't there enough graves for us in Egypt? What have you done to us? Why did you make us leave Egypt? ¹² Didn't we tell you this would happen while we were still in Egypt? We said, 'Leave us alone! Let us be slaves to the Egyptians. It's better to be a slave in Egypt than a corpse in the wilderness!'"

¹³ But Moses told the people, "Don't be afraid. Just stand still and watch the Lord rescue you today. The Egyptians you see today will never be seen again. ¹⁴ The Lord himself will fight for you. Just stay calm."

When the Israelites saw the Egyptian army coming, they were terrified.[113] They called out to the Lord for help. But they forgot all the things that God had done to get them out of Egypt. They were angry with Moses for leading them out of

---

111. **shore** - the edge of a sea or lake
112. **camped** - set up a place to stay for a short time
113. **terrified** - very, very afraid

HIS STORY: THE RESCUE

Egypt. Moses told them to just wait and see what God would do. They were trapped.[114] They could not go forward into the Red Sea. And the Egyptian army was coming up behind them. Only God could save them.

EXODUS 14:15-31

¹⁵ Then the Lord said to Moses, "Why are you crying out to me? Tell the people to get moving! ¹⁶ Pick up your staff and raise your hand over the sea. Divide the water so the Israelites can walk through the middle of the sea on dry ground. ¹⁷ And I will harden the hearts of the Egyptians, and they will charge in after the Israelites. My great glory will be displayed through Pharaoh and his troops, his chariots, and his charioteers. ¹⁸ When my glory is displayed through them, all Egypt will see my glory and know that I am the Lord!"

¹⁹ Then the angel of God, who had been leading the people of Israel, moved to the rear of the camp. The pillar of cloud also moved from the front and stood behind them. ²⁰ The cloud settled between the Egyptian and Israelite camps. As darkness fell, the cloud turned to fire, lighting up the night. But the Egyptians and Israelites did not approach each other all night.

²¹ Then Moses raised his hand over the sea, and the Lord opened up a path through the water with a strong east wind. The wind blew all that night, turning the seabed into dry land. ²² So the people of Israel walked through the middle of the sea on dry ground, with walls of water on each side!

²³ Then the Egyptians—all of Pharaoh's horses, chariots, and charioteers—chased them into the middle of the sea. ²⁴ But just before dawn the Lord looked down on the Egyptian army from the pillar of fire and cloud, and he threw their forces into total confusion. ²⁵ He twisted their chariot wheels, making their chariots difficult to drive. "Let's get out of here—away from these Israelites!" the Egyptians shouted. "The Lord is fighting for them against Egypt!"

²⁶ When all the Israelites had reached the other side, the Lord said to Moses, "Raise your hand over the sea again. Then the waters will rush back and cover the Egyptians and their chariots and charioteers." ²⁷ So as the sun began to rise, Moses raised his hand over the sea, and the water rushed back into its usual place. The Egyptians tried to escape, but

---

114. **trapped** - having no way to escape

SESSION 11: GOD RESCUED THE ISRAELITES AND MADE AN AGREEMENT WITH THEM

> the Lord swept them into the sea. ²⁸ Then the waters returned and covered all the chariots and charioteers—the entire army of Pharaoh. Of all the Egyptians who had chased the Israelites into the sea, not a single one survived.
>
> ²⁹ But the people of Israel had walked through the middle of the sea on dry ground, as the water stood up like a wall on both sides. ³⁰ That is how the Lord rescued Israel from the hand of the Egyptians that day. And the Israelites saw the bodies of the Egyptians washed up on the seashore. ³¹ When the people of Israel saw the mighty power that the Lord had unleashed against the Egyptians, they were filled with awe before him. They put their faith in the Lord and in his servant Moses.

God saved his people even though they did not deserve[115] his mercy at all. He told Moses to raise his hand and then God made a dry path through the sea. God is the creator of oceans, seas, rivers, lakes and water so he could make a dry path through the sea. All the Israelites with all their animals walked along this path that God had made.

The Egyptians followed the Israelites into the path God had made through the sea. In the morning, the Lord made the Egyptians' chariots[116] very hard to drive. The Egyptians were afraid because now they could see that God was fighting against them. But it was too late. The water came crashing in and all the Egyptians were killed. The Israelites could see the bodies of the Egyptians wash up on the shore. They believed God when they saw his great power. God rescues people who are trapped and who turn to him for help.

In Exodus Chapters 16 and 17, God's story tells us about the time immediately after the Israelites had crossed the Red Sea. They were in the wilderness where there were no people and no food or water. They got angry with Moses and Aaron and they forgot that God was the only one who could help them. They thought that life was better in Egypt and that they would starve[117] to death in the wilderness.

Even though the Israelites did not trust him, God took care of them. He gave them food to eat. He made birds come to their camp that they could kill and eat. He gave them food called 'manna' which was on the ground each morning when

---

115. **deserve** - to earn something by something you have done
116. **chariot** - a small cart with two wheels that was pulled along by horses
117. **starve** - to die because you don't have any food to eat

HIS STORY: THE RESCUE

they woke up. They made bread out of this manna that God gave them. Later, when there was only a little water for them to drink, they started to complain[118] again. But God gave them the water that they needed. He gave them more than enough for all the people and all their animals.

God kept leading the Israelites day and night. He brought them to Mount Sinai.

EXODUS 19:1,2

¹ Exactly two months after the Israelites left Egypt, they arrived in the wilderness of Sinai. ² After breaking camp at Rephidim, they came to the wilderness of Sinai and set up camp there at the base of Mount Sinai.

They set up camp there in the wilderness in front of Mount Sinai. Remember that God had said many years before that this would be a sign to Moses that God was with him and the Israelites? God said he would bring Moses and the Israelites back to this mountain to worship him. And that is what happened. God always does what he says he will do.

God brought the Israelites to Mount Sinai to make an agreement[119] with them as a people. Another word for an agreement in English is *covenant*. A covenant is an agreement that is often written down in a contract.[120] Another older English word that means the same thing is *testament*.

EXODUS 19:3-8

³ Then Moses climbed the mountain to appear before God. The Lord called to him from the mountain and said, "Give these instructions to the family of Jacob; announce it to the descendants of Israel: ⁴ 'You have seen what I did to the Egyptians. You know how I carried you on eagles' wings and brought you to myself. ⁵ Now if you will obey me and keep my covenant, you will be my own special treasure from among all the peoples on earth; for all the earth belongs to me. ⁶ And you will be my kingdom of priests, my holy nation.' This is the message you must give to the people of Israel."

⁷ So Moses returned from the mountain and called together the elders of the people and told them everything the Lord had commanded him. ⁸ And all the people responded

---

118. **complain** - to say that you are not happy about something or to say bad things about someone because of something they have done
119. **agreement** - for two people or groups of people to say that they promise to do the things that they've said they will do
120. **contract** - something that is written down that two people or groups of people agree to

SESSION 11: GOD RESCUED THE ISRAELITES AND MADE AN AGREEMENT WITH THEM

together, "We will do everything the Lord has commanded." So Moses brought the people's answer back to the Lord.

Moses climbed up the mountain to speak to God. God told Moses to tell the Israelites that he was their Father and their Lord who had rescued them from slavery in Egypt. He said that they would be his special people on the earth. They would be his people, and they would be part of his work on earth. But he said that they must obey all that he was going to tell them to do. This would be the agreement he would make with them. When Moses told all of this to the Israelites, they said they would do whatever the Lord said.

The Israelites did not know what would be in God's agreement. Before, they had failed[121] to believe him and to do what he had said. So they should not have agreed that they would do whatever God asked. They should have remembered that their lives were full of sin. They should have asked God to help them. They should have remembered that sin and Satan were in control of their lives, and that they deserved death for their sins. They should have remembered that only God could save them by sending them the promised Rescuer.

In Exodus Chapter 19, you can read all that God told Moses that the people should do to get ready to hear what he would say. He wanted them to prepare in every way in order to hear what his agreement with them would be. He wanted them to know how important this covenant with them would be. God said they should set a boundary[122] around the mountain. He said that no person or animal could cross that boundary. If any person or animal did go over it, they would have to be killed.

God was showing the Israelites that because he was there, this mountain was a holy[123] place. He would come there to tell them what his agreement was. Only God is perfect and his agreement would also be perfect. God wanted to remind the Israelites that they were sinners and they could not just come to him without his help. If they crossed over the boundary God had made around the mountain, they would die. God always does what is real and true. So their relationship with him had to be real and true as well. They were his enemies, so they could not just come to him in the way they wanted to come. They had to come to him in the way he said. Then their relationship with him would be a real and a true one.

---

121. **failed** - were not able to do something
122. **boundary** - a line that marks an area
123. **holy place** - a place set apart for God

HIS STORY: THE RESCUE

On the morning of the third day, a cloud covered the top of the mountain. The Israelites could hear thunder and see lightning flashing. The whole mountain was smoking and the ground was shaking. Moses led the terrified people right up to the boundary. Then, God told Moses to come up and he went up into the smoke on the mountain.

Then God spoke to Moses again on the mountain.

EXODUS 20:1-17

¹ Then God gave the people all these instructions:

² "I am the Lord your God, who rescued you from the land of Egypt, the place of your slavery.

³ "You must not have any other god but me.

⁴ "You must not make for yourself an idol of any kind or an image of anything in the heavens or on the earth or in the sea. ⁵ You must not bow down to them or worship them, for I, the Lord your God, am a jealous God who will not tolerate your affection for any other gods. I lay the sins of the parents upon their children; the entire family is affected—even children in the third and fourth generations of those who reject me. ⁶ But I lavish unfailing love for a thousand generations on those who love me and obey my commands.

⁷ "You must not misuse the name of the Lord your God. The Lord will not let you go unpunished if you misuse his name.

⁸ "Remember to observe the Sabbath day by keeping it holy. ⁹ You have six days each week for your ordinary work, ¹⁰ but the seventh day is a Sabbath day of rest dedicated to the Lord your God. On that day no one in your household may do any work. This includes you, your sons and daughters, your male and female servants, your livestock, and any foreigners living among you. ¹¹ For in six days the Lord made the heavens, the earth, the sea, and everything in them; but on the seventh day he rested. That is why the Lord blessed the Sabbath day and set it apart as holy.

¹² "Honor your father and mother. Then you will live a long, full life in the land the Lord your God is giving you.

¹³ "You must not murder.

¹⁴ "You must not commit adultery.

¹⁵ "You must not steal.

¹⁶ "You must not testify falsely against your neighbor.

SESSION 11: GOD RESCUED THE ISRAELITES AND MADE AN AGREEMENT WITH THEM

> [17] "You must not covet your neighbor's house. You must not covet your neighbor's wife, male or female servant, ox or donkey, or anything else that belongs to your neighbor."

Moses came back down from the mountain and told the Israelite people what God had said. God had given ten commandments[124] to the Children of Israel. Later, he would give them many other laws on how they should live and how they should come to him. But these first ten commandments were the most basic[125] and important ones for them to understand.

God reminded them that he is their Lord who rescued them from slavery in Egypt. He had a right to be their Law Maker because he is the Creator and because he rescued them and took care of them.

The 1st commandment. God said that they should have no other god but him. This means that no person, no thing, no want, and no idea should be more important than God. They should not trust in anyone else to help them or take care of them. They should not trust in themselves or in anything else. If they did that even once, then they would be disobeying God's 1st commandment and they would fail to uphold their part of their agreement with him.

The 2nd commandment. God said that they should not make *idols*. Idols are man-made things that people worship like gods. Many other nations at that time worshiped man-made idols. People who do not listen to God often turn to

---

124. **commandment** - a rule from God that must be obeyed
125. **basic** - the starting point or the foundation (for all the other rules)

HIS STORY: THE RESCUE

man-made things and worship them. Many people spend their lives thinking about and working to get man-made things. If the Israelites did that even once, they would be disobeying God's 2nd commandment and their agreement with God would be broken.

The 3rd commandment. God said that they should not misuse[126] his name. God wanted them to remember who he really is. He did not want them to use his name in a bad way. And he did not want them to use his name without thinking about it. He wanted them to remember that he was their Lord and the one who had saved them. The Egyptians and other people of that time often used the names of their gods in chants.[127] They would say the name of a god and think that saying it would protect them from harm. God wanted the Israelites to always remember the truth about who he really is. The way that they spoke about him or used his name would show what they really thought about him. If they forgot this even once, then they would have disobeyed God's 3rd commandment.

The 4th commandment. God told them that they should keep one day in each week holy. This day would be called the *Sabbath*. This day would be set aside for him. In the Hebrew language, 'Sabbath' means *rest*. God rested after the sixth day of creation. God wanted the Israelites to stop and rest and take one day off from their normal work so they could remember God, their Creator. By doing so, they would be agreeing with God that he is the one in control of their lives. God knew that they might get busy with their lives and forget about him. So he asked them to set aside one day each week to remember him. If they even forgot about God for a moment, then they would be breaking this commandment that God gave that they should remember him.

The 5th commandment. God said that they should honor[128] their fathers and mothers. Later in God's story, it says that God wants parents to teach their children about him. So God knew that children must honor their parents or they would not honor him. He wanted each generation to know, love and respect him. If any of the Israelites treated their parents badly, even once, then they would have disobeyed God's 5th commandment.

The 6th commandment. God said they could not murder.[129] All life comes from God. God loves people and their lives are very valuable to him. He wanted

---

126. **misuse** - to use something in the wrong way
127. **chant** - a song or phrase that people think will make things happen if they repeat it
128. **honor** - to give someone love and respect for something they have done
129. **murder** - the killing of one human being by another

SESSION 11: GOD RESCUED THE ISRAELITES AND MADE AN AGREEMENT WITH THEM

the Israelites to value human life as much as he does. He said that one person should not take another person's life. Later in God's story, he says that to hate a person is the same as if you had killed them. So if the Israelites hated someone even once, they would have broken God's 6th commandment.

The 7th commandment. God said that they should not commit adultery.[130] God created marriage as the best way for people to live and for children to be raised. Any sex outside of marriage goes against what God wanted. Later, God's story says that to look at someone and have sexual thoughts is the same as if you had sex with them. If the Israelites did this even once, they would have disobeyed God's 7th commandment.

The 8th commandment. God said that they should not steal. God wanted them to know that they should not take anything that belongs to any other person. It could be money or other things that people own. But it also meant that they should not take something away from another person in any other way as well. They should not just think about themselves and get what they want by taking it from someone else. Later, God's story says that people should think about what other people need first, before thinking about themselves. If the Israelites thought about their own needs first and took anything from another person, even one time, they would have disobeyed God's 8th commandment.

The 9th commandment. God says that they should not speak falsely about others. God does not lie; he always tells the truth. Satan is a liar and he hates truth. So God told the Israelites that they should not tell lies about other people. God knows that Satan uses lies to harm people and to cause problems between them. If the Israelites told even one lie or said something that was not totally true, they would have disobeyed God's 9th commandment.

The 10th commandment. God tells them not to 'covet' other people's things. To covet something is to want something that belongs to someone else. God was the one who had taken care of the Israelites and had given them everything they needed. He rescued them and took care of them when they were in the wilderness. If they coveted other people's things, it would have shown that they were not happy with what God had given them. Also, if they wanted other people's things, it would have shown that they thought that their needs were more important than other people's. Coveting does not just mean wanting more money or more stuff, but also wanting to have power over other people, or just wanting to have more than other people. If the Israelites even once wanted

---

130. **commit adultery** - sex between a married person and someone who is not their husband or wife

HIS STORY: THE RESCUE

something that did not belong to them, they would have broken God's 10th commandment.

So these were God's laws that Moses brought down from the mountain. God had told the people what they had to do as part of his agreement with them, but it would be an impossible[131] task! They would never have been able to obey even one of God's laws all of the time!

God wanted them to see that it was impossible for them to obey all of his laws. God is perfect and the laws that he made showed how a perfect group of people should live together. But, the Israelites were not perfect. They had been born outside of the garden of Eden into a world of sin and death. They were sinners. They could not follow his laws even if they had tried to. God wanted them to know that they needed him to rescue them from death. He wanted a relationship with them that was true and real. The truth was that they needed him to rescue them. They could not pay for their own sins by following God's laws. They would not be able to pay for their sins with their own efforts.

This was what God was trying to say to people from the very beginning. Adam and Eve were naked and ashamed. Only God could make clothes for them out of animal skins. The fig leaves that they found for themselves were not enough. The clothing God made for them showed that they deserved death. The animals had died in their place. Cain tried to come to God in his own way. But God did not accept Cain's offering. Cain did not agree with God that there must be death to pay for his sins. Noah and his family had only one door to enter the boat. God told them how to build the boat and he was the one to close the one door behind them. Death was outside the boat, but Noah and his family were safe inside. God was the one who rescued them. They had no way to escape but God saved them. Isaac had no hope except for God giving a sheep to die in his place. And the Israelites had no way to escape from Pharaoh's army by the Red Sea. So God made a way for them to cross over safely and he rescued them from their enemies.

Now God had given his laws to the Israelites. They wanted his help and protection.[132] They wanted a special relationship with him. He said that they would be the nation through which the promised Rescuer would come. All the families of the earth would be blessed through them. And so the Israelites were happy to agree to God's contract. They thought that they would have no trouble

---

131. **impossible** - something that cannot be done
132. **protection** - to keep safe from harm or injury

SESSION 11: GOD RESCUED THE ISRAELITES AND MADE AN AGREEMENT WITH THEM

following all of God's laws. They thought that they could do it and that he would be happy with them. But this was not real or true. They should have known that this would be impossible for them to do. God is perfectly holy and he always does what is right. They could never live perfect lives following his laws. They needed God to rescue them from death and from being separated[133] from him forever.

1. God led the Israelites to the Red Sea where they could not escape from their enemies. Why did he do that? What was he showing about himself?
2. Did the Israelites have faith in God? Did they believe what God said?
3. God helped the Israelites in the wilderness. He led them and gave them food and water. Why did he do that?
4. How did God show that his laws were important?
5. Did God think that the Israelites could follow his laws?
6. Could any person follow all of God's laws? Why or why not?
7. Why did God give the Israelites his laws if he knew they would not be able to obey them?

---

133. **separated** - to be apart from, or away from, something

SESSION 12

GOD TOLD THE ISRAELITES HOW TO WORSHIP HIM

The Israelites said they were happy to make an agreement with God. When Moses came back down the mountain with God's laws, the Israelites said again that they would do everything God said.

EXODUS 24:3

³ Then Moses went down to the people and repeated all the instructions and regulations the Lord had given him. All the people answered with one voice, "We will do everything the Lord has commanded."

Then God told Moses to go up on the mountain again.

EXODUS 24:12

¹² Then the Lord said to Moses, "Come up to me on the mountain. Stay there, and I will give you the tablets of stone on which I have inscribed the instructions and commands so you can teach the people."

This time, God gave Moses a copy of his laws written on large flat stones. God wanted his perfect laws to be carved[134] into stone. He did not want them to be

---

134. **carved** - to cut into something with something sharp to leave a deep mark

HIS STORY: THE RESCUE

lost or changed. He wanted the Israelites to remember what they had agreed to do.

God also told Moses something amazing. God said he was going to come and live with the Israelites. They had agreed to God's contract and he said he was going to be part of their community.[135] The Israelites were nomadic – this means that they moved around from place to place and lived in tents. The place God would live among them had to be made so that it could be moved from place to place. God told Moses that they must make a large meeting tent where he could stay. In English, the word for this tent is 'tabernacle.'

This tabernacle would be a special place. God told Moses every single small thing that should be done in order to make it. He told Moses very clearly what furniture[136] and what other things should be inside it. He also told Moses how it should be decorated.[137] God wanted the Israelites to see clearly how holy and perfect he is. He wanted to show them that sinful human beings cannot just come to God in their own way. He wanted them to understand that they had to come to him in the way that he said. So he told them very, very clearly how to make this special place where he would live with his people.

God knew that the Israelites would not be able to follow his laws. He knew that they could not do what they had agreed to do. Yes, they were God's chosen people, but like all people born outside of the garden, they were sinners. They could not change that or fix that themselves. They were born into a world of sin, and sin was part of who they were. Like all people, they could not live perfectly and follow all of God's laws. God is the only one who is perfect. The Israelites could not do what God's laws said. They needed God to rescue them. But they did not understand that then.

Now God had made an agreement, a covenant, with the Israelites. He would live among them. The tabernacle would be a place where they could come to him. It would be one place where all the people – around two million people – could come to God precisely how he wanted. It was a very important and special place. God told them exactly[138] how they should make it. You can read later in your Bible in Exodus Chapters 25 to 27 all the things God said about how to build the tabernacle. We will look now at just some of the things that God said about it.

---

135. **community** - a group of people living together in the same area
136. **furniture** - things for people to use in a room, like tables, chairs and lamps
137. **decorate** - to make something look better by adding curtains or paint or designs to it
138. **exactly** - he told them every small detail

SESSION 12: GOD TOLD THE ISRAELITES HOW TO WORSHIP HIM

God told them to use animal skins and materials made of animal hair for the outside walls and the roof of the tabernacle. These are the same things that the Israelites used to make their own tents that they lived in.

God said there should be a large area with tent walls around it to mark the edge of the tabernacle, about 46 m x 23 m.[139] Inside those tent walls, there should be one tent that was about 14 m x 4.5 m[140] with two rooms inside it. The first room, the bigger one, should be called the Holy Place. The Holy Place would be next to another room called the Most Holy Place. This room would be half as big as the Holy Place.

The Most Holy Place would be God's place, set apart for him. God is spirit – he does not have a body like us – and so he does not need a house or a tent to live in. But God wanted his people to know that he was with them. That is why he wanted them to build the tabernacle.

God said that they should hang a very thick curtain[141] between the two rooms. The curtain was there to remind the people that they could not just come to God in their own way. He is holy and they were not holy. The curtain should remind them of their sin that kept them separated from God. Their sin was like the curtain that was between them and the Most Holy Place where God was.

God said that a special wooden box covered in gold should be put inside the Most Holy Place. This would be the only thing inside the Most Holy Place. In English, this box is called an 'ark.' An ark is a strong box and anything that is

139. **43 m x 23 m** - 141 ft. x 75 ft.
140. **14 m x 4.5 m** - 46 ft. x 15 ft.
141. **curtain** - a piece of material held at the top to make a screen

HIS STORY: THE RESCUE

put inside it will be safe. God's laws that were written on the flat stones would be kept inside this golden box. These laws were the agreement that the Israelites had made with God. This golden box was called the Ark of the Covenant. God said that the box should have a special lid on it. This lid would cover the flat stones with the laws written on them that were inside. God said that just above the box would be the place where he would stay. That would be his place over the golden box with the laws inside. He said that place would be a place of mercy, where wrong things would be made right.

God knew that the people could never obey his laws. He knew that they could not pay for their sins. But he wanted to make a way for them to come to him. He did not want them to die because of their sins. He loves people and he wanted to rescue the Israelites and be with them. He wanted them to have a relationship with him that was real and true. The golden box with the laws inside showed how perfect God's laws were. It showed that God's perfect laws would never change. But because God loves people, he would make a way to "cover" his laws – just like the lid on the golden box covered the laws written in stone. He did not want the people to have to pay for their sins with their own deaths. God had promised to send the Rescuer to deal with sin forever. But until that time, God was making a temporary[142] way for his people to come to him in the tabernacle.

God said they should make a large altar – a place for burning offerings. This altar should be made of brass.[143] It should be placed inside the area with the tent walls around it. God said that people should bring animals there to be killed. He said that the person who brought the animal should put their hand on the head of the animal. Then, they should ask God to accept the animal's death in place of their own. God wanted them to always remember that they deserved death for their sins, but that he had made a way for them to come to him and to live.

There were many other decorations, furniture and objects that God told them to put in the tabernacle. God told them how to make everything and what materials everything should be made out of. All of the things in the tabernacle were there to remind the people of the important things about God.

God told Moses that a group of men called priests[144] would take care of the tabernacle. The priests would make sure that the offerings were done correctly.

---

142. **temporary** - something that is only for a short amount of time
143. **brass** - a yellow metal made up of copper and zinc
144. **priest** - someone who helps other people to worship God

SESSION 12: GOD TOLD THE ISRAELITES HOW TO WORSHIP HIM

They would help the people to do everything the way that God said it should be done. God said that Moses' brother, Aaron, would be the first high priest. The high priest would be the leader of the priests. Aaron's sons would work with him. Later, new priests would come from Aaron's family too. You can read all the things God said about the priests in Exodus Chapters 28 and 29. God told the Israelites very, very clearly many things about the priests. He told them how to make special, beautiful clothing for the priests. He told them exactly how these men should do the work he wanted them to do. He gave them many instructions[145] about how they should make their offerings.

God said that the high priest had a special job to do. On one day each year, the high priest should go into the Most Holy Place. This day was called the *Day of Atonement*. Atonement means to pay for something that you have done wrong. God said that on that day, the high priest should take the blood of an animal into God's special place. The priest should sprinkle[146] the blood on the lid of the Ark of the Covenant. God said that they should do this each year, just like he told them to. Then God would not punish the Israelites for all the times that they broke his laws in that year.

God knows everything that has ever happened and that will ever happen. So he knew that the Children of Israel would not be able to obey the laws he had given them. He wanted them to understand that they needed him to save them. But even when Moses was still up on the mountain with God, the Israelites were already breaking God's laws.

You can read the whole story about what they did later in Exodus Chapter 32. Moses was up on the mountain for a long time. While the Israelites were waiting for him, they melted[147] down a large amount of gold. With the gold, they made the shape of a calf.[148] Then they worshiped the golden calf and thanked it for bringing them out of Egypt. They forgot that it was God who had brought them out of Egypt. They were worshiping an idol[149] instead of God.

God knew that they would break his laws, so he made another way for them to come to him. He said they could offer animals at the tabernacle. By doing that, they would show that they knew that they should die for their sins. But the

---

145. **instructions** - directions or orders about how to do something
146. **sprinkle** - to cover something with small drops (of the blood)
147. **melted** - heated the gold so they could make another shape out of it
148. **calf** - a young cow
149. **idol** - something that people make out of metal or wood that they worship as a god

animals would die in their place. They should do that and wait for the Rescuer to come. He would defeat Satan and pay for people's sins once and for all.

After the tabernacle was finished, the Israelites started to move again.

EXODUS 40:36-38

36 Now whenever the cloud lifted from the Tabernacle, the people of Israel would set out on their journey, following it. 37 But if the cloud did not rise, they remained where they were until it lifted. 38 The cloud of the Lord hovered over the Tabernacle during the day, and at night fire glowed inside the cloud so the whole family of Israel could see it. This continued throughout all their journeys.

God came and lived with them. During the day, the people of Israel could see that God was with them. God put a cloud above the tabernacle. And at night, they could see that he was still there. God put a fire inside the cloud at night so they could all see that he was still with them. When this cloud moved up, the people knew that God was telling them to move on.

One day, ten or eleven months after they had first arrived at Mount Sinai, the cloud moved up.

NUMBERS 10:11

11 In the second year after Israel's departure from Egypt—on the twentieth day of the second month—the cloud lifted from the Tabernacle of the Covenant.

With God leading them, they traveled through the wilderness. They reached the border[150] area of Canaan. This was the land that God had promised to Abraham hundreds of years before. They set up camp at a place called Kadesh Barnea.

The land of Canaan is the area that we now call Israel, the Palestinian territories,[151] Lebanon, and the western parts of Jordan and Syria. This was the land that God promised to the Israelite nation. But when they got to the border, there were many tribes already living there. These tribes were *Semitic* people. Semitic means that they were descendants of Noah's son, Shem. Some of these tribes were trying to get more land, money and power. They fought with the other tribes. These tribes did not listen to God or follow what he said. They worshiped idols as well. They did not believe he was the Creator. God had told

---

150. **border** - the outside edge of something
151. **territories** - areas of land that are ruled by a state or country

SESSION 12: GOD TOLD THE ISRAELITES HOW TO WORSHIP HIM

Abraham many years before that these tribes would be punished for turning away from him. God knew what the land of Canaan would be like when the Israelites arrived there. He knew that there would already be tribes of people living there.

While the Israelites were camped at Kadesh Barnea, some interesting things happened. You can read about it later for yourself. But we will move ahead in the story a little bit now. God told Moses to choose twelve men – one man from each of the Israelite tribes. He told them to go into Canaan and come back to tell the people what they had found there.

NUMBERS 13:21-29

²¹ So they went up and explored the land from the wilderness of Zin as far as Rehob, near Lebo-hamath. ²² Going north, they passed through the Negev and arrived at Hebron, where Ahiman, Sheshai, and Talmai—all descendants of Anak—lived. (The ancient town of Hebron was founded seven years before the Egyptian city of Zoan.) ²³ When they came to the valley of Eshcol, they cut down a branch with a single cluster of grapes so large that it took two of them to carry it on a pole between them! They also brought back samples of the pomegranates and figs. ²⁴ That place was called the valley of Eshcol (which means "cluster"), because of the cluster of grapes the Israelite men cut there.

²⁵ After exploring the land for forty days, the men returned ²⁶ to Moses, Aaron, and the whole community of Israel at Kadesh in the wilderness of Paran. They reported to the whole community what they had seen and showed them the fruit they had taken from the land. ²⁷ This was their report to Moses: "We entered the land you sent us to explore, and it is indeed a bountiful country—a land flowing with milk and honey. Here is the kind of fruit it produces. ²⁸ But the people living there are powerful, and their towns are large and fortified. We even saw giants there, the descendants of Anak! ²⁹ The Amalekites live in the Negev, and the Hittites, Jebusites, and Amorites live in the hill country. The Canaanites live along the coast of the Mediterranean Sea and along the Jordan Valley."

The twelve men went in to the land of Canaan for nearly six weeks. They went to different areas in the land. They saw that the land was very good for growing things. They brought back a huge bunch of grapes to show the people. But they

HIS STORY: THE RESCUE

also told the people that the tribes in the land were very strong. They said there were huge people in the land and that their towns had very strong walls. But two of the men who had entered Canaan told the people not to be afraid. Their names were Caleb and Joshua. They believed that God would help them to defeat the people who were living there.

NUMBERS 13:30

³⁰ But Caleb tried to quiet the people as they stood before Moses. "Let's go at once to take the land," he said. "We can certainly conquer it!"

But the people did not listen to Caleb and Joshua. They were afraid. They listened to the other ten men who had gone into Canaan. They thought about Egypt and they wanted to go back there. They got angry and wanted to kill Caleb and Joshua. They did not want Moses and Aaron to be their leaders any more.

God had promised that the Israelites would live in the land of Canaan. But they did not believe what God said. Because the Children of Israel did not believe what God said, he told them that their generation would not go and live in the promised land. God said that they would move around in the wilderness for 40 years and then die in the wilderness. But he said that their children's generation would go into the land that he had promised.

God's story tells us more about the Israelites while they were in the wilderness. You can read in Numbers Chapter 20 about a time when they ran out of water. They did not ask God for help. Instead, they complained and blamed Moses and Aaron for leading them out to die in the wilderness.

Not very long after this, the Israelites again started to complain about God and Moses. They said that they did not have good food and drink in the wilderness. They said that the manna that God had given them for food was horrible.[152]

NUMBERS 21:4-9

⁴ Then the people of Israel set out from Mount Hor, taking the road to the Red Sea to go around the land of Edom. But the people grew impatient with the long journey, ⁵ and they began to speak against God and Moses. "Why have you brought us out of Egypt to die here in the wilderness?" they complained. "There is nothing to eat here and nothing to drink. And we hate this horrible manna!"

⁶ So the Lord sent poisonous snakes among the people, and

---

152. **horrible** - very bad or unpleasant

SESSION 12: GOD TOLD THE ISRAELITES HOW TO WORSHIP HIM

> many were bitten and died. ⁷ Then the people came to Moses and cried out, "We have sinned by speaking against the Lord and against you. Pray that the Lord will take away the snakes." So Moses prayed for the people.
>
> ⁸ Then the Lord told him, "Make a replica of a poisonous snake and attach it to a pole. All who are bitten will live if they simply look at it!" ⁹ So Moses made a snake out of bronze and attached it to a pole. Then anyone who was bitten by a snake could look at the bronze snake and be healed!

God sent poisonous[153] snakes to the place where the Israelites were camped. When the snakes bit a person, that person would die. The people knew that God did this to them because they had spoken against God and against Moses. They asked Moses to talk to God and ask for his help. God told Moses to make a bronze snake and put it on a pole. God said that any person who had been bitten by a poisonous snake could look at the bronze snake on the pole. If they looked at it, then God would heal[154] them.

God sent the snakes to show the Israelites that they needed him. They had no way to escape the bite of the snakes. But God made a way for them to live. If they did not do what he said, they would die.

God promised Adam and Eve that he would send the Rescuer to end the power of Satan. The Rescuer would save people from having to pay for their sins. The bronze snake was an example of what the Rescuer would do for all people later on. We will hear all about that later in God's story.

---

153. **poisonous** - something with poison in it that can kill people
154. **heal** - to make someone well again

HIS STORY: THE RESCUE

1. God very clearly told the Children of Israel how to build the tabernacle. Why did he do that?

2. God knew that the Israelites would not obey his laws. But he still went to live with them and he gave them a way to come to him. Why do you think he did that?

3. How did he say the Israelites should come to him?

4. How did God show that he was with the Israelites?

5. What did the bronze snake on a pole show the people about God?

SESSION 13

GOD TOOK THE ISRAELITES INTO CANAAN

God said that the generation of people that he had brought out of Egypt would not enter the promised land of Canaan. He said that because when the Israelites were in Kadesh Barnea, they did not believe him. They spoke against God and against Moses. God said they would not go into the land, and that is what happened. Because they did not believe what God said was true, the Israelites of that generation died in the wilderness.

But Joshua and Caleb had listened to God. They had told the people to trust in God. So they were the only two people from that generation to enter the promised land. God told Moses to make Joshua the new leader of the Israelites.

NUMBERS 27:18-23

18 The Lord replied, "Take Joshua son of Nun, who has the Spirit in him, and lay your hands on him. 19 Present him to Eleazar the priest before the whole community, and publicly commission him to lead the people. 20 Transfer some of your authority to him so the whole community of Israel will obey him. 21 When direction from the Lord is needed, Joshua will stand before Eleazar the priest, who will use the Urim—one of the sacred lots cast before the Lord—to determine his will.

HIS STORY: THE RESCUE

> This is how Joshua and the rest of the community of Israel will determine everything they should do."
>
> 22 So Moses did as the Lord commanded. He presented Joshua to Eleazar the priest and the whole community. 23 Moses laid his hands on him and commissioned him to lead the people, just as the Lord had commanded through Moses.

Not long after that, God told Moses to go to the top of a mountain overlooking[155] Canaan.

DEUTERONOMY 34:1-8

> 1 Then Moses went up to Mount Nebo from the plains of Moab and climbed Pisgah Peak, which is across from Jericho. And the Lord showed him the whole land, from Gilead as far as Dan; 2 all the land of Naphtali; the land of Ephraim and Manasseh; all the land of Judah, extending to the Mediterranean Sea; 3 the Negev; the Jordan Valley with Jericho—the city of palms—as far as Zoar. 4 Then the Lord said to Moses, "This is the land I promised on oath to Abraham, Isaac, and Jacob when I said, 'I will give it to your descendants.' I have now allowed you to see it with your own eyes, but you will not enter the land."
>
> 5 So Moses, the servant of the Lord, died there in the land of Moab, just as the Lord had said. 6 The Lord buried him in a valley near Beth-peor in Moab, but to this day no one knows the exact place. 7 Moses was 120 years old when he died, yet his eyesight was clear, and he was as strong as ever. 8 The people of Israel mourned for Moses on the plains of Moab for thirty days, until the customary period of mourning was over.

God told Moses to remember his promise to Abraham, Isaac and Jacob. He said that this land was what he had promised to give to their descendants. God showed Moses the land, but Moses could not go in. Moses died there and the Israelites mourned[156] for 30 days.

God's story tells us about many things that happened as he helped the Israelites move into Canaan. We can't discuss all of them here, but you can read about them later in your Bible. Joshua led the Israelites in many battles against the tribes who were living in Canaan. Some of the time, they trusted in God to help

---

155. **overlooking** - from the top you can see over the whole land
156. **mourned** - to feel sorry because of the death of someone

SESSION 13: GOD TOOK THE ISRAELITES INTO CANAAN

them and he did help them to beat their enemies. But sometimes they did not believe God would help them. Because they did not always believe him, they had a very difficult time. They had many enemies living all around them. They did not listen to God, so they could not take over the whole land like he had wanted. Many enemies who wanted to kill the Israelites lived near them.

Also, because God's people lived among the other tribes, they started to act like them.

JUDGES 2:7-13

⁷ And the Israelites served the Lord throughout the lifetime of Joshua and the leaders who outlived him—those who had seen all the great things the Lord had done for Israel.

⁸ Joshua son of Nun, the servant of the Lord, died at the age of 110. ⁹ They buried him in the land he had been allocated, at Timnath-serah in the hill country of Ephraim, north of Mount Gaash.

¹⁰ After that generation died, another generation grew up who did not acknowledge the Lord or remember the mighty things he had done for Israel.

¹¹ The Israelites did evil in the Lord's sight and served the images of Baal. ¹² They abandoned the Lord, the God of their ancestors, who had brought them out of Egypt. They went after other gods, worshiping the gods of the people around them. And they angered the Lord. ¹³ They abandoned the Lord to serve Baal and the images of Ashtoreth.

After Joshua died, the next generation of Israelites forgot about God. They started to worship false gods. God's enemy, Satan, was leading them to forget about God. He didn't want them to follow God. He didn't want God's rescue plan to work out. The Israelites forgot that only God could save them. They tried to find another way to save themselves by asking for help from false gods. God's story says that *they angered the Lord*. God had a plan to rescue all people through the children of Israel. But they forgot about him. So when they forgot about him, he let their enemies defeat them in battle.[157]

This happened many times over the next few hundred years. The Israelite people turned away from God and worshiped other gods. When they did that, God let their enemies win. He even let their enemies take some of their land. Then,

---

157. **battle** - in wars or fights

HIS STORY: THE RESCUE

when their enemies defeated them, the Israelites would turn back to the Lord and repent.[158]

At this time, God helped some of the Israelites to become leaders over their people. God raised up these leaders to help the Israelite tribes fight their enemies.

JUDGES 2:16-19

> [16] Then the Lord raised up judges to rescue the Israelites from their attackers. [17] Yet Israel did not listen to the judges but prostituted themselves by worshiping other gods. How quickly they turned away from the path of their ancestors, who had walked in obedience to the Lord's commands.
>
> [18] Whenever the Lord raised up a judge over Israel, he was with that judge and rescued the people from their enemies throughout the judge's lifetime. For the Lord took pity on his people, who were burdened by oppression and suffering. [19] But when the judge died, the people returned to their corrupt ways, behaving worse than those who had lived before them. They went after other gods, serving and worshiping them. And they refused to give up their evil practices and stubborn ways.

The English word used for these leaders is 'judges.' Another word that is sometimes used for them is 'deliverers,' which means 'rescuers.' God brought these leaders to the Israelite people to help them. Even though the people kept turning against God, he always helped them when they came back to him. God had a plan that he had promised long ago. He would not give up on the Israelite people and he would not give up on his plan. He was going to send a Rescuer who would destroy the power of Satan, sin and death.

The last of the judges was called Samuel. He spoke the words of God to Israel for many years. Someone who speaks the words of God is called a *prophet*. When Samuel was old, there was nobody to take over from him.

1 SAMUEL 8:1-7

> [1] As Samuel grew old, he appointed his sons to be judges over Israel. [2] Joel and Abijah, his oldest sons, held court in Beersheba. [3] But they were not like their father, for they were greedy for money. They accepted bribes and perverted justice.
>
> [4] Finally, all the elders of Israel met at Ramah to discuss the

---

158. **repent** - to agree with God that you have sinned against him

SESSION 13: GOD TOOK THE ISRAELITES INTO CANAAN

> matter with Samuel. ⁵ "Look," they told him, "you are now old, and your sons are not like you. Give us a king to judge us like all the other nations have."
>
> ⁶ Samuel was displeased with their request and went to the Lord for guidance. ⁷ "Do everything they say to you," the Lord replied, "for they are rejecting me, not you. They don't want me to be their king any longer.

The people asked Samuel to give them a king. Samuel thought that this was a sinful idea. Why? Because God was the leader of the Israelites. God was the one who had led them out of Egypt. He was the one who had helped them. Samuel talked to the Lord about it. The Lord said that the people were rejecting him, God, as their king. They wanted a king like all the other nations around them. They did not want God to lead them anymore.

God let them have a king because that was what they wanted. Their first king was called Saul. He started out well. Then he began to become angry at the Lord's words that were spoken by Samuel.

1 SAMUEL 13:13,14

> ¹³ "How foolish!" Samuel exclaimed. "You have not kept the command the Lord your God gave you. Had you kept it, the Lord would have established your kingdom over Israel forever. ¹⁴ But now your kingdom must end, for the Lord has sought out a man after his own heart. The Lord has already appointed him to be the leader of his people, because you have not kept the Lord's command."

Saul did not listen to the words of God that Samuel spoke. So God found another leader for his people. His name was David. When David was young, he was a shepherd. There are many stories about David's life in the Bible. When he was young, he fought against a giant[159] called Goliath. David trusted God and he beat Goliath.

David was Israel's greatest and most famous king. David had a very close relationship with God. Just like all people, David was a sinner and he did not always do the right thing. But he always talked to God about his sins. He always knew that he should die for his sins, but that God had made a way for him to

---

159. **giant** - a huge, very tall man

131

HIS STORY: THE RESCUE

come to him. David is a great example of a person who wanted to have a close relationship with the Lord.

God made David the King of Israel. God also made David one of his storytellers – someone who spoke the words of God. David was a prophet. David was also a very good musician.[160] He wrote many songs about God and about his relationship with God. Another word for the songs that worship God is 'psalms.' Many of David's songs are written down in the Book of Psalms. You can read these songs later in your Bible. When David wrote his songs, he was very open and honest[161] about how he felt. God made sure that these songs are in the Bible for us to read today. God wants to have a close relationship with every person. David's songs show us an example of God's close relationship with a person that he loved very much.

King David led the nation of Israel well. They enjoyed a time of peace and they grew strong. The Israelites did not need to move around anymore. David lived in a beautiful palace.[162] He wanted the Lord to have a beautiful place to live in too. David did not think that the tabernacle tent was a good enough place for God anymore.

2 SAMUEL 7:1-17

¹ When King David was settled in his palace and the Lord had given him rest from all the surrounding enemies, ² the king summoned Nathan the prophet. "Look," David said, "I am living in a beautiful cedar palace, but the Ark of God is out there in a tent!"

³ Nathan replied to the king, "Go ahead and do whatever you have in mind, for the Lord is with you."

⁴ But that same night the Lord said to Nathan,

⁵ "Go and tell my servant David, 'This is what the Lord has declared: Are you the one to build a house for me to live in? ⁶ I have never lived in a house, from the day I brought the Israelites out of Egypt until this very day. I have always moved from one place to another with a tent and a Tabernacle as my dwelling. ⁷ Yet no matter where I have gone with the Israelites, I have never once complained to Israel's tribal leaders, the shepherds of my people Israel. I have never asked them, "Why haven't you built me a beautiful cedar house?"'

---

160. **musician** - someone who plays music and writes songs
161. **honest** - to speak the truth and not to hide anything
162. **palace** - a large and beautiful building where a king or ruler lives

SESSION 13: GOD TOOK THE ISRAELITES INTO CANAAN

[8] "Now go and say to my servant David, 'This is what the Lord of Heaven's Armies has declared: I took you from tending sheep in the pasture and selected you to be the leader of my people Israel. [9] I have been with you wherever you have gone, and I have destroyed all your enemies before your eyes. Now I will make your name as famous as anyone who has ever lived on the earth! [10] And I will provide a homeland for my people Israel, planting them in a secure place where they will never be disturbed. Evil nations won't oppress them as they've done in the past, [11] starting from the time I appointed judges to rule my people Israel. And I will give you rest from all your enemies.

"'Furthermore, the Lord declares that he will make a house for you—a dynasty of kings! [12] For when you die and are buried with your ancestors, I will raise up one of your descendants, your own offspring, and I will make his kingdom strong. [13] He is the one who will build a house—a temple—for my name. And I will secure his royal throne forever. [14] I will be his father, and he will be my son. If he sins, I will correct and discipline him with the rod, like any father would do. [15] But my favor will not be taken from him as I took it from Saul, whom I removed from your sight. [16] Your house and your kingdom will continue before me for all time, and your throne will be secure forever.'"

[17] So Nathan went back to David and told him everything the Lord had said in this vision.

Nathan the prophet spoke the words of God. Through Nathan, God told David that it was a good idea to build a house for God. But God said that David should not build it; instead, it was David's son who would build it. God also said that David's *throne will be secure forever*. God was making a promise that the Rescuer would come from David's family. The Promised One, who would come to defeat Satan, would be a direct descendant of David. This was the same promise that God had made to Abraham, Isaac and Jacob. God was saying that he would still carry out his plan and that he had not forgotten his promise.

King David started to collect all the gold, silver, special timber and other materials to build God's house. The word we use for this house of God is 'temple.' The temple would be built in Jerusalem, the main city of Israel. David's son, Solomon, was the one who would build the temple, just like God said. This is what Solomon said about it.

HIS STORY: THE RESCUE

2 CHRONICLES 2:5,6

⁵ "This must be a magnificent Temple because our God is greater than all other gods. ⁶ But who can really build him a worthy home? Not even the highest heavens can contain him! So who am I to consider building a Temple for him, except as a place to burn sacrifices to him?

Solomon built the temple in Jerusalem. It was a huge and beautiful building made of stone, wood, gold and silver. It used the same plan for the rooms and had the same furniture as the tabernacle. When it was finished, the people offered many animal sacrifices[163] to God. God went into the temple and the people could see a very bright light. The bright light was in the Most Holy Place in the temple. God was showing them that he was there in the temple. God wanted to live with his people. He wanted them to know he was there with them.

When David and Solomon were kings of Israel, there was a time of peace. Israel became powerful and rich. But after David and Solomon were dead, Israel split into two kingdoms[164] – the northern and southern kingdoms. These two kingdoms were called Israel and Judah. Over time, each kingdom had about 20 kings that came to power. Most of these kings did not follow God. They followed other gods and did the things that the nations around them did. God was very sad that the people of Israel did not follow him. But he never gave up on them. He kept trying and trying to speak to them, to correct them and to punish them. He wanted them to return to him. Whenever they came back to him and asked him for help, he did help them.

God tells us in his story about many things that happened to Israel over the next 500 years. The people of Israel did not always follow God. Many times they worshiped other gods and turned away from God. They did not obey God's laws and they did not keep their agreement with him. But God always tried to speak to them in many ways. He loved them and he wanted them to remember him. He wanted to have a real and close relationship with them.

The main way that God spoke to Israel and Judah during this time was through his prophets. Some of the most well known prophets from this time were Isaiah, Jeremiah, Ezekiel and Daniel. They told the people not to follow other gods.

---

163. **sacrifice** - to kill an animal or to give something else as an offering to God
164. **kingdom** - an area and a group of people who are ruled by one king

SESSION 13: GOD TOOK THE ISRAELITES INTO CANAAN

They said that a time was coming when the people would be judged[165] for what they were doing. You can read what each of these prophets said in the books of the Bible named after them.

Jonah was another prophet of God during this time. God sent him to speak to the nations around Israel. He told them that terrible things would happen if they did not turn to the true Creator God. You can read about what happened to Jonah in the Book of Jonah in the Bible.

Some people did listen to the prophets and turn back to God. And sometimes one of the kings would guide the people to turn back to God. But that did not happen very often. During these 500 years, most people forgot about God. They kept offering sacrifices to God in the temple, but they did not really know or love God. This is what God said about them.

ISAIAH 29:13

> [13] And so the Lord says,
> "These people say they are mine.
> They honor me with their lips,
> but their hearts are far from me.
> And their worship of me
> is nothing but man-made rules learned by rote.

God is always real and true in everything he does. He wants to have real and true relationships with people. He knew that the people offering sacrifices in the temple did not really follow him. They were doing things that he said were *man-made rules*. God always knows what people are really thinking. The people offered sacrifices and followed rules, but they did not really believe that what God said was true. They did not think about God as if he were a real person that they could know and love. They did not want a true relationship with God.

The prophet Isaiah delivered a message from God to Israel, the northern kingdom. He said that the Assyrians would defeat them in war if they did not repent. The Assyrians were a very strong enemy nation but Israel did not listen to God's message. So the Assyrians took over Israel's northern city of Samaria around 722 BC. Then Israel was ruled by the Assyrians. Thousands of Israelite people were taken away as slaves. Then, the Assyrians brought other people to live in the northern areas of Canaan. These people did not know the true, Creator God. They worshiped other gods.

---

165. **judged** - to be told how you will be punished or rewarded for what you have done

HIS STORY: THE RESCUE

The prophet Jeremiah, and other prophets, delivered messages from God to the southern kingdom of Judah. He told them to repent. He said they should remember the agreement that they had made with God. If they did not, then the very strong nation of Babylon would destroy them. Judah did not listen to God's message. The Babylonians came and tore down the temple in Jerusalem. They took down the stone walls that were around Jerusalem. Many people from Judah were taken away to Babylon. God's story tells us about this time. You can read about it in your own Bible later in 2 Kings 25:1-12.

After these terrible things happened, many of the Israelites wanted to turn back to God. They read the laws that God had given them. After a generation, some of the Israelite people in Assyria and Babylon came back to Canaan. Later, they rebuilt the walls of Jerusalem and they rebuilt the temple. These people were called 'Jews.' This name probably comes from the name Judah, which was the most important tribe of the 12 tribes of Israel.

God wanted the Jews to be an example to other nations. They should not have been like the people around them. But the Jews did not want a real relationship with God. They tried to follow all of God's laws but that was impossible. They also added many new laws that they had made up themselves. They thought this would please God and pay for their sins. They did not believe that only God could save them. Of course, God knew that this would happen. Many years before, when God was talking to Moses, he said:

DEUTERONOMY 31:20

> 20 For I will bring them into the land I swore to give their ancestors—a land flowing with milk and honey. There they will become prosperous, eat all the food they want, and become fat. But they will begin to worship other gods; they will despise me and break my covenant.

In about 400 BC, Alexander the Great came and took over the land of Canaan. He was a leader from Greece. At that time, the Greek culture and language had spread over a huge area around the Mediterranean Sea. After Alexander died, there were many wars fought in the area. There were wars in the land where the Jews lived. In around 60 BC, the army of Rome came and took over the land where the Israelites lived. The people were ruled by the Romans and they had to pay a lot of tax money to Rome.

The Jews at that time still offered sacrifices to God in the temple. They tried to follow the laws that God had given them and the laws that they had made up themselves. They thought of God just like he was an idol. They did not know him or love him for who he really is. They did not believe the true things about God that God had told them. But God did not give up on them. God loved them and wanted them to remember who he truly is. He wanted them to have a real relationship with him. But it had to be because of who he really is and because of who they really were. Any other kind of relationship would have been a lie. And God does not lie. Here are some things God said through the prophet Isaiah.

ISAIAH 51:12-16

¹² "I, yes I, am the one who comforts you.
So why are you afraid of mere humans,
who wither like the grass and disappear?
¹³ Yet you have forgotten the Lord, your Creator,
the one who stretched out the sky like a canopy
and laid the foundations of the earth.
Will you remain in constant dread of human oppressors?
Will you continue to fear the anger of your enemies?
Where is their fury and anger now?
It is gone!
¹⁴ Soon all you captives will be released!
Imprisonment, starvation, and death will not be your fate!
¹⁵ For I am the Lord your God,
who stirs up the sea, causing its waves to roar.
My name is the Lord of Heaven's Armies.
¹⁶ And I have put my words in your mouth
and hidden you safely in my hand.
I stretched out the sky like a canopy
and laid the foundations of the earth.
I am the one who says to Israel,
'You are my people!'"

Even though his people had forgotten him, God did not forget them. And God did not forget his plan to rescue people from Satan, sin and death. But how would he do it?

HIS STORY: THE RESCUE

1. The generation of Israelites who came out of Egypt did not go into the Promised Land. Why?
2. How did the people demonstrate that they had turned away from God?
3. When the people turned away from God, what did God do?
4. The Jews tried to follow God's laws – so why was God not happy about that?
5. Did God change his rescue plan because the Israelites forgot about him?

SESSION 14

GOD SENT JOHN TO GET ISRAEL READY FOR THE RESCUER

About 340 years before the Romans arrived, God sent one of his prophets to the Jews. His name was Malachi. Malachi was the last prophet who had his words written down in the Old Testament. Through Malachi, God reminded the Jewish people of his promise to send a Rescuer. He said that the Promised One would come soon.

MALACHI 3:1,2

¹ "Look! I am sending my messenger, and he will prepare the way before me. Then the Lord you are seeking will suddenly come to his Temple. The messenger of the covenant, whom you look for so eagerly, is surely coming," says the Lord of Heaven's Armies.

² "But who will be able to endure it when he comes? Who will be able to stand and face him when he appears? For he will be like a blazing fire that refines metal, or like a strong soap that bleaches clothes.

HIS STORY: THE RESCUE

But God said that just before the Rescuer would come, another prophet would come first. He would bring a message from God that would get the people ready for the Rescuer's arrival.

MALACHI 4:5,6

⁵ "Look, I am sending you the prophet Elijah before the great and dreadful day of the Lord arrives. ⁶ His preaching will turn the hearts of fathers to their children, and the hearts of children to their fathers. Otherwise I will come and strike the land with a curse."

After Malachi died, God did not send another prophet for 400 years. God did not talk to his people for 400 years. He wanted them to wait for the Rescuer to come.

The first part of God's story that we call the Old Testament was written in the Hebrew language. The Old Testament ends with the words of God's prophet, Malachi. The second part of God's story is called the New Testament. We will hear more about the men who wrote down the words of God in the New Testament later. The New Testament was written in the Greek language.

Many things happened in the world in the 400 years after Malachi. The Greek language spread throughout the whole region.¹⁶⁶ Many groups of people could now talk to each other in Greek. Because of that, many ideas spread very far. Also, the Romans built many, many roads. It became easier for people to go from city to city. During this time, the Hebrew people spread out and settled in many places around the Mediterranean Sea. They took God's story with them. They took the idea that there is one God, not many gods. Many small towns and cities had Jewish people living in them. They knew God's true story that told about God's promises about the Rescuer. Other people heard about God's true story because the Jewish people were living among them.

Now we will read in God's story what happened next. The land of Israel and Judah had been under the rule of the Romans for a long time. The Jewish people were waiting for the Rescuer to come. They called him *Messiah*. In the Hebrew language, Messiah means 'God's promised Rescuer.'

Two of the Jewish people waiting for the Messiah were a man called Zechariah and his wife, Elizabeth.

---

166. **region** - a large area with many countries and groups of people

SESSION 14: GOD SENT JOHN TO GET ISRAEL READY FOR THE RESCUER

LUKE 1:5-25

⁵ When Herod was king of Judea, there was a Jewish priest named Zechariah. He was a member of the priestly order of Abijah, and his wife, Elizabeth, was also from the priestly line of Aaron. ⁶ Zechariah and Elizabeth were righteous in God's eyes, careful to obey all of the Lord's commandments and regulations. ⁷ They had no children because Elizabeth was unable to conceive, and they were both very old.

⁸ One day Zechariah was serving God in the Temple, for his order was on duty that week. ⁹ As was the custom of the priests, he was chosen by lot to enter the sanctuary of the Lord and burn incense. ¹⁰ While the incense was being burned, a great crowd stood outside, praying.

¹¹ While Zechariah was in the sanctuary, an angel of the Lord appeared to him, standing to the right of the incense altar. ¹² Zechariah was shaken and overwhelmed with fear when he saw him. ¹³ But the angel said, "Don't be afraid, Zechariah! God has heard your prayer. Your wife, Elizabeth, will give you a son, and you are to name him John. ¹⁴ You will have great joy and gladness, and many will rejoice at his birth, ¹⁵ for he will be great in the eyes of the Lord. He must never touch wine or other alcoholic drinks. He will be filled with the Holy Spirit, even before his birth. ¹⁶ And he will turn many Israelites to the Lord their God. ¹⁷ He will be a man with the spirit and power of Elijah. He will prepare the people for the coming of the Lord. He will turn the hearts of the fathers to their children, and he will cause those who are rebellious to accept the wisdom of the godly."

¹⁸ Zechariah said to the angel, "How can I be sure this will happen? I'm an old man now, and my wife is also well along in years."

¹⁹ Then the angel said, "I am Gabriel! I stand in the very presence of God. It was he who sent me to bring you this good news! ²⁰ But now, since you didn't believe what I said, you will be silent and unable to speak until the child is born. For my words will certainly be fulfilled at the proper time."

²¹ Meanwhile, the people were waiting for Zechariah to come out of the sanctuary, wondering why he was taking so long. ²² When he finally did come out, he couldn't speak to them. Then they realized from his gestures and his silence that he must have seen a vision in the sanctuary.

HIS STORY: THE RESCUE

> ²³ When Zechariah's week of service in the Temple was over, he returned home. ²⁴ Soon afterward his wife, Elizabeth, became pregnant and went into seclusion for five months. ²⁵ "How kind the Lord is!" she exclaimed. "He has taken away my disgrace of having no children."

Zechariah was a priest in the temple. One day, he was doing his work there. One of God's spirit messengers, an angel, came to talk to him. The angel showed himself in human form to speak to Zechariah. The angel said that Zechariah and Elizabeth would have a son and that they should call him John. In the Hebrew and Aramaic languages, John means 'God has shown grace.'[167]

The angel told Zechariah what John's work would be. John was the prophet that Malachi said would come just before the Rescuer came. John's message would help people to get ready for the Promised One. The angel said, *he will prepare*[168] *the people for the coming of the Lord*. The angel said that the Rescuer would be the Lord himself. Somehow, God would appear among his people in a special way. How would he do that?

John was born to Zechariah and Elizabeth even though they were both old. God said they would have a son and that is what happened. A few days after John was born, God the Spirit gave Zechariah the special ability[169] to speak for God.

LUKE 1:67-79

> ⁶⁷ Then his father, Zechariah, was filled with the Holy Spirit and gave this prophecy:
>
> ⁶⁸ "Praise the Lord, the God of Israel,
> because he has visited and redeemed his people.
> ⁶⁹ He has sent us a mighty Savior
> from the royal line of his servant David,
> ⁷⁰ just as he promised
> through his holy prophets long ago.
> ⁷¹ Now we will be saved from our enemies
> and from all who hate us.
> ⁷² He has been merciful to our ancestors
> by remembering his sacred covenant—
> ⁷³ the covenant he swore with an oath
> to our ancestor Abraham.

---

167. **grace** - when God loves people or forgives people or saves people when they have not done anything themselves to earn it or get it
168. **prepare** - to get ready for something
169. **ability** - to be able to do something

SESSION 14: GOD SENT JOHN TO GET ISRAEL READY FOR THE RESCUER

> [74] We have been rescued from our enemies
> so we can serve God without fear,
> [75] in holiness and righteousness
> for as long as we live.
>
> [76] "And you, my little son,
> will be called the prophet of the Most High,
> because you will prepare the way for the Lord.
> [77] You will tell his people how to find salvation
> through forgiveness of their sins.
> [78] Because of God's tender mercy,
> the morning light from heaven is about to break upon us,
> [79] to give light to those who sit in darkness and in the shadow
> of death, and to guide us to the path of peace."

Zechariah said that God's promises about the Messiah were about to come true. God had made a promise to Abraham that all the families of the earth would be blessed through Abraham's family. God was going to do what he had said he would do. Zechariah said, *"Praise the Lord, the God of Israel, because he has visited and redeemed his people."* Redeemed means that someone else has paid the price for something that you owe. Zechariah said that that was what God was going to do.

Zechariah also said that when John grew up, he would tell people about their sins and how they could be forgiven[170] for them. John would get people ready for the Rescuer to come.

Zechariah said that because of God's mercy, the morning light of heaven was about to come. The light would *give light to those who sit in darkness and in the shadow of death*. Since the time that Adam and Eve had listened to the lies of Satan, darkness had ruled the earth. All the people of the earth lived in darkness away from the light of knowing God. They lived in *the shadow of death* because when they died they would go to the place of death. Now God said that his light was about to come.

So far, all through God's story he has kept trying to speak the truth to people. They could see all the things around them that he had created for them. He had spoken to them many times. He had made an agreement with them and had given them his laws. He had lived among his people, the Israelites. He had sent his prophets, and their words had been written down. But Satan had been

---

170. **forgiven** - to be made free of a debt that you owe to someone else for doing something wrong to them

HIS STORY: THE RESCUE

working against God and telling lies about him. And people had chosen to believe Satan and not to believe God.

John's work was to tell the people of Israel that God was about to come. God was going to come into the darkness. He was going to bring light and truth. He was going to show that Satan had told lies to people. And God was going to show who he really is in a way that had never happened before. He was going to come and find those people who would listen to him. He was going to tell his story to them, and to show them who he really is, in a whole new way. This thing that was going to happen soon[171] was the most important thing that had ever happened and that will ever happen.

In the northern part of the land of Israel was a town called Nazareth. A young woman called Mary lived there. She was engaged[172] to a man called Joseph. Joseph was a descendant of King David. Mary was a sinner like all people. But Mary knew she was a sinner and that she was separated from God. She knew that she needed God to save her. She was one of the Jewish people who were waiting for the Rescuer to come.

God sent an angel to talk to Mary. He told her that God had chosen her to be the mother of the Rescuer.

LUKE 1:26-33

> 26 In the sixth month of Elizabeth's pregnancy, God sent the angel Gabriel to Nazareth, a village in Galilee, 27 to a virgin named Mary. She was engaged to be married to a man named Joseph, a descendant of King David. 28 Gabriel appeared to her and said, "Greetings, favored woman! The Lord is with you!"
>
> 29 Confused and disturbed, Mary tried to think what the angel could mean. 30 "Don't be afraid, Mary," the angel told her, "for you have found favor with God! 31 You will conceive and give birth to a son, and you will name him Jesus. 32 He will be very great and will be called the Son of the Most High. The Lord God will give him the throne of his ancestor David. 33 And he will reign over Israel forever; his Kingdom will never end!"

The angel told Mary that when her son was born she should give him the name Jesus. Jesus is the English word for the name Yeshua. In the Hebrew language,

---

171. **soon** - in a short amount of time
172. **engaged** - promised to marry someone

SESSION 14: GOD SENT JOHN TO GET ISRAEL READY FOR THE RESCUER

Yeshua means 'Yahweh saves,' or 'God rescues.' The angel said that Jesus would be the *Son of the Most High*. He would be the Son of God.

Remember before that we said that God is three people in one. He is God the Father, God the Son and God the Spirit. The angel told Mary that her son would be the Son of God. God is a spirit, and does not have a body. God can be at any time or at any place he wants to be. God is the all-powerful Creator. Now the angel told Mary that God was going to be born as a human baby. Jesus would be a human baby but he would not be like any other baby before. This baby would be God. The angel also told Mary that her son would reign[173] as a king forever.

About 600 years before, God had said that these things would happen. Here is what he said through his prophet Isaiah.

ISAIAH 9:6

⁶ For a child is born to us,
a son is given to us.
The government will rest on his shoulders.
And he will be called:
Wonderful Counselor, Mighty God,
Everlasting Father, Prince of Peace.

God said that *a child is born to us, a son is given to us*. He would be called things that would show he is wonderful, wise, powerful, eternal and that he would bring peace.

Mary did not understand how she could have a baby. She had never had sex with a man. She was a virgin. The angel told her that it would be something that God would make happen.

LUKE 1:34-36

³⁴ Mary asked the angel, "But how can this happen? I am a virgin."

³⁵ The angel replied, "The Holy Spirit will come upon you, and the power of the Most High will overshadow you. So the baby to be born will be holy, and he will be called the Son of God. ³⁶ What's more, your relative Elizabeth has become pregnant in her old age! People used to say she was barren, but she has conceived a son and is now in her sixth month.

---

173. **reign** - to rule as a king

HIS STORY: THE RESCUE

God was the one who gave life to people in the beginning. He is the only one who can start life. He said he would give Mary a son. He would make the child grow inside of her and it would be born in the normal way. But her baby would not be a normal human child. He would not have a human father. He would not be a descendant of Adam, so he would not be born a sinner like all other people. He would be the perfect Son of God.

Mary listened to what the angel said. She believed that God would do everything just as the angel said he would.

One of God's storytellers at that time was called Matthew. Matthew wrote about the life of Jesus in the Book of Matthew in the Bible. He started by telling about the family of Jesus. Matthew called him *Jesus the Messiah*.

MATTHEW 1:1

¹ This is a record of the ancestors of Jesus the Messiah, a descendant of David and of Abraham

Remember that in the Hebrew language, Messiah means 'God's promised Rescuer'. So when Matthew called him Jesus the Messiah, he meant that Jesus is God's Promised One, and that he had special work to do.

Fifteen hundred years before, Moses had given the Israelites a message from God. He said that one day God would bring a prophet from among the Israelites. Remember that a prophet is someone who speaks the words of God.

DEUTERONOMY 18:15-18

¹⁵ "Moses continued, "The Lord your God will raise up for you a prophet like me from among your fellow Israelites. You must listen to him. ¹⁶ For this is what you yourselves requested of the Lord your God when you were assembled at Mount Sinai. You said, 'Don't let us hear the voice of the Lord our God anymore or see this blazing fire, for we will die.'

¹⁷ "Then the Lord said to me, 'What they have said is right. ¹⁸ I will raise up a prophet like you from among their fellow Israelites. I will put my words in his mouth, and he will tell the people everything I command him.

God said that he would put his words in the mouth of this prophet. He also said that this prophet would tell the people everything that God told him to say. Jesus is the One that God was talking about. Many years before, God said something else about the Promised One who would come. David wrote it down in one of his songs, or psalms.

PSALMS 110:4

⁴ The Lord has taken an oath and will not break his vow: "You are a priest forever in the order of Melchizedek."

Melchizedek was a special priest who lived in the time of Abraham. David said that the Promised One would also be a special priest. Remember that the work of the high priests was to bring the blood of animals to sprinkle on the lid of the Ark of the Covenant. They did this once every year. They had to do it every year, generation after generation, to cover the sins of the people. Later in God's story we will see that Jesus is God's special chosen Priest. He would make an offering that was far greater than any other priest had ever given.

About 700 years before Jesus was born, God's prophet Isaiah wrote this about him.

ISAIAH 9:7

⁷ His government and its peace
will never end.
He will rule with fairness and justice from the throne of his ancestor David for all eternity.
The passionate commitment of the Lord of Heaven's Armies will make this happen!

Isaiah said that a descendant of David's would come and rule *with fairness and justice*[174] *from the throne of his ancestor David for all eternity.* Jesus was God's chosen king to rule all of creation. He was the one that Isaiah had written about.

So Jesus, the Christ, would be chosen by God to be his Prophet, Priest and King.

We have only read here about a few of the things that Moses, David and Isaiah said about Jesus. But there are many other things written about him in the Old Testament. Many things were said about the family of Jesus, about his birth, about his life, about what kind of a person he would be and about how he would die. God does not live in time like we do. He knows what is going to happen in the future. He put those things about Jesus in his story a long time before they happened. God knows everything. And when God says that something will happen, it always does happen.

---

174. **justice** - to be fair and true

HIS STORY: THE RESCUE

1. What were some of the things that happened in the world during the 400 years after Malachi?

2. How do you think Zechariah and Elizabeth felt when they heard that the Messiah was about to come?

3. Why did Matthew call him Jesus the Messiah?

4. What are some other things that the Old Testament prophets said about Jesus, the Promised One?

SESSION 15

JESUS WAS BORN AND GREW UP. JESUS WAS BAPTIZED

Now God's story tells us about when Jesus the Messiah was born.

MATTHEW 1:18-25

18 This is how Jesus the Messiah was born. His mother, Mary, was engaged to be married to Joseph. But before the marriage took place, while she was still a virgin, she became pregnant through the power of the Holy Spirit. 19 Joseph, to whom she was engaged, was a righteous man and did not want to disgrace her publicly, so he decided to break the engagement quietly.

20 As he considered this, an angel of the Lord appeared to him in a dream. "Joseph, son of David," the angel said, "do not be afraid to take Mary as your wife. For the child within her was conceived by the Holy Spirit. 21 And she will have a son, and you are to name him Jesus, for he will save his people from their sins."

22 All of this occurred to fulfill the Lord's message through his prophet:

23 "Look! The virgin will conceive a child!
She will give birth to a son, and they will call him Immanuel, which means 'God is with us.'"

HIS STORY: THE RESCUE

> ²⁴ When Joseph woke up, he did as the angel of the Lord commanded and took Mary as his wife. ²⁵ But he did not have sexual relations with her until her son was born. And Joseph named him Jesus.

Mary was engaged to a man called Joseph. The Jewish law said that being engaged to someone meant that they had made a very strong agreement to get married. People who were engaged could not just break up easily. They would have to get divorced[175] to break their engagement. While Joseph and Mary were engaged, she lived in her family home. Later, after she and Joseph were married, Mary would move into Joseph's house.

Joseph and Mary had not had sex. But Joseph found out that Mary was pregnant.[176] So he thought that Mary had slept with[177] another man. When a Jewish woman did that, it was very, very bad. Sometimes the people would kill a woman who did that. But God's story says that Joseph was a good man and he did not want to *disgrace her publicly*. This means he did not want all the people to find out because then Mary would be very ashamed. So Joseph decided to quietly break off their engagement.

But it was part of God's plan that Joseph would marry Mary. God knew that Joseph would take care of Mary and her special child. So God sent an angel to talk to Joseph and to tell him about Mary's child. God's angel told Joseph clearly that Mary had not broken her engagement agreement. He said that Mary was pregnant because God had made it happen, not a man. The angel told Joseph that the baby boy should be called Jesus. Remember that in the Hebrew language, Jesus is *Yeshua* and it means 'Yahweh saves.' The angel said he would be called Jesus because he would save his people from their sins.

The angel also said the baby would be called *Immanuel*. This name comes from two Hebrew words for 'God' and 'with us.' So Immanuel means 'God with us'. The prophet Isaiah wrote all of this about 700 years earlier:

ISAIAH 7:14

> ¹⁴ All right then, the Lord himself will give you the sign. Look! The virgin will conceive a child! She will give birth to a son and will call him Immanuel (which means 'God is with us').

---

175. **divorce** - a legal ruling by a judge or court to break a marriage agreement
176. **pregnant** - going to have a baby
177. **slept with** - had sex with

SESSION 15: JESUS WAS BORN AND GREW UP. JESUS WAS BAPTIZED

Joseph believed that what God's angel had told him was true. So he did what the angel said to do. He married Mary but he did not have sex with her until after her baby was born. When the baby was born, he named him Jesus.

God's story, written down by Matthew, now tells us about what happened when Jesus was born. Joseph and Mary were away from their hometown of Nazareth when the time came for the baby to be born. The Romans were doing a census - getting information about all the people they ruled over. They told everyone to go to his own town to register for the census. Joseph belonged to the family line of David, so he had to go to Bethlehem, which was the town of David. So Jesus was born in the town of Bethlehem. Today, Bethlehem is a city in the West Bank area of Palestine.

MATTHEW 2:1-18

¹ Jesus was born in Bethlehem in Judea, during the reign of King Herod. About that time some wise men from eastern lands arrived in Jerusalem, asking, ² "Where is the newborn king of the Jews? We saw his star as it rose, and we have come to worship him."

³ King Herod was deeply disturbed when he heard this, as was everyone in Jerusalem. ⁴ He called a meeting of the leading priests and teachers of religious law and asked, "Where is the Messiah supposed to be born?"

⁵ "In Bethlehem in Judea," they said, "for this is what the prophet wrote:

⁶ 'And you, O Bethlehem in the land of Judah,
are not least among the ruling cities of Judah,
for a ruler will come from you
who will be the shepherd for my people Israel.'"

⁷ Then Herod called for a private meeting with the wise men, and he learned from them the time when the star first appeared. ⁸ Then he told them, "Go to Bethlehem and search carefully for the child. And when you find him, come back and tell me so that I can go and worship him, too!"

⁹ After this interview the wise men went their way. And the star they had seen in the east guided them to Bethlehem. It went ahead of them and stopped over the place where the child was. ¹⁰ When they saw the star, they were filled with joy! ¹¹ They entered the house and saw the child with his mother, Mary, and they bowed down and worshiped him. Then they opened their treasure chests and gave him gifts of gold, frankincense, and myrrh.

¹² When it was time to leave, they returned to their own country by another route, for God had warned them in a dream not to return to Herod.

¹³ After the wise men were gone, an angel of the Lord appeared to Joseph in a dream. "Get up! Flee to Egypt with the child and his mother," the angel said. "Stay there until I tell you to return, because Herod is going to search for the child to kill him."

¹⁴ That night Joseph left for Egypt with the child and Mary, his mother, 15 and they stayed there until Herod's death. This fulfilled what the Lord had spoken through the prophet: "I called my Son out of Egypt."

¹⁶ Herod was furious when he realized that the wise men had outwitted him. He sent soldiers to kill all the boys in and around Bethlehem who were two years old and under, based on the wise men's report of the star's first appearance.
¹⁷ Herod's brutal action fulfilled what God had spoken through the prophet Jeremiah:

¹⁸ "A cry was heard in Ramah—
weeping and great mourning.
Rachel weeps for her children,
refusing to be comforted,
for they are dead."

Some wise men from the east of Palestine came to Jerusalem. They were following a star that they saw in the sky where they lived. The star was a sign that the wise men knew about. They knew that this special star in the sky meant that a baby had been born who would be *King of the Jews*. So the wise men came to Jerusalem to find out about this baby.

At that time, there was a king who ruled over the Jewish lands. His name was King Herod. The Romans had made him King of the Jews. Herod heard what the wise men had said about a baby being born who would be King of the Jews. Herod thought that this baby might grow up and take over his place as the king. He got together all the Jewish religious experts.[178] These were the chief[179] priests and the scribes.[180] Herod asked them where the Messiah would be born. The religious experts told Herod about something that was written in

---

178. **Jewish religious experts** - people who know all the rules and laws of the Jews
179. **chief** - the leader
180. **scribes** - Jewish religious leaders who were experts in Jewish law and could read and write

SESSION 15: JESUS WAS BORN AND GREW UP. JESUS WAS BAPTIZED

the Old Testament. It said that a leader and shepherd of Israel would be born in Bethlehem. Herod told the wise men to go to Bethlehem to find the child. He said he wanted to worship the new king. He told them to come back and tell him when they had found the child in Bethlehem.

The wise men followed the star to the house where Jesus was. They gave gifts to him and worshiped him as the new king. God told the wise men in a dream that they should not go back to Herod. So they went home by another way.

One of God's angels told Joseph that Herod was looking for them. The angel said that Joseph should quickly go with Mary and Jesus to Egypt. They went away just in time. Herod was very angry and did not want this new king to take over. So he told his people to kill all the boys in Bethlehem who were two years old or younger. God knew this would happen. It had been written about by the prophet Jeremiah. We can be sure that Satan wanted all these boy babies to die. Satan did not want the Rescuer to come. He knew about God's plan to send a man who would destroy him and his rule over the people of the earth. Satan wanted to stop God's rescue plan.

Later, after Herod had died, God told Joseph that it was time to leave Egypt. So Joseph, Mary and Jesus went back to Israel. They went back to their hometown of Nazareth. One of the men who wrote God's story at that time was called Luke. He wrote about how God was with Jesus as he grew up in Nazareth.

LUKE 2:40

⁴⁰ There the child grew up healthy and strong. He was filled with wisdom, and God's favor was on him.

Luke also wrote about a time when Jesus was twelve years old. He went with Joseph and Mary to Jerusalem to go to the Passover festival. This was a festival that was held once each year in Jerusalem. At the Passover festival, the Jewish people remembered how God had killed the firstborn son and animal in every Egyptian house. They remembered how he had passed over the houses of the Israelites who had put blood on the doorposts of their houses.

LUKE 2:41-52

⁴¹ Every year Jesus' parents went to Jerusalem for the Passover festival. ⁴² When Jesus was twelve years old, they attended the festival as usual. ⁴³ After the celebration was over, they started home to Nazareth, but Jesus stayed behind in Jerusalem. His parents didn't miss him at first, ⁴⁴ because they assumed he was among the other travelers. But when

HIS STORY: THE RESCUE

he didn't show up that evening, they started looking for him among their relatives and friends.

⁴⁵ When they couldn't find him, they went back to Jerusalem to search for him there. ⁴⁶ Three days later they finally discovered him in the Temple, sitting among the religious teachers, listening to them and asking questions. ⁴⁷ All who heard him were amazed at his understanding and his answers.

⁴⁸ His parents didn't know what to think. "Son," his mother said to him, "why have you done this to us? Your father and I have been frantic, searching for you everywhere."

⁴⁹ "But why did you need to search?" he asked. "Didn't you know that I must be in my Father's house?" ⁵⁰ But they didn't understand what he meant.

⁵¹ Then he returned to Nazareth with them and was obedient to them. And his mother stored all these things in her heart.

⁵² Jesus grew in wisdom and in stature and in favor with God and all the people.

After the festival in Jerusalem was finished, Joseph and Mary started to go back to Nazareth. They were with a large group of other Jewish people. So they did not notice that Jesus was not with the group. At the end of the day, they saw that Jesus was not with them. So they went back to Jerusalem and found him. Jesus was sitting in the temple talking to the Jewish religious leaders. God's story says that Joseph and Mary and everyone else was *amazed at his understanding and his answers*. They were very surprised[181] because Jesus knew God's written words so well. They were amazed[182] that he knew so much when he was only a twelve-year-old boy. Jesus knew these things because he was the Son of God.

Mary asked Jesus why he had done this. Jesus asked her why they had looked for him. He said they should have known he would be in his Father's house. Jesus wanted them to remember who he really is – the Son of God. The temple was the house of God among the Jewish people. Jesus said he was in his Father's house. He was telling them that God is his Father.

Now God's story tells us more about John. Remember that God had given John the job of getting the people of Israel ready for the Messiah. Matthew wrote about the things that John said to the people.

---

181. **surprised** - to see something that you do not expect to see
182. **amazed** - to be very, very surprised about something you see

SESSION 15: JESUS WAS BORN AND GREW UP. JESUS WAS BAPTIZED

MATTHEW 3:1-6

¹ In those days John the Baptist came to the Judean wilderness and began preaching. His message was, ² "Repent of your sins and turn to God, for the Kingdom of Heaven is near." ³ The prophet Isaiah was speaking about John when he said,

"He is a voice shouting in the wilderness,
'Prepare the way for the Lord's coming!
Clear the road for him!'"

⁴ John's clothes were woven from coarse camel hair, and he wore a leather belt around his waist. For food he ate locusts and wild honey. ⁵ People from Jerusalem and from all of Judea and all over the Jordan Valley went out to see and hear John. ⁶ And when they confessed their sins, he baptized them in the Jordan River.

John lived in the wilderness in an area that is east and north of Jerusalem. He lived near the Jordan River. He dressed in clothing made from the hair of camels.[183] He ate wild honey and locusts. He spoke the word of God to the people. People from far away heard about John. Many people came to hear what John was saying. John told them to *repent*. Repent means to change your way of thinking and see yourself in the same way that God sees you. John was telling the people to stop trying to follow all of God's laws, because that was impossible. God wanted the people to see that they were sinners and that they needed him to rescue them. God wanted them to remember that they needed him to save them from having to pay for their sins. He sent John to tell the people these things.

The prophet Isaiah wrote about John. Matthew repeated the words of God that Isaiah had written many years before: *"Prepare the way for the Lord's coming! Clear the road for him!"* This message was about John and his work to get the people of Israel ready for the Rescuer to come.

God's story says that more and more people came to listen to John's message. They came from Jerusalem and from all over the Jordan Valley. Many people listened to what John said and believed it was true. They agreed that they were sinners and that they needed God to save them. After they accepted what John said, the Bible says that *he baptized them in the Jordan River*. This means that John helped them to go under the water and then come up again. They did

---

183. **camels** - large hairy animals with long necks and long legs that can live in very dry places

HIS STORY: THE RESCUE

this as a sign that they had repented. They had agreed with God that they were sinners and they were waiting for God to rescue them. They were ready and waiting for the Messiah to come.

MATTHEW 3:7-10

⁷ But when he saw many Pharisees and Sadducees coming to watch him baptize, he denounced them. "You brood of snakes!" he exclaimed. "Who warned you to flee the coming wrath?
⁸ Prove by the way you live that you have repented of your sins and turned to God. ⁹ Don't just say to each other, 'We're safe, for we are descendants of Abraham.' That means nothing, for I tell you, God can create children of Abraham from these very stones. ¹⁰ Even now the ax of God's judgment is poised, ready to sever the roots of the trees. Yes, every tree that does not produce good fruit will be chopped down and thrown into the fire.

Not everyone who came to hear John believed what he said. Matthew wrote that many Pharisees and Sadducees came to hear John. The Pharisees were religious leaders of the Jewish people. They taught the people to try to follow all the laws of God and the laws that the Jews had made up themselves. The Sadducees were the religious leaders of the Jewish temple and the priests. They thought that God would be happy with them just because they were the descendants of Abraham. The Pharisees and Sadducees had a lot of power over the people.

John knew that the Pharisees and Sadducees did not agree with God. He spoke to them and said they were like snakes who were trying to crawl away from God's anger. God knows what people are really thinking. He knew that these religious men did not really believe that they were sinners or that they needed God to rescue them. John spoke the words of God to them. He said that God would cut them down like fruit trees that did not have any fruit.

When John was baptizing people, he spoke about someone who was going to come soon.

MATTHEW 3:11,12

¹¹ "I baptize with water those who repent of their sins and turn to God. But someone is coming soon who is greater than I am—so much greater that I'm not worthy even to be his slave and carry his sandals. He will baptize you with the Holy Spirit and with fire. ¹² He is ready to separate the chaff from the wheat with his winnowing fork. Then he will clean up the

SESSION 15: JESUS WAS BORN AND GREW UP. JESUS WAS BAPTIZED

threshing area, gathering the wheat into his barn but burning the chaff with never-ending fire."

John said that he was baptizing them in the water of the Jordan River. He said that this was just to show that the people had repented - that they agreed with God that they were sinners. But John said that the Promised One would be much greater than him. The One who was coming would baptize people with the Holy Spirit and with fire. The meaning of this is made clear later in God's story.

John said that the coming One would separate the people into those who really believed that what God said was true and those who did not really believe God. He said that the Messiah would send the people who did not believe God to be burned up by a fire that never goes out. This means that those people who did not believe the things that God said would be punished forever.

MATTHEW 3:13-17

¹³ Then Jesus went from Galilee to the Jordan River to be baptized by John. ¹⁴ But John tried to talk him out of it. "I am the one who needs to be baptized by you," he said, "so why are you coming to me?"

¹⁵ But Jesus said, "It should be done, for we must carry out all that God requires." So John agreed to baptize him.

¹⁶ After his baptism, as Jesus came up out of the water, the heavens were opened and he saw the Spirit of God descending like a dove and settling on him. ¹⁷ And a voice from heaven said, "This is my dearly loved Son, who brings me great joy."

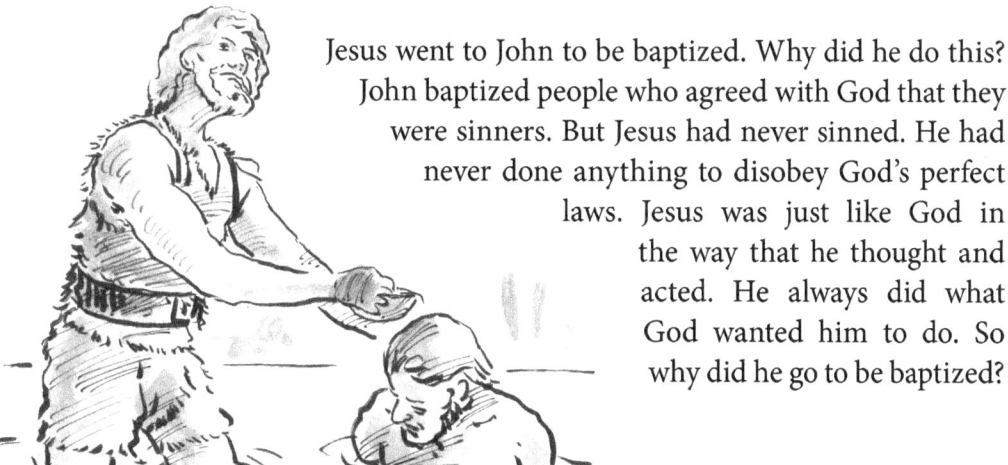

Jesus went to John to be baptized. Why did he do this? John baptized people who agreed with God that they were sinners. But Jesus had never sinned. He had never done anything to disobey God's perfect laws. Jesus was just like God in the way that he thought and acted. He always did what God wanted him to do. So why did he go to be baptized?

HIS STORY: THE RESCUE

John asked Jesus the same question. John said that Jesus was the one who should baptize him.

Jesus told John that he must be baptized because it was what God wanted. Even though Jesus did not need to repent, he wanted to do everything that God said. If he did not do this, people could say that he did not obey God in every way. So John baptized him.

Matthew wrote about what happened just after Jesus came up out of the water. God's Spirit came down like a dove[184] and landed on Jesus. This was a sign that Jesus would live his life always being close to God. He would always trust God to guide him and to take care of him. God's Spirit would give him wisdom and strength to do the work that God wanted him to do.

God the Father saw that Jesus was obeying everything that he had said. He wanted the people to know what he thought about Jesus. He said, *"This is my dearly loved Son, who brings me great joy."* God was totally happy with everything about Jesus and he loved him very much.

Another man who wrote about the life of Jesus in God's story was called John. This is a different John to the one who was baptizing people in the Jordan River. John wrote about something that happened the day after Jesus was baptized.

²⁹ The next day John saw Jesus coming toward him and said, "Look! The Lamb of God who takes away the sin of the world!

JOHN 1:29

John called Jesus *the Lamb of God who takes away the sin of the world*. For over a thousand years, the people of Israel had killed lambs in the tabernacle and in the temple. Once every year, the blood of lambs was sprinkled on the top of the Ark of the Covenant in the Most Holy Place in the Temple. God had told the people to do this to show that they agreed with him that they should die for their sins. The animals died in their place so that they did not have to die. So why did John call Jesus 'the Lamb of God'?

John was saying clearly that Jesus would be sacrificed to pay for sin. His sacrifice would not just be for the sins of the people of Israel, but it would take away the sins of the whole world.

---

184. **dove** - a bird that is a sign or symbol of peace

SESSION 15: JESUS WAS BORN AND GREW UP. JESUS WAS BAPTIZED

1. God's story says that an angel came to speak to Joseph. What are angels?
2. What do the names Jesus and Immanuel tell us about Jesus and the work he would do?
3. What does it mean when someone repents?
4. Why did Jesus want John to baptize him?
5. When John called Jesus the Lamb of God, what did he mean by that?
6. Do you think Jewish people understood what John meant by calling Jesus the 'Lamb of God'? Why or why not?

SESSION 16

JESUS STARTED HIS WORK

Matthew wrote in God's story about something that happened to Jesus.

MATTHEW 4:1-11

¹ Then Jesus was led by the Spirit into the wilderness to be tempted there by the devil. ² For forty days and forty nights he fasted and became very hungry.

³ During that time the devil came and said to him, "If you are the Son of God, tell these stones to become loaves of bread."

⁴ But Jesus told him, "No! The Scriptures say,
'People do not live by bread alone,
but by every word that comes from the mouth of God.'"

⁵ Then the devil took him to the holy city, Jerusalem, to the highest point of the Temple, ⁶ and said, "If you are the Son of God, jump off! For the Scriptures say,

'He will order his angels to protect you.
And they will hold you up with their hands
so you won't even hurt your foot on a stone.'"

⁷ Jesus responded, "The Scriptures also say, 'You must not test the Lord your God.'"

HIS STORY: THE RESCUE

> ⁸ Next the devil took him to the peak of a very high mountain and showed him all the kingdoms of the world and their glory. ⁹ "I will give it all to you," he said, "if you will kneel down and worship me."
>
> ¹⁰ "Get out of here, Satan," Jesus told him. "For the Scriptures say,
>
> 'You must worship the Lord your God
> and serve only him.'"
>
> ¹¹ Then the devil went away, and angels came and took care of Jesus.

God's Spirit was guiding Jesus. After Jesus was baptized, God's Spirit led him to go by himself into the wilderness. Jesus stayed in the wilderness for 40 days without eating any food. Jesus had a body, just like we do, so he was very, very hungry. Satan came to talk to Jesus. Matthew calls Satan *the devil*. This is just other name for Satan.

Jesus had not eaten any food for about six weeks. He was very weak and hungry, and he was alone in the wilderness. We don't know how Satan looked or if he showed himself in a body to Jesus. But God's story says that Satan started to talk with Jesus. Satan said, *"If you are the Son of God, tell these stones to become loaves of bread."* Satan knew that Jesus was very, very hungry. He wanted Jesus to think of himself and to make food for himself. He wanted Jesus to do something that God had not told him to do. Satan wanted Jesus to listen to him and not to listen to God. He was trying to trick Jesus. This was just like Satan had done with Adam and Eve. But Jesus knew what Satan was trying to do. So Jesus spoke some words that are written in God's story in the Old Testament in the Book of Deuteronomy.

DEUTERONOMY 8:3

> ³ Yes, he humbled you by letting you go hungry and then feeding you with manna, a food previously unknown to you and your ancestors. He did it to teach you that people do not live by bread alone; rather, we live by every word that comes from the mouth of the Lord.

Jesus would not use his great power to help himself. The work that God wanted him to do was for other people, not for himself. And Jesus would not be guided by God's Enemy. The words he spoke from Deuteronomy were first spoken by Moses many years before. When he spoke those words, Moses was remembering

SESSION 16: JESUS STARTED HIS WORK

how God took the Israelites into the wilderness for 40 years. At that time, God was showing the Israelites that they should trust him to take care of them. He wanted them to know that things like food are not the most important things in life. God wanted them to trust him in every way to take care of them. God is the one who gives life and he wants people to know that he can take care of them.

Then God's story says that Satan took Jesus to the highest point on the roof of the temple in Jerusalem. We don't know how he did that, but we know it is true. Satan is very powerful and he can do things like that. Then Satan spoke to Jesus again. He told Jesus to jump off the temple to see if God's angels would save him. Satan used some of God's words about Jesus that are written in Psalms.

PSALMS 91:11,12

¹¹ For he will order his angels
to protect you wherever you go.
¹² They will hold you up with their hands
so you won't even hurt your foot on a stone.

Satan wanted Jesus to jump off to see if God would save him. If Jesus had jumped off the temple it would have shown that he did not really trust God. If he had jumped, he would have been testing to see if God really loved him or not. Satan used God's words but he was trying to trick Jesus.

But Jesus did not listen to Satan. He knew that God loved him and that God would always take care of him. Jesus did not have to make God show that he cared for him. He spoke to Satan and repeated some more of Moses' words that are written in the Old Testament: *"The Scriptures also say, 'You must not test the Lord your God'."* Moses had spoken these words when the Israelites were trying to make God give them water in the wilderness. Moses and Jesus were saying that it is wrong to test God like that. It is wrong to try to make God do something that we think he should do. God always does the right thing. So people can just wait and trust him to do the right thing. And that is what Jesus did.

Now it says that Satan took Jesus up on a high mountain. They could see *all the kingdoms of the world and their glory.* Satan was showing Jesus all of the power and wealth that people had made. Since Adam and Eve had disobeyed God in the garden, Satan had become the false ruler of earth. He said to Jesus that he could give him all the power and the wealth of the earth. Satan asked Jesus to lie or kneel down on the ground and worship him, then Jesus could have all of those things.

HIS STORY: THE RESCUE

Jesus did not listen to Satan at all. He knew that God had other work for him to do. He did not choose to have all the power and wealth on the earth. He just wanted to do what God wanted him to do. He told Satan to go away. Then he spoke some more of God's words from Deuteronomy: *"Get out of here, Satan," Jesus told him. "For the Scriptures say, 'You must worship the Lord your God and serve only him.'"*

In the beginning, Satan showed that he wanted people to worship him and not to worship God. Satan tricked Adam and Eve. They listened to him and they disobeyed God. But Jesus did not listen to Satan. He thought only about the work that God wanted him to do. Jesus knew that the work that God wanted him to do would be very difficult. But he chose to do God's work anyway. Jesus showed that he would not disobey God.

Jesus was sent by God to be God's Lamb; to save people from their sins. He was going to be the Rescuer of all the people of the world. He could only do that work if he did not ever sin, if he did not ever disobey God. Only a perfect man could be God's special, chosen Prophet, Priest and King. Only a perfect man could save people from Satan, sin and death. That is why Satan was trying to get Jesus to disobey God. Satan did not want Jesus to be able to do the work that God wanted him to do.

But this is God's story and it is God's rescue plan. And God always does what he says he will do. Jesus is the Son of God and so he always does what he says he will do, too.

After Jesus told Satan to go away, he did go away. Then God's story says that God's angels came to take care of Jesus. In the fight against Satan, Jesus won. He used the true words of God and he used his faith in God to defeat Satan.

Now we will read from God's story in the Book of Mark. Mark was another man who was alive at the same time as Jesus. God chose four men to write down all the things that happened to Jesus in his life. Their words are written in the first four books of the New Testament – Matthew, Mark, Luke and John. These men were guided by God's Spirit. The things that they wrote were exactly what he wanted them to say. These four books in God's story give a very clear picture of the life and work of Jesus the Messiah.

SESSION 16: JESUS STARTED HIS WORK

MARK 1:14,15

¹⁴ Later on, after John was arrested, Jesus went into Galilee, where he preached God's Good News. ¹⁵ "The time promised by God has come at last!" he announced. "The Kingdom of God is near! Repent of your sins and believe the Good News!"

Mark wrote that John was arrested.[185] John was the one who God sent to get people ready for Jesus to come. He was the one who had baptized Jesus. God's story tells us that he was arrested because he said something against King Herod and the way Herod was living. Herod kept John in prison for a while, then, he had John killed by having his head cut off. John had done the work that God had given him to do. He told the people to repent. If they had agreed with God that they needed him to save them, John baptized them. John had done God's work of getting the people ready for the Messiah.

At this time, Jesus was about 30 years old. Mark wrote that *Jesus went into Galilee, where he preached*[186] *God's Good News.* God's good news was that Jesus was the Messiah that the Jewish people had been waiting for. Jesus went to towns and villages in the area of Galilee, which is in northern Palestine. Jesus told the people to repent, just like John had told them. Jesus wanted them to know that they could not do anything to escape[187] death for their sins. Only God could pay back the debt that they owed to him for disobeying him. Only God could make a way back to himself so that people could have a real and true relationship with him again.

Jesus said, *"The time promised by God has come at last! ... The Kingdom of God is near!"* He meant that the way to escape had arrived. Satan had ruled the earth since the beginning when people turned away from God. But now, Jesus was saying that Satan's rule would be broken. God had made many promises that a Rescuer would come. Now Jesus said that the kingdom of God was near. God wanted to have a close and real relationship with people. He wanted to be their Leader and their King. He wanted them to know him and to enjoy following him. He had a plan to rescue the people. And all of this was going to happen because Jesus had come. Jesus told the people to believe this good news from God.

---

185. **arrested** - put into prison or jail
186. **preached** - he taught people things about God
187. **escape** - to get away from something

HIS STORY: THE RESCUE

MARK 1:16-20

¹⁶ One day as Jesus was walking along the shore of the Sea of Galilee, he saw Simon and his brother Andrew throwing a net into the water, for they fished for a living. ¹⁷ Jesus called out to them, "Come, follow me, and I will show you how to fish for people!" ¹⁸ And they left their nets at once and followed him.

¹⁹ A little farther up the shore Jesus saw Zebedee's sons, James and John, in a boat repairing their nets. ²⁰ He called them at once, and they also followed him, leaving their father, Zebedee, in the boat with the hired men.

Mark wrote about how Jesus asked some men to follow him. He went up to Simon and Andrew. These men were brothers who caught fish in a big lake in Galilee. It is called the Sea of Galilee. Jesus told Simon and Andrew that he would teach them how to *fish for people*. Jesus meant he would teach them how to bring people to God, and to him, the Rescuer. They left their work on the boats and followed him.

Further along the shore were another two brothers, James and John. They were fixing their fishing nets. Jesus called them and they followed him as well. Part of the work Jesus would do for the next three years would be to teach these men. There would be some others too who would follow him like that. He wanted to have some men who knew about the work that God had given him to do.

Mark wrote about how Jesus started to show who he really was. He began to show people that he was God's Son, the promised Messiah.

MARK 1:21-39

²¹ Jesus and his companions went to the town of Capernaum. When the Sabbath day came, he went into the synagogue and began to teach. ²² The people were amazed at his teaching, for he taught with real authority—quite unlike the teachers of religious law.

²³ Suddenly, a man in the synagogue who was possessed by an evil spirit cried out, ²⁴ "Why are you interfering with us, Jesus of Nazareth? Have you come to destroy us? I know who you are—the Holy One of God!"

²⁵ But Jesus reprimanded him. "Be quiet! Come out of the man," he ordered. ²⁶ At that, the evil spirit screamed, threw the man into a convulsion, and then came out of him.

²⁷ Amazement gripped the audience, and they began to

SESSION 16: JESUS STARTED HIS WORK

discuss what had happened. "What sort of new teaching is this?" they asked excitedly. "It has such authority! Even evil spirits obey his orders!" [28] The news about Jesus spread quickly throughout the entire region of Galilee.

[29] After Jesus left the synagogue with James and John, they went to Simon and Andrew's home. [30] Now Simon's mother-in-law was sick in bed with a high fever. They told Jesus about her right away. [31] So he went to her bedside, took her by the hand, and helped her sit up. Then the fever left her, and she prepared a meal for them.

[32] That evening after sunset, many sick and demon-possessed people were brought to Jesus. [33] The whole town gathered at the door to watch. [34] So Jesus healed many people who were sick with various diseases, and he cast out many demons. But because the demons knew who he was, he did not allow them to speak.

[35] Before daybreak the next morning, Jesus got up and went out to an isolated place to pray. [36] Later Simon and the others went out to find him. [37] When they found him, they said, "Everyone is looking for you."

[38] But Jesus replied, "We must go on to other towns as well, and I will preach to them, too. That is why I came." [39] So he traveled throughout the region of Galilee, preaching in the synagogues and casting out demons.

Jesus was in Capernaum, a fishing village on the northern shore of the Sea of Galilee. This area was where Simon, Andrew, James and John lived. Jesus went to the synagogue there to teach on the Sabbath day. The synagogue was the Jewish meeting house. The Sabbath day is the Jewish day of rest. The people there were amazed at how Jesus explained[188] what Moses and the other prophets had written.

The people in the synagogue had been taught before by the scribes. The scribes were men who made copies of God's words. They were experts in the laws of the Jewish religion. They were always trying to get people to follow all of God's laws and all of the other laws that they had made up themselves. So when these people in the synagogue heard Jesus teach, it was different to how the scribes had taught. Jesus *taught with real authority*. This means that when he spoke,

---

188. **explained** - to tell about something and what it really means

HIS STORY: THE RESCUE

he was very clear and very powerful in what he said. *Authority* means that you have the right to say something. Jesus had the right to speak the words of God, because he was the Son of God.

A man who was there in the synagogue had one of Satan's evil spirits living in him. Remember how in the beginning, many angels followed Satan? Some of these angels who had followed Satan were able to live in people and make them do what Satan wanted them to do. The evil spirit living in this man called out to Jesus. The evil spirit was very afraid of Jesus. He knew who Jesus really was. He said, *"I know who You are - the Holy One of God!"* He asked Jesus if he had come to destroy them.

Jesus wanted to be the one to show people who he really was. He did not want the evil spirit to tell people about him. So Jesus told the spirit to be quiet and to leave the man. When the spirit left the man it threw him into a convulsion[189] and called out loudly. The people were even more amazed. They saw that even the evil spirits had to obey what Jesus said. God is much, much more powerful than the evil spirits. They had to do what he said.

Jesus went to many towns and villages. He spoke to groups of people and also to individuals. Jesus wanted people to see that he was really God's Son. Mark wrote about some more things that happened to Jesus.

MARK 1:40-42

⁴⁰ A man with leprosy came and knelt in front of Jesus, begging to be healed. "If you are willing, you can heal me and make me clean," he said.

⁴¹ Moved with compassion, Jesus reached out and touched him. "I am willing," he said. "Be healed!" ⁴² Instantly the leprosy disappeared, and the man was healed.

A man with a very bad skin disease came to Jesus. He asked Jesus to help him. This man probably had leprosy. Leprosy was a very a bad sickness that could easily be passed on to other people. So people with leprosy had to live outside the town and not live near healthy people. God's story says that Jesus was *moved with compassion*. That means that Jesus cared for this man very much and wanted to help him. Jesus reached out and touched the man. Jesus touched him and then he was healed. His sickness was totally gone.

---

189. convulsion - to fall on the ground and have your body shake without being able to stop it

SESSION 16: JESUS STARTED HIS WORK

Wherever Jesus went, he healed people who were sick or who had evil spirits living in them. Matthew, Mark, Luke and John wrote about the many times that Jesus healed and helped people. But the real work of Jesus was not just to heal people of the sicknesses of their bodies. The work of God that Jesus came to do was to heal people from the payment for their sin. The man with leprosy had no way to heal himself. Only God could save him. Only Jesus could heal him. This was a real example to people of how only God could rescue them.

1. What was Satan trying to get Jesus to do? Why?
2. How did Jesus defeat Satan when Satan tried to get him to disobey God?
3. Jesus healed many sick people. What was he trying to show people about himself?
4. Why did the evil spirits obey what Jesus told them to do?

169

SESSION 17

JESUS SAID THAT PEOPLE MUST BE BORN AGAIN

We will read more about God's story from what John wrote. This John is the fisherman, the brother of James, whom Jesus called to follow him. John wrote about something that happened to Jesus.

JOHN 3:1-19

¹ There was a man named Nicodemus, a Jewish religious leader who was a Pharisee. ² After dark one evening, he came to speak with Jesus. "Rabbi," he said, "we all know that God has sent you to teach us. Your miraculous signs are evidence that God is with you."

³ Jesus replied, "I tell you the truth, unless you are born again, you cannot see the Kingdom of God."

⁴ "What do you mean?" exclaimed Nicodemus. "How can an old man go back into his mother's womb and be born again?"

⁵ Jesus replied, "I assure you, no one can enter the Kingdom of God without being born of water and the Spirit. ⁶ Humans can reproduce only human life, but the Holy Spirit gives birth to spiritual life. ⁷ So don't be surprised when I say, 'You must be born again.' ⁸ The wind blows wherever it wants. Just as you can hear the wind but can't tell where it comes from or

> where it is going, so you can't explain how people are born of the Spirit."
>
> [9] "How are these things possible?" Nicodemus asked.
>
> [10] Jesus replied, "You are a respected Jewish teacher, and yet you don't understand these things? [11] I assure you, we tell you what we know and have seen, and yet you won't believe our testimony. [12] But if you don't believe me when I tell you about earthly things, how can you possibly believe if I tell you about heavenly things? [13] No one has ever gone to heaven and returned. But the Son of Man has come down from heaven. [14] And as Moses lifted up the bronze snake on a pole in the wilderness, so the Son of Man must be lifted up, [15] so that everyone who believes in him will have eternal life.
>
> [16] "For this is how God loved the world: He gave his one and only Son, so that everyone who believes in him will not perish but have eternal life. [17] God sent his Son into the world not to judge the world, but to save the world through him.
>
> [18] "There is no judgment against anyone who believes in him. But anyone who does not believe in him has already been judged for not believing in God's one and only Son. [19] And the judgment is based on this fact: God's light came into the world, but people loved the darkness more than the light, for their actions were evil.

John describes a time that Jesus talked with a man called Nicodemus. Nicodemus was a Pharisee – a Jewish religious leader. Nicodemus came to talk to Jesus one night. He probably came at night so that the other Jewish religious leaders would not see him talking to Jesus.

The Jewish leaders did not like what Jesus was teaching the people. Large groups of people were coming to hear Jesus speak. Jesus told the people that God had given him the job of making a way back to God. The Jewish leaders had been telling the people to follow all of the Jewish religious laws. They told the people that if they followed all the laws, God would be happy with them. The Jewish leaders got power over the people by telling them to follow all of the Jewish laws. They learned all of the words of all of the laws. They were experts in what the laws said. They had power over the people because they were experts in the laws.

Jesus told the people that every person was a sinner. He told them that they needed God to rescue them. The Jewish leaders thought that if people listened

SESSION 17: JESUS SAID THAT PEOPLE MUST BE BORN AGAIN

to Jesus, they would stop listening to them. They thought that Jesus would make them lose their power over the people.

The Jewish leaders told lies about Jesus. They said that Satan was helping him to make the evil spirits obey him. They went to him and asked him about God's laws. They wanted to try to get him to make a mistake and say the wrong thing. But Jesus knew all of God's words and he could answer all of their questions. The people were starting to listen to Jesus and not to listen to the Jewish leaders.

So that is probably why Nicodemus came to talk to Jesus at night. He didn't want the other Jewish religious leaders to know that he went to talk with Jesus. Nicodemus talked to Jesus and called him *Rabbi*. A Rabbi is a Jewish man who teaches people about God. Nicodemus said that Jesus had come from God and that God must be with him because of the amazing things that Jesus had done.

Jesus said that for Nicodemus to be one of God's people, and under God's rule, he had to be *born again*. But what did that mean? Nicodemus did not understand. He asked Jesus how someone could be born again.

Jesus said that the only way to escape the rule of Satan and sin and death, and to be one of God's people, you have to be born again. He said it was not being born again in your body, but in your spirit. He said that being born again was something that God's Spirit would do. Jesus talked about the Spirit of God like a strong wind. He said that the wind can go wherever it wants to go. Jesus meant that being born again is something that only God's Spirit can do for people. It does not matter if a person is a religious expert or not. It only matters what a person really thinks. God knows what people really believe. He knows if people really think that only God can rescue them.

When a person is born the first time, they are born outside the garden, like Cain and Abel. They have sin with them and in them. They cannot escape it. Everyone who has only been born once is under the rule of God's Enemy. And that is the same for Abraham's descendants, like Nicodemus.

Nicodemus still did not understand. Jesus asked him why a Jewish teacher like Nicodemus did not understand things about God. Jesus said that he understood and could speak about all things about God. Jesus came from God, and so the things he said were true.

Jesus called himself the *Son of Man*. He called himself that because he is the Son of God who had become a man. He came to earth to do the work of God, but he was also a real man. And he told Nicodemus that he would be lifted up like the

HIS STORY: THE RESCUE

bronze snake that Moses had lifted up. Remember that when the Israelites were in the desert, some poisonous snakes came, and if they bit people, they would die. God told Moses to make a bronze snake and put it on a pole. When the Israelites looked at it they would not die. Jesus said that he was going to be lifted up just like that bronze snake. Nicodemus knew God's story very well, so he would have known this story very well. But what Jesus was telling him now was new. Jesus said that the bronze snake was an example of himself and his work.

Jesus said that when he is lifted up, everyone who believes in him will have eternal[190] life. The Israelites who had been bitten by the snakes had no way to save themselves from death. That is like all the people of the world who have no way to save themselves. They have been born into the world of sin and death and they are all sinners. Their sin will mean that when they die they will not be with God, but they will be in a place of punishment and death. But Jesus said that those who believe in him would be born again into God's family and be given eternal life.

Jesus then told Nicodemus that God loves the whole world. He said that because of his love he has sent his Son as the Messiah, the Rescuer – Jesus. God did this so that no one who believes in him will have to pay for his or her sins. They will not have to die and be separated from God. Jesus said that God will save them, rescue them, and give them life forever with him.

Mark wrote about something else that happened in the life and work of Jesus, God's Son. Jesus went to many towns in the countryside of Judea. Then he went back to the town of Capernaum. He stayed in that area for the next few years with some other men who were with him.

MARK 2:1-12

¹ When Jesus returned to Capernaum several days later, the news spread quickly that he was back home. ² Soon the house where he was staying was so packed with visitors that there was no more room, even outside the door. While he was preaching God's word to them, ³ four men arrived carrying a paralyzed man on a mat. ⁴ They couldn't bring him to Jesus because of the crowd, so they dug a hole through the roof above his head. Then they lowered the man on his mat, right down in front of Jesus. ⁵ Seeing their faith, Jesus said to the paralyzed man, "My child, your sins are forgiven."

⁶ But some of the teachers of religious law who were sitting

---

190. **eternal** - something that goes on forever and does not stop

SESSION 17: JESUS SAID THAT PEOPLE MUST BE BORN AGAIN

> there thought to themselves, [7] "What is he saying? This is blasphemy! Only God can forgive sins!"
>
> [8] Jesus knew immediately what they were thinking, so he asked them, "Why do you question this in your hearts? [9] Is it easier to say to the paralyzed man 'Your sins are forgiven,' or 'Stand up, pick up your mat, and walk'? [10] So I will prove to you that the Son of Man has the authority on earth to forgive sins." Then Jesus turned to the paralyzed man and said, [11] "Stand up, pick up your mat, and go home!"
>
> [12] And the man jumped up, grabbed his mat, and walked out through the stunned onlookers. They were all amazed and praised God, exclaiming, "We've never seen anything like this before!"

The people of Capernaum had heard that Jesus was there. Many people came to the house where Jesus was. He sat and talked with them. He clearly explained the things that the prophets had written. He spoke with authority. Some Jewish religious leaders were there too. They were not happy about the things that Jesus was saying. They were not happy that many people wanted to hear what Jesus said. The house was full of people. Nobody else could come in the door because so many people were already in the house.

Some men carried a man to the house where Jesus was. This man was paralyzed. That means that he could not move or walk. The other men could not bring the paralyzed man into the house. So they took him up to the roof of the house. They made a hole in the roof and let the man down into the house through the hole. They believed that Jesus could heal the man, so they let him down through the roof. Jesus knew that the men believed that he could heal the man. They knew that Jesus was the Son of God. Jesus said to the man, *"My child, your sins are forgiven."*

The teachers of religious law in the house were very angry. They heard what Jesus had said. They knew that only God could forgive sins. Now, Jesus said that this man's sins were forgiven. These religious leaders did not believe that Jesus was God's Son. So they did not think that Jesus should say that this man's sins were forgiven.

Jesus told them that he did have the authority to forgive sins. Why? Because he is God's Son. Then Jesus told the man to get up. Jesus said that and then the man

HIS STORY: THE RESCUE

did get up. He got up and he walked out. Everyone who was there was amazed. Many of the people there thanked God for what he had done.

Later, near the lake, Jesus saw a tax collector[191] sitting near the road. His name was Levi. He was getting money from people to give to the Roman government. The Jewish people did not like men like this. They worked for the Romans and they took a lot of money from people. Jesus asked Levi to follow him.

MARK 2:13-17

> [13] Then Jesus went out to the lakeshore again and taught the crowds that were coming to him. [14] As he walked along, he saw Levi son of Alphaeus sitting at his tax collector's booth. "Follow me and be my disciple," Jesus said to him. So Levi got up and followed him.
>
> [15] Later, Levi invited Jesus and his disciples to his home as dinner guests, along with many tax collectors and other disreputable sinners. (There were many people of this kind among Jesus' followers.) [16] But when the teachers of religious law who were Pharisees saw him eating with tax collectors and other sinners, they asked his disciples, "Why does he eat with such scum?"
>
> [17] When Jesus heard this, he told them, "Healthy people don't need a doctor—sick people do. I have come to call not those who think they are righteous, but those who know they are sinners."

Levi left his work as a tax collector and he followed Jesus. Later, Levi was called Matthew. He was the man who wrote down all the things that Jesus did in his life. What he wrote is in the Book of Matthew in the Bible.

Jesus and his close followers[192] went to eat at Levi's house. There were many other people there. God's story says these people were *tax collectors and sinners*. These were people that the Jewish leaders thought were bad people. Some of them worked for the Romans and they did not follow the Jewish laws. The Jewish religious leaders, the Pharisees, saw that Jesus was eating with people like that. The Pharisees would never eat with people like that. It was against their Jewish laws to do that. They asked why Jesus would eat with bad people like that.

---

191. **tax collector** - someone who has the work of getting money for the government from people
192. **followers** - people who follow someone else; to follow means to listen to them and to be with them and to believe what they say

SESSION 17: JESUS SAID THAT PEOPLE MUST BE BORN AGAIN

Jesus said to them, *"Healthy people don't need a doctor—sick people do. I have come to call not those who think they are righteous[193], but those who know they are sinners."* He said that only people who know that they are sick would go to the doctor. And he said only people who know that they are sinners would come to him. People who think that they can follow all of God's laws would not come to him. People like that would not come because they did not think that they needed God to rescue them.

The Jewish religious leaders were hoping that Jesus would break one of their laws. Then they could say he was a bad man because he had broken God's law.

MARK 3:1-6

¹ Jesus went into the synagogue again and noticed a man with a deformed hand. ² Since it was the Sabbath, Jesus' enemies watched him closely. If he healed the man's hand, they planned to accuse him of working on the Sabbath.

³ Jesus said to the man with the deformed hand, "Come and stand in front of everyone." ⁴ Then he turned to his critics and asked, "Does the law permit good deeds on the Sabbath, or is it a day for doing evil? Is this a day to save life or to destroy it?" But they wouldn't answer him.

⁵ He looked around at them angrily and was deeply saddened by their hard hearts. Then he said to the man, "Hold out your hand." So the man held out his hand, and it was restored! ⁶ At once the Pharisees went away and met with the supporters of Herod to plot how to kill Jesus.

Mark wrote about a time that Jesus was at the synagogue on the Sabbath day. There was a man there with a paralyzed hand. The religious leaders were watching carefully. They wanted Jesus to do something to break the Jewish laws. The Jews had many laws about the Sabbath day. Their laws said that people could not do any work at all on the Sabbath day. They wanted Jesus to heal the man so that they could say that Jesus had done some work on the Sabbath day. They wanted to accuse him of breaking God's law.

Jesus knew what the religious leaders were thinking. He knew that they were hoping he would break the Jewish law. So he asked them some questions. He asked if it was the law to do good things on the Sabbath or to do bad things. They did not answer him.

---

193. **righteous** - to be right with God because you have followed all his laws

HIS STORY: THE RESCUE

God's story says that Jesus was angry and very sad about what the Jewish leaders were thinking. They did not know the real meaning of the laws that God had given them. And they had added many laws that they had made up themselves. They did not know what God is really like. They thought that they could follow all of God's laws. But that was impossible.

Jesus asked the man to put out his hand. Jesus healed the man's hand. The religious leaders saw Jesus heal the man. But they still did not believe that Jesus was God's Son. Then the Pharisees went out to talk to the followers of King Herod about how they could kill Jesus.

Mark wrote about how people from very far away started to come to see Jesus. People came from all over Palestine and from other places. They came from as far north as modern-day Lebanon. Very large numbers of people came to see Jesus. They had heard about the amazing things he had done. They wanted to be healed from their sicknesses. They wanted to hear what Jesus was saying about God.

MARK 3:7-12

⁷ Jesus went out to the lake with his disciples, and a large crowd followed him. They came from all over Galilee, Judea, ⁸ Jerusalem, Idumea, from east of the Jordan River, and even from as far north as Tyre and Sidon. The news about his miracles had spread far and wide, and vast numbers of people came to see him.

⁹ Jesus instructed his disciples to have a boat ready so the crowd would not crush him. ¹⁰ He had healed many people that day, so all the sick people eagerly pushed forward to touch him. ¹¹ And whenever those possessed by evil spirits caught sight of him, the spirits would throw them to the ground in front of him shrieking, "You are the Son of God!" ¹² But Jesus sternly commanded the spirits not to reveal who he was.

The evil spirits knew who Jesus really was. They said that Jesus was the Son of God. But Jesus did not want the evil spirits to tell the people who he really was.

Jesus had many followers. But he chose twelve men to be his very close companions.

SESSION 17: JESUS SAID THAT PEOPLE MUST BE BORN AGAIN

MARK 3:13-19

¹³ Afterward Jesus went up on a mountain and called out the ones he wanted to go with him. And they came to him. ¹⁴ Then he appointed twelve of them and called them his apostles. They were to accompany him, and he would send them out to preach, ¹⁵ giving them authority to cast out demons. ¹⁶ These are the twelve he chose:

Simon (whom he named Peter),
¹⁷ James and John (the sons of Zebedee, but Jesus nicknamed them "Sons of Thunder"),
¹⁸ Andrew,
Philip,
Bartholomew,
Matthew,
Thomas,
James (son of Alphaeus),
Thaddaeus,
Simon (the zealot),
¹⁹ Judas Iscariot (who later betrayed him).

Jesus named these twelve men *apostles*. An apostle is someone chosen by God to do special work. Jesus said these apostles would be with him. He said that they would be sent out to preach. And that they would have the authority to tell Satan's evil spirits to leave people.

Jesus had come into the world to defeat God's Enemy. He had already begun his work. But God always wants people to work with him. He wants people to fight with him against Satan and to work with him on his rescue plan. So Jesus chose these twelve apostles to work with him.

One of the twelve apostles was Judas Iscariot. Jesus is God so he knows everything that people are thinking. He knows everything that is going to happen. He knew that later Judas Iscariot would betray[194] him. But God had a rescue plan and Judas was going to be part of God's plan. So even though Jesus knew that Judas would betray him, he chose him as one of the apostles. Jesus knew that it was part of God's plan.

Mark and the other apostles went everywhere with Jesus. Mark wrote about one evening[195] when they were going over the Sea of Galilee in a boat.

---

194. **betray** - to help someone's enemies to catch or hurt them
195. **evening** - the time at the end of the day, from about 6 pm until bedtime

HIS STORY: THE RESCUE

MARK 4:35-41

35 As evening came, Jesus said to his disciples, "Let's cross to the other side of the lake." 36 So they took Jesus in the boat and started out, leaving the crowds behind (although other boats followed). 37 But soon a fierce storm came up. High waves were breaking into the boat, and it began to fill with water.

38 Jesus was sleeping at the back of the boat with his head on a cushion. The disciples woke him up, shouting, "Teacher, don't you care that we're going to drown?"

39 When Jesus woke up, he rebuked the wind and said to the waves, "Silence! Be still!" Suddenly the wind stopped, and there was a great calm. 40 Then he asked them, "Why are you afraid? Do you still have no faith?"

41 The disciples were absolutely terrified. "Who is this man?" they asked each other. "Even the wind and waves obey him!"

That day, Jesus had been teaching large groups of people. He had been teaching them all day on the shore of the lake. Late in the afternoon, Jesus told his apostles that they should go over to the other side of the lake. So Jesus and the apostles started to cross the lake in a boat. There were other boats near them too. Jesus went to the back of the boat and went to sleep.

The Sea of Galilee is a very big lake. Very bad storms[196] can happen quickly on the lake. That evening, when Jesus was on the boat, a huge storm started. The wind was very strong. Big waves were coming into the boat. The apostles were afraid that the boat would sink.[197] Some of these men were fishermen and they had been on the lake many times. They were very afraid of this storm so it must have been a very, very big storm. They woke up Jesus and said to him, *"Teacher! Don't you care that we're going to drown?"*

Jesus got up and spoke to the wind and to the sea. He told the wind and the sea to be quiet and to be still. When Jesus said that, the wind and the sea were very calm.[198] Then Jesus asked the men in the boat why they were afraid. He said, *"Do you still have no faith?"* Jesus wanted them to believe that he was really who he said he was – God's Son.

---

196. **storms** – dangerous or bad weather
197. **sink** - fill up with water and go down under the water
198. **calm** - quiet and peaceful and still

SESSION 17: JESUS SAID THAT PEOPLE MUST BE BORN AGAIN

1. What did the Pharisees think about God's laws?
2. What did Jesus mean when he said that Nicodemus must be born again?
3. Why did Jesus say he was like the bronze snake that Moses lifted up?
4. What is an 'apostle'?
5. Why did Jesus choose Judas even though he knew that Judas would betray him?

SESSION 18

JESUS SHOWED HIS GREAT POWER

The apostles saw what Jesus had done. Jesus had showed them his great power. They saw that Jesus had power over the wind and the sea. Only the Creator of the wind and the sea could have power over them. The men saw what Jesus had done and they were afraid because they saw how much power Jesus really had.

Then Mark wrote about what happened when their boat reached the other side of the lake. Jesus met a man there who had many, many evil spirits living in him. You can read in your Bible later about what happened. It is written in Mark 5:1-20. The evil spirits knew who Jesus really was. They called him *"Jesus, Son of the Most High God."* And Jesus showed that he was much more powerful than Satan and his evil followers. Jesus healed the man and told the evil spirits to get out of him. He sent them into a group of 2000 pigs. Then the pigs ran into the lake and died. The people who lived there were very afraid of Jesus when they saw what he did. They wanted him to go away. The man who Jesus had freed from the evil spirits wanted to be with Jesus. But Jesus told him to go to tell his family what God had done for him.

Jesus went back over the Sea of Galilee. John wrote about what happened next.

HIS STORY: THE RESCUE

JOHN 6:1-15

¹ After this, Jesus crossed over to the far side of the Sea of Galilee, also known as the Sea of Tiberias. ² A huge crowd kept following him wherever he went, because they saw his miraculous signs as he healed the sick. ³ Then Jesus climbed a hill and sat down with his disciples around him. ⁴ (It was nearly time for the Jewish Passover celebration.) ⁵ Jesus soon saw a huge crowd of people coming to look for him. Turning to Philip, he asked, "Where can we buy bread to feed all these people?"

⁶ He was testing Philip, for he already knew what he was going to do.

⁷ Philip replied, "Even if we worked for months, we wouldn't have enough money to feed them!"

⁸ Then Andrew, Simon Peter's brother, spoke up. ⁹ "There's a young boy here with five barley loaves and two fish. But what good is that with this huge crowd?"

¹⁰ "Tell everyone to sit down," Jesus said. So they all sat down on the grassy slopes. (The men alone numbered about 5,000.)
¹¹ Then Jesus took the loaves, gave thanks to God, and distributed them to the people. Afterward he did the same with the fish. And they all ate as much as they wanted. ¹² After everyone was full, Jesus told his disciples, "Now gather the leftovers, so that nothing is wasted." ¹³ So they picked up the pieces and filled twelve baskets with scraps left by the people who had eaten from the five barley loaves.

¹⁴ When the people saw him do this miraculous sign, they exclaimed, "Surely, he is the Prophet we have been expecting!" ¹⁵ When Jesus saw that they were ready to force him to be their king, he slipped away into the hills by himself.

Jesus saw that a huge crowd[199] of people was coming to see him. God's story says that he went up on to a mountain with his *disciples*.[200] Sometimes in the Bible, *disciples* means the twelve men Jesus had chosen. Sometimes it means other people who were following him around. It was just before the Jewish Passover festival. Remember that this was the time each year when the Jewish people remembered what God had done for them in Egypt? They remembered the time

---

199. **crowd** - a very, very large group of people
200. **disciples** - the men who were close followers of Jesus

SESSION 18: JESUS SHOWED HIS GREAT POWER

that God had saved them from death when they put blood around the doors of their houses. God had passed over the houses that had the blood on them. So each year, the Jewish people had a celebration[201] to remember the time God passed over them.

So Jesus and his disciples were sitting up on the mountain. Jesus saw a huge crowd of people coming. Philip was one of the disciples who was there with Jesus. Jesus asked Philip where they could buy food for all the people who were coming.

John wrote that Jesus already knew what was going to happen. He asked Philip about the food to *test him*. Jesus wanted the disciples to learn more about who he really is. He wanted them to know that they could ask him for help. He wanted to show them that he could take care of anything. But Philip did not remember that. He said that even a lot of money would not buy enough food for all the people. Then Andrew said there was a young boy with five small bread loaves[202] and two fish. But Andrew said that this little bit of food would not be enough to feed all of the people.

Jesus said that all the people should sit down on the grass. God's story says that there were about 5000 men there. But there were also women and children there. So it was a huge crowd of people.

Jesus thanked God his Father for the food they were going to eat. Then he took the bread loaves and *distributed them to the people*. Distributed means that he passed it out to people. Then he did the same thing with the fish. He gave people as much as they wanted to eat. After everyone had eaten all they could eat, there was still a lot of food left over. Jesus was only given a small amount of food, but he was able to keep giving out food until all the people had eaten. Jesus could do that because he is God - he could make more food where there was not enough food before.

The crowd were amazed by what Jesus had done. They said that Jesus must be God's Prophet. They wanted Jesus to be their king. Jesus knew why the people wanted him to be their king. He knew that most of the people only wanted him to give them food and to heal people who were sick. They did not want a real relationship with God. And they did not believe that Jesus had come to save them from their debt of sin before God. God had special work for Jesus to do. God had a plan and Jesus was a part of that plan. Jesus knew that being a

201. **celebration** - a time when people get together to remember something good that has happened
202. **loaves** - pieces of bread that are shaped and baked and then cut up for eating

HIS STORY: THE RESCUE

king on earth was not part of God's plan. So he went away and climbed up a mountain by himself.

John wrote about what happened that night.

JOHN 6:16-21

¹⁶ That evening Jesus' disciples went down to the shore to wait for him. ¹⁷ But as darkness fell and Jesus still hadn't come back, they got into the boat and headed across the lake toward Capernaum. ¹⁸ Soon a gale swept down upon them, and the sea grew very rough. ¹⁹ They had rowed three or four miles when suddenly they saw Jesus walking on the water toward the boat. They were terrified, ²⁰ but he called out to them, "Don't be afraid. I am here!" ²¹ Then they were eager to let him in the boat, and immediately they arrived at their destination!

After all the people had eaten, the disciples waited for Jesus on the shore. But it got dark and he still did not come. So the disciples got into a boat and went back across the lake to Capernaum. A big storm came up and *the sea grew very rough.*²⁰³ They rowed²⁰⁴ the boat for a long time to try to get across the lake.

Then they saw Jesus walking on the sea. He came near their boat and they were afraid. They were afraid because people can't walk on water, but Jesus was walking on the water. They could see how powerful he really was and they were afraid. But Jesus told them not to be afraid. They brought him in to the boat and then the boat came safely to the shore.

The next morning, the crowd from the day before came to Capernaum looking for Jesus. They asked him how he got there. They knew that he did not go in the boat with his disciples.

---

203. **rough** - the sea had a lot of waves going up and down and from side to side
204. **rowed** - pushed the boat along with paddles or oars

SESSION 18: JESUS SHOWED HIS GREAT POWER

JOHN 6:22-35

²² The next day the crowd that had stayed on the far shore saw that the disciples had taken the only boat, and they realized Jesus had not gone with them. ²³ Several boats from Tiberias landed near the place where the Lord had blessed the bread and the people had eaten. ²⁴ So when the crowd saw that neither Jesus nor his disciples were there, they got into the boats and went across to Capernaum to look for him. ²⁵ They found him on the other side of the lake and asked, "Rabbi, when did you get here?"

²⁶ Jesus replied, "I tell you the truth, you want to be with me because I fed you, not because you understood the miraculous signs. ²⁷ But don't be so concerned about perishable things like food. Spend your energy seeking the eternal life that the Son of Man can give you. For God the Father has given me the seal of his approval."

²⁸ They replied, "We want to perform God's works, too. What should we do?"

²⁹ Jesus told them, "This is the only work God wants from you: Believe in the one he has sent."

³⁰ They answered, "Show us a miraculous sign if you want us to believe in you. What can you do? ³¹ After all, our ancestors ate manna while they journeyed through the wilderness! The Scriptures say, 'Moses gave them bread from heaven to eat.'"

³² Jesus said, "I tell you the truth, Moses didn't give you bread from heaven. My Father did. And now he offers you the true bread from heaven. ³³ The true bread of God is the one who comes down from heaven and gives life to the world."

³⁴ "Sir," they said, "give us that bread every day."

³⁵ Jesus replied, "I am the bread of life. Whoever comes to me will never be hungry again. Whoever believes in me will never be thirsty.

Jesus knew why the people were looking for him. He knew it was because they wanted him to make more food for them. They wanted to see him show his power. They asked him how they could do those things too. But Jesus did not send them away. He tried to help them to understand the truth. Jesus said that they should believe in the One that God had sent. He was talking about himself.

HIS STORY: THE RESCUE

He wanted them to know that he was the Son of God and that God had sent him.

The people said that they would believe him if he made them more food to eat. They said that Moses gave their ancestors bread from heaven. This was the bread called manna that God had given the Israelites in the wilderness. Jesus told them that it was God who gave the manna, not Moses. Then Jesus said that now God wanted to give them *the true bread from heaven*. He said that the true bread from heaven was *the one who comes down from heaven and gives life to the world*. Jesus was talking about himself.

Jesus said *"I am the bread of life."* He said that any person who believed in him would never be hungry or thirsty again.

When God first created people, they had a real and close relationship with him. When people are separated from God, they feel a need to be close to God. Even if they don't understand it, people need God. He is the only one who can really take care of people and really love people. He is their Father and their Creator. When people are separated from God, it is like they are hungry and thirsty for God. If people do not eat or drink, they will be hungry and thirsty and then they will die. If people are separated from God, they will die too. So that is what Jesus was saying when he called himself the bread of life. He meant that if people believed in him they would not be hungry or thirsty for God again. He was the One that God had sent to bring life to the world.

Mark describes how one day some Pharisees and teachers of religious law came from Jerusalem to see Jesus.

MARK 7:1-7

¹ One day some Pharisees and teachers of religious law arrived from Jerusalem to see Jesus. ² They noticed that some of his disciples failed to follow the Jewish ritual of hand washing before eating. ³ (The Jews, especially the Pharisees, do not eat until they have poured water over their cupped hands, as required by their ancient traditions. ⁴ Similarly, they don't eat anything from the market until they immerse their hands in water. This is but one of many traditions they have clung to—such as their ceremonial washing of cups, pitchers, and kettles.)

⁵ So the Pharisees and teachers of religious law asked him, "Why don't your disciples follow our age-old tradition? They eat without first performing the hand-washing ceremony."

SESSION 18: JESUS SHOWED HIS GREAT POWER

> ⁶ Jesus replied, "You hypocrites! Isaiah was right when he prophesied about you, for he wrote,
>
> 'These people honor me with their lips,
> but their hearts are far from me.
> ⁷ Their worship is a farce,
> for they teach man-made ideas as commands from God.'

The Pharisees and the scribes saw that some of his disciples did not wash their hands before eating their bread. The Pharisees and religious Jews had many laws about washing. They had very strict[205] laws about washing their hands before eating any food. Mark explained these laws on washing.

So the Pharisees and religious experts from Jerusalem saw that the men who were following Jesus had disobeyed one of their Jewish laws. They asked Jesus why his disciples did not follow *our age-old tradition*. A tradition is something that people do because people have been doing that same thing for many years. The traditions that the Pharisees were talking about were laws that they had made up themselves. These were things that they made up and followed. They thought that if they did that, then God would be pleased with them.

Jesus called them *hypocrites*. 'Hypocrites' are people who say they will do something and then they don't do it. The religious Jews were trying to make God happy with them by following many laws. But they did not really want to have a relationship with God. They did not understand who God really is. They did not believe all the things that God had said. They were acting like God was just an idol. So Jesus called them hypocrites. He spoke some of the words of the prophet Isaiah. Isaiah wrote about people who say that they love God but don't really mean it.

Then Jesus spoke to the crowd of people who were there.

MARK 7:14-23

> ¹⁴ Then Jesus called to the crowd to come and hear. "All of you listen," he said, "and try to understand. ¹⁵ It's not what goes into your body that defiles you; you are defiled by what comes from your heart."
>
> ¹⁷ Then Jesus went into a house to get away from the crowd, and his disciples asked him what he meant by the parable he had just used. ¹⁸ "Don't you understand either?" he asked.

---

205. **strict** - a strong law that should not be broken or disobeyed

HIS STORY: THE RESCUE

> "Can't you see that the food you put into your body cannot defile you? [19] Food doesn't go into your heart, but only passes through the stomach and then goes into the sewer." (By saying this, he declared that every kind of food is acceptable in God's eyes.)
>
> [20] And then he added, "It is what comes from inside that defiles you. [21] For from within, out of a person's heart, come evil thoughts, sexual immorality, theft, murder, [22] adultery, greed, wickedness, deceit, lustful desires, envy, slander, pride, and foolishness. [23] All these vile things come from within; they are what defile you."

Jesus asked the crowd to come and listen to him. He talked about eating and drinking. He talked about that because the Jews had many laws about eating and drinking. They had many laws about what food they could eat, how they should cook it, who should cook it, and how they should eat it. Jesus said that food or drink could not make someone good or evil. He said that what goes into a person from outside could not defile[206] them. Jesus said that it is *what comes from inside that defiles you.*

He meant that people are sinners because of what comes out of our hearts. Jesus was telling the religious Jews that they could not escape their sin. They tried to follow very strict laws about washing and eating and drinking. But following those laws could not change who they really were inside. They were born into the world of sin and death. Jesus said that people do evil things and think evil things all the time. And they do those evil things because of who they really are inside. Jesus was trying to get the religious Jews to see who they really were. They were trying to follow God's laws and all their other laws. But Jesus said that this was not going to help them. They were evil inside. He wanted them to know that they were sinners and that they needed God to rescue them.

Luke recorded a story that Jesus had told. Jesus used stories when he was teaching people. In English, we call these stories 'parables.' A parable is a story that is told as an example of something. Jesus told this parable to some people who thought that they were righteous. These people thought that God would be happy with them because of the good things that they did. They thought that they were good and that everyone else was bad.

---

206. **defile** - to make something dirty or not acceptable to God

SESSION 18: JESUS SHOWED HIS GREAT POWER

LUKE 18:9-14

⁹ Then Jesus told this story to some who had great confidence in their own righteousness and scorned everyone else: ¹⁰ "Two men went to the Temple to pray. One was a Pharisee, and the other was a despised tax collector. ¹¹ The Pharisee stood by himself and prayed this prayer: 'I thank you, God, that I am not like other people—cheaters, sinners, adulterers. I'm certainly not like that tax collector! ¹² I fast twice a week, and I give you a tenth of my income.'

¹³ "But the tax collector stood at a distance and dared not even lift his eyes to heaven as he prayed. Instead, he beat his chest in sorrow, saying, 'O God, be merciful to me, for I am a sinner.'

¹⁴ I tell you, this sinner, not the Pharisee, returned home justified before God. For those who exalt themselves will be humbled, and those who humble themselves will be exalted."

Jesus told the parable about two men who went to the temple to pray. One was a Pharisee, and the other was a tax collector. The Pharisee stood by himself and prayed to God. He thanked God that he was not like other people. He said other people were sinners and that he was not. He saw the tax collector there, and he said to God that he was not like that tax collector who was a sinner. The tax collector stood a long way away. He was too ashamed to look up when he prayed to God. He was very, very sad because he knew that he was a sinner. He knew that he was separated from God because of his sin. He knew that only God could save him. So he asked God to save him.

At the end of his parable, Jesus said: *"I tell you, this sinner, not the Pharisee, returned home justified before God."* Jesus was explaining what God thinks about these two different kinds of people. Both of the men in the story were sinners. All people have been born into the world of sin and death and all people disobey God's perfect laws. So what was different about the two men in Jesus' story?

Jesus said that the tax collector was justified,[207] but that the Pharisee was not justified. The tax collector understood the truth about God. He knew that he could never follow God's laws even if he really tried. He was very, very sad about his sin. He knew that he was separated from God because of it. So he asked God to help him. The tax collector had a real and true relationship with God. He knew who God really is and what God really thinks. He believed that all the

---

207. **justified** - to be put into a right relationship with God again because he has paid for your sin

HIS STORY: THE RESCUE

things that God had said were true. So Jesus said that he was *justified* – that he did not have to pay for his sin with death, and that he was in a right relationship with God.

The Pharisee was a man who tried very hard to follow all of the Jewish laws. So he did not believe that he was a sinner. He did not believe that he was separated from God by his sin. He did not come to God in the way that God told people to come. He did not have a real and true relationship with God. He thought that he could follow all of God's perfect laws. But that is impossible. Jesus said that the Pharisee was not justified. He did not believe the truth about God or about himself. So he could not have a relationship with God. He would have to pay for his sins.

1. Why was Jesus able to stop the big storm on the Sea of Galilee?
2. What did Jesus mean when he asked the men in the boat, "Do you still have no faith?"
3. What was Jesus trying to show Philip when he asked him about getting food for the huge crowd of people?
4. Why did Jesus say, "I am the bread of life"?
5. In the parable that Jesus told, he said that the Pharisee was not justified. What did he mean?
6. Why was the tax collector 'justified'?

SESSION 19

JESUS IS THE ONLY DOOR TO ETERNAL LIFE

Mark wrote that Jesus and his disciples left Galilee. They went north to the area around Caesarea Philippi. This was a town at the base of Mount Hermon. As they were walking, Jesus asked them a question.

MARK 8:27-30

²⁷ Jesus and his disciples left Galilee and went up to the villages near Caesarea Philippi. As they were walking along, he asked them, "Who do people say I am?"

²⁸ "Well," they replied, "some say John the Baptist, some say Elijah, and others say you are one of the other prophets."

²⁹ Then he asked them, "But who do you say I am?"

Peter replied, "You are the Messiah."

³⁰ But Jesus warned them not to tell anyone about him.

Jesus already knew the answer to his question. He asked the question so that his disciples would think about who he really is.

The disciples told Jesus that some people had said that he was *John the Baptist*. This was the one who had baptized people in the Jordan River and that King

HIS STORY: THE RESCUE

Herod had killed. These people thought that John had come back to life after Herod had killed him. Other people had said that Jesus was Elijah. Elijah was an Old Testament prophet. The disciples said that some other people had said that Jesus was another prophet. Jesus had clearly said that he was God's Son. He had shown people his great power by the many amazing things he had done. But still, many people did not believe that Jesus was God's Son.

Then Jesus asked his disciples, *"But who do you say I am?"* Jesus was asking the disciples if they believed what he had said about himself. Jesus had told them that he was the One that God had sent. They had also seen all the amazing things he had done.

So Jesus asked who they thought he was. Peter said *"You are the Messiah."* Before, Peter's name was Simon. He was one of the fishermen that Jesus had asked to follow him. But Jesus said now his name would be Peter. Peter said that Jesus was the Messiah. Remember that *Messiah* means the Chosen One from God, the One that God had promised long ago? Messiah means the Prophet, the great High Priest and the eternal King from the family of David. Peter was just a fisherman from Capernaum. But he had been with Jesus for some time now. He had seen the life of Jesus every day. He had heard Jesus explain things about God. He had seen the amazing things that Jesus had done. So Peter and the other disciples knew who Jesus really was. They knew that he was the Messiah. But the Jews had been waiting for the Messiah to come to be a great king on earth. They did not understand the real work that God had given Jesus, the Messiah, to do.

Jesus told them not to tell anyone about him. He didn't want people to follow him just because they wanted a new king on earth. He didn't come to do the work of a king on earth. He wanted people to know who he really was - the Lamb of God. Then Jesus started to tell his disciples what would happen to him.

MARK 8:31-33

³¹ Then Jesus began to tell them that the Son of Man must suffer many terrible things and be rejected by the elders, the leading priests, and the teachers of religious law. He would be killed, but three days later he would rise from the dead. ³² As he talked about this openly with his disciples, Peter took him aside and began to reprimand him for saying such things.

³³ Jesus turned around and looked at his disciples, then reprimanded Peter. "Get away from me, Satan!" he said. "You are seeing things merely from a human point of view, not from God's."

SESSION 19: JESUS IS THE ONLY DOOR TO ETERNAL LIFE

Jesus called himself the Son of Man. Remember how he used that name for himself because he is the Son of God who came as a real man? Jesus told them clearly that he would suffer many things. He said that the Jewish religious leaders would reject[208] him and then kill him. He said that they would kill him but three days later he would rise from the dead. Jesus meant that he would come to life again after three days.

Peter took Jesus aside and started to reprimand[209] him. Peter was telling Jesus not to say the things he was saying. He knew that Jesus was the Messiah but he did not know what that meant. Jesus was telling them what it really meant. They thought the Messiah would be a great king on earth. But Jesus was telling them that he would have to suffer and die.

When Peter told Jesus not to say those things, Jesus reprimanded Peter. He said, *"Get away from me, Satan! ... You are seeing things merely from a human point of view, not from God's."*

Jesus spoke very strongly to Peter. He did that because Peter was saying things that Satan wants people to believe. Satan wants people to think that they are not separated from God. Satan wants them to think that somehow everything will be OK. Satan doesn't want people to know that they have been born into a world of sin and death.

The only way to get back to a real relationship with God is if there is a payment of death for sin. This is the only true and real way that people can come to God. People must know that they are separated from God by their sin. And they have to believe that only God can help them. That is the truth about the way that things really are. But Satan wants people to think that they can come to God without any payment for sin. That's not how things really are in God's true rescue story. It isn't true. People must to come to God in a real way, and understand how things really are. God loves people and wants to save them from death. But they have to come to him in the way he made for them to come; there is no other way.

That is why Jesus spoke strongly to Peter. Jesus had come to earth to do the work of God. That work would mean that he would suffer and die. So Jesus would not listen to any other way of doing things. He did not want to be a great king on

---

208. **reject** - to not listen to someone, to not like or love someone, to not agree with someone or to say that what someone says is wrong
209. **reprimand** - to tell someone to stop what they are doing

earth with many followers. He just wanted to do the work that God had given him to do.

MARK 8:34-9:1

34 Then, calling the crowd to join his disciples, he said, "If any of you wants to be my follower, you must give up your own way, take up your cross, and follow me. 35 If you try to hang on to your life, you will lose it. But if you give up your life for my sake and for the sake of the Good News, you will save it. 36 And what do you benefit if you gain the whole world but lose your own soul? 37 Is anything worth more than your soul? 38 If anyone is ashamed of me and my message in these adulterous and sinful days, the Son of Man will be ashamed of that person when he returns in the glory of his Father with the holy angels."

9:1 Jesus went on to say, "I tell you the truth, some standing here right now will not die before they see the Kingdom of God arrive in great power!"

Jesus called over a crowd of people to listen to him speak. He wanted to tell them what it really means to be one of his followers. He said that people who followed him would have to give up many things. They would have to stop doing what they wanted in their lives. They would have to believe what he said about himself. They would have to decide to follow him. Jesus said, *"if you give up your life for my sake and for the sake of the Good News, you will save it."* He meant that if people believed what Jesus said about himself and followed him, their lives would be saved.

Mark wrote about something that happened six days later.

MARK 9:2-10

2 Six days later Jesus took Peter, James, and John, and led them up a high mountain to be alone. As the men watched, Jesus' appearance was transformed, 3 and his clothes became dazzling white, far whiter than any earthly bleach could ever make them. 4 Then Elijah and Moses appeared and began talking with Jesus.

5 Peter exclaimed, "Rabbi, it's wonderful for us to be here! Let's make three shelters as memorials—one for you, one for Moses, and one for Elijah." 6 He said this because he didn't really know what else to say, for they were all terrified.

7 Then a cloud overshadowed them, and a voice from the

SESSION 19: JESUS IS THE ONLY DOOR TO ETERNAL LIFE

> cloud said, "This is my dearly loved Son. Listen to him." ⁸ Suddenly, when they looked around, Moses and Elijah were gone, and they saw only Jesus with them.
>
> ⁹ As they went back down the mountain, he told them not to tell anyone what they had seen until the Son of Man had risen from the dead. ¹⁰ So they kept it to themselves, but they often asked each other what he meant by "rising from the dead."

Jesus asked Peter, James and John to walk with him up a high mountain. God's story doesn't say which mountain this was. But some people say it was Mount Tabor in Galilee. While they were there on the mountain, Jesus *was transformed.*²¹⁰ His clothes became very, very white and were dazzling.²¹¹ Then, Peter, James and John saw Moses and Elijah talking with Jesus.

The disciples were terrified. Peter was amazed and afraid. He did not know what to say. So he said that they should build three tabernacles on the mountain. He thought that people could come to worship Jesus, Moses and Elijah in that place. Right then, a cloud came over them. A voice came out of the cloud and said *"This is my dearly loved Son. Listen to him."* When they looked again, only Jesus was there. On their way down the mountain, Jesus told them not to tell anyone about what had happened. He said they should wait until after he had risen from the dead.

Peter, James and John had seen who Jesus really was. Before, he had just looked like a man to them. But they had seen that he was also the Son of God living in a human body. And God had spoken to them from the cloud. God the Father had said that Jesus was his Son and that they should listen to him. They did not tell anyone what happened, just like Jesus had said. God's story says that they talked about what *rising from the dead* meant. They did not understand.

Jesus wanted people to understand who he really was. He wanted them to know what work God had for him to do. He used many examples to try to help people to understand these things. John wrote about one example Jesus used.

JOHN 10:7-11

> ⁷ So he explained it to them: "I tell you the truth, I am the gate for the sheep. ⁸ All who came before me were thieves and robbers. But the true sheep did not listen to them. ⁹ Yes, I am the gate. Those who come in through me will be saved. They

---

210. **transformed** - to change very much
211. **dazzling** - so bright that it is hard to look at

> will come and go freely and will find good pastures. ¹⁰ The thief's purpose is to steal and kill and destroy. My purpose is to give them a rich and satisfying life.
>
> ¹¹ "I am the good shepherd. The good shepherd sacrifices his life for the sheep.

Jesus said, *"I am the gate for the sheep."* The people there knew what he was talking about. They had many sheep in their area. So they knew how sheep were looked after. The shepherds would take their sheep out to graze. Sometimes they took them far away from the towns and villages. At night, the shepherd would put the sheep inside an area with a stone fence around it. A good shepherd would not leave the sheep alone at night. He would stay there with them. He would sleep in the doorway of the stone fence. He would do this so that the sheep could not get out and thieves[212] could not get in. The sheep would be safe inside at night.

So the people there knew what a good shepherd was. They knew what Jesus was talking about when he said he was *the gate of the sheep*. But Jesus wasn't talking about real sheep. He was talking about people. He was saying that people are like sheep. They need a shepherd to take care of them. And Jesus said that if people *"come in through me"*, they would be saved. Jesus was saying that he is the way to come to God. He said that anyone who came to God in that way – through him – would be saved. God would take care of them and they would be safe from God's Enemy. Jesus said, *"My purpose is to give them a rich and satisfying life. I am the good shepherd. The good shepherd sacrifices his life for the sheep."*

Jesus also said that he would *sacrifice his life for the sheep*. He meant that he would die to rescue people. Jesus was saying that he loves people so much that he would die for them.

A little later, John wrote about something else that Jesus said about himself.

> ⁶ Jesus told him, "I am the way, the truth, and the life. No one can come to the Father except through me.

JOHN 14:6

---

212. **thieves** - people who take things that belong to other people

SESSION 19: JESUS IS THE ONLY DOOR TO ETERNAL LIFE

When he said this, Jesus was speaking to his disciples. Jesus said that he is *the way* that people can come to God. He said that there was no other way to come to God except through him.

Jesus also said that he is *the truth*. Jesus is God's Son and he came to earth as a man to do the work that God wanted him to do. That is the truth. God always speaks the truth and Jesus always spoke the truth. Jesus always lived in a true way. He said he was the truth. People must understand who Jesus really was so they can understand the truth about God and everything else. If they don't know who Jesus was they cannot understand the truth.

Jesus also said that he is *the life*. Jesus meant that real life can only happen because of him. People are alive for a short time on earth. Then they die and will be separated from God forever because of their sin. But God wants people to live forever with him. God wants people to have real life – eternal life. Jesus said that he is the life because he would be the only way for people to come to God and have a real, eternal life with God.

1. Why did Jesus ask his disciples, "Who do you say that I am?"
2. Why did Jesus reprimand Peter?
3. What did Jesus really mean when he said, "I am the gate for the sheep"?
4. What did Jesus mean when he said, "I am the way, the truth and the life"?

SESSION 20

JESUS BROUGHT A MAN BACK TO LIFE

John wrote about something amazing that happened in a village called Bethany. This village was very close to Jerusalem in Judea. It was on the Mount of Olives which is right next to Jerusalem. Two sisters and their brother lived there. Their names were Mary, Martha and Lazarus. Luke wrote about Mary and Martha before in God's story. They were close friends and followers of Jesus and so was their brother, Lazarus.

At that time, the Jewish leaders wanted Jesus to stop teaching. They wanted to find him and kill him. Many people were following Jesus, and the Jewish leaders wanted that to stop.

JOHN 11:1-16

¹ A man named Lazarus was sick. He lived in Bethany with his sisters, Mary and Martha. ² This is the Mary who later poured the expensive perfume on the Lord's feet and wiped them with her hair. Her brother, Lazarus, was sick. ³ So the two sisters sent a message to Jesus telling him, "Lord, your dear friend is very sick."

⁴ But when Jesus heard about it he said, "Lazarus's sickness will not end in death. No, it happened for the glory of God so

HIS STORY: THE RESCUE

that the Son of God will receive glory from this." ⁵ So although Jesus loved Martha, Mary, and Lazarus, ⁶ he stayed where he was for the next two days. ⁷ Finally, he said to his disciples, "Let's go back to Judea."

⁸ But his disciples objected. "Rabbi," they said, "only a few days ago the people in Judea were trying to stone you. Are you going there again?"

⁹ Jesus replied, "There are twelve hours of daylight every day. During the day people can walk safely. They can see because they have the light of this world. 10 But at night there is danger of stumbling because they have no light." 11 Then he said, "Our friend Lazarus has fallen asleep, but now I will go and wake him up."

¹² The disciples said, "Lord, if he is sleeping, he will soon get better!" ¹³ They thought Jesus meant Lazarus was simply sleeping, but Jesus meant Lazarus had died.

¹⁴ So he told them plainly, "Lazarus is dead. ¹⁵ And for your sakes, I'm glad I wasn't there, for now you will really believe. Come, let's go see him."

¹⁶ Thomas, nicknamed the Twin, said to his fellow disciples, "Let's go, too—and die with Jesus."

Mary and Martha sent a message to Jesus. They told him that their brother was sick. Jesus is God, so he knew what would happen. He said that this sickness happened *"for the glory of God so that the Son of God will receive glory from this."* To give someone *glory* means that you see something amazing that they have done and you praise them for it. Jesus said that he would *receive glory*[213] through this sickness.

Jesus was in another place at that time. He got the message from Mary and Martha that Lazarus was sick. But then he stayed for two more days in the place where he was. After two days, he said to his disciples, *"Let's go back to Judea."* But the disciples did not want to go to Judea. Judea was a province[214] in Israel where the city of Jerusalem was. Jerusalem was where many Jewish religious leaders were. They wanted to arrest and kill Jesus. The disciples said to Jesus that if he returned to Jerusalem, the Jews might try to kill him.

---

213. **glory** - for people to see who Jesus really was and to praise and worship him for it
214. **province** - an area at that time that had a Roman governor

SESSION 20: JESUS BROUGHT A MAN BACK TO LIFE

Jesus said he wanted to go and *wake* Lazarus up. The disciples thought that Jesus meant that Lazarus was just asleep. So they said that it was good for Lazarus to sleep so he could get well. But Jesus told them clearly that Lazarus was dead. He said that he was glad he wasn't there. He knew what was going to happen. Jesus knew that when the disciples saw what he would do, that they would believe he was the One sent from God.

One of the disciples called Thomas said, *"Let's go too - and die with Jesus."* Thomas wanted them all to go with Jesus. But he thought that the Jews would kill them all. So Jesus and the disciples went to Bethany.

JOHN 11:17-32

¹⁷ When Jesus arrived at Bethany, he was told that Lazarus had already been in his grave for four days. ¹⁸ Bethany was only a few miles down the road from Jerusalem, ¹⁹ and many of the people had come to console Martha and Mary in their loss.

²⁰ When Martha got word that Jesus was coming, she went to meet him. But Mary stayed in the house. ²¹ Martha said to Jesus, "Lord, if only you had been here, my brother would not have died. ²² But even now I know that God will give you whatever you ask."

²³ Jesus told her, "Your brother will rise again."

²⁴ "Yes," Martha said, "he will rise when everyone else rises, at the last day."

²⁵ Jesus told her, "I am the resurrection and the life. Anyone who believes in me will live, even after dying. ²⁶ Everyone who lives in me and believes in me will never ever die. Do you believe this, Martha?"

²⁷ "Yes, Lord," she told him. "I have always believed you are the Messiah, the Son of God, the one who has come into the world from God." ²⁸ Then she returned to Mary. She called Mary aside from the mourners and told her, "The Teacher is here and wants to see you." ²⁹ So Mary immediately went to him.

³⁰ Jesus had stayed outside the village, at the place where Martha met him. ³¹ When the people who were at the house consoling Mary saw her leave so hastily, they assumed she was going to Lazarus's grave to weep. So they followed her there.

HIS STORY: THE RESCUE

> ³² When Mary arrived and saw Jesus, she fell at his feet and said, "Lord, if only you had been here, my brother would not have died."

Jesus and the disciples arrived in Bethany. But when they got there, Lazarus had already been put in a tomb.²¹⁵ His body had been in the tomb for four days. There were a lot of people there. Bethany was very close to Jerusalem, so many Jews were there too.

Martha went out of the house to meet Jesus. She said that if Jesus had been there before, Lazarus would not have died. But then she said that Jesus could ask God to help and that God would help. Jesus told Martha that her brother would *rise again*. Jesus meant that he would bring Lazarus back to life. But Martha thought Jesus was talking about a time far in the future. She said, *"he will rise when everyone else rises, at the last day."* Martha knew that God's story described the end of time when all people that have died will rise again. God will judge them at that time. But that is not what Jesus was talking about.

Jesus said to Martha *"I am the resurrection²¹⁶ and the life. Anyone who believes in me will live, even after dying."* Jesus was saying that he was the One who brings people back to life. He said that anyone who believed in him would never die. Martha said that she believed that Jesus was the Messiah, the Son of God, the One who was sent to the world by God.

Martha went into the house to get Mary. She told Mary that Jesus wanted to see her. Mary went to where Jesus was. The Jews who were there followed Mary. Mary was crying and she said, *"Lord, if only you had been here, my brother would not have died."* Mary thought that it was too late, even for Jesus, to save her brother.

JOHN 11:33-37

> ³³ When Jesus saw her weeping and saw the other people wailing with her, a deep anger welled up within him, and he was deeply troubled. ³⁴ "Where have you put him?" he asked them.
>
> They told him, "Lord, come and see." ³⁵ Then Jesus wept.
> ³⁶ The people who were standing nearby said, "See how much he loved him!" ³⁷ But some said, "This man healed a blind man. Couldn't he have kept Lazarus from dying?"

---

215. **tomb** - a stone room where dead bodies are kept; a big stone is put at the door to close it
216. **resurrection** - to come to life again after being dead

SESSION 20: JESUS BROUGHT A MAN BACK TO LIFE

Jesus saw Mary crying and he saw the Jews crying. He was angry and very sad. Jesus was sad because God does not want people to die. God made people in the beginning to have a real relationship with him forever. Jesus was angry because many people there did not believe that he could save Lazarus from death. Jesus asked where they had put the body of Lazarus.

JOHN 11:38-44

38 Jesus was still angry as he arrived at the tomb, a cave with a stone rolled across its entrance. 39 "Roll the stone aside," Jesus told them.

But Martha, the dead man's sister, protested, "Lord, he has been dead for four days. The smell will be terrible."

40 Jesus responded, "Didn't I tell you that you would see God's glory if you believe?" 41 So they rolled the stone aside. Then Jesus looked up to heaven and said, "Father, thank you for hearing me. 42 You always hear me, but I said it out loud for the sake of all these people standing here, so that they will believe you sent me." 43 Then Jesus shouted, "Lazarus, come out!" 44 And the dead man came out, his hands and feet bound in graveclothes, his face wrapped in a headcloth. Jesus told them, "Unwrap him and let him go!"

Jesus arrived at the tomb. It was in a cave[217] with a stone over the door. Jesus told them to move the stone away. Martha said that the body had already been there for four days and so it would smell terrible. Jesus told her to remember something that he had told her before. He said that if she believed, she would see the glory of God. He meant that she would see God do something amazing. And when she saw what God had done, she would worship God.

They took the stone away from the cave. Then Jesus spoke to God, his Father. He thanked his Father for listening to him. He said that so the crowd could hear him. He wanted the people to know that God had sent him. Then he shouted[218] in a loud voice, *"Lazarus, come out!"* After Jesus called out, Lazarus came out of the tomb. Lazarus was wrapped[219] up in cloth.[220] When the Jews put a dead body in a tomb, they wrapped it in cloth first. Jesus told them to take the cloth off Lazarus and let him go.

---

217. **cave** - a room inside a stone area under the ground or next to a cliff
218. **shouted** - he called out in a loud voice
219. **wrapped** - to put material or cloth all over and around something
220. **cloth** - material or fabric that clothes are made out of

HIS STORY: THE RESCUE

Lazarus had been dead and Jesus had brought Lazarus back to life. He showed the people who he really was. Before, Jesus said he is the *life* and that he is the *resurrection*. He is the one who brings people back to life from death.

John wrote about what happened next. Many Jews who were there saw what Jesus had done. Many of them believed that God had sent Jesus. But other people went to tell the Jewish religious leaders about it.

JOHN 11:45-54

⁴⁵ Many of the people who were with Mary believed in Jesus when they saw this happen. ⁴⁶ But some went to the Pharisees and told them what Jesus had done. ⁴⁷ Then the leading priests and Pharisees called the high council together. "What are we going to do?" they asked each other. "This man certainly performs many miraculous signs. ⁴⁸ If we allow him to go on like this, soon everyone will believe in him. Then the Roman army will come and destroy both our Temple and our nation."

⁴⁹ Caiaphas, who was high priest at that time, said, "You don't know what you're talking about! ⁵⁰ You don't realize that it's better for you that one man should die for the people than for the whole nation to be destroyed."

⁵¹ He did not say this on his own; as high priest at that time he was led to prophesy that Jesus would die for the entire nation. ⁵² And not only for that nation, but to bring together and unite all the children of God scattered around the world.

⁵³ So from that time on, the Jewish leaders began to plot Jesus' death. ⁵⁴ As a result, Jesus stopped his public ministry among the people and left Jerusalem. He went to a place near the wilderness, to the village of Ephraim, and stayed there with his disciples.

The leaders of the priests and the Pharisees met together. When they met together, their group was called the high council. This was the highest court

SESSION 20: JESUS BROUGHT A MAN BACK TO LIFE

of the Jews, where important things were talked about. They were very worried about Jesus. They thought that everyone would believe in him. They did not want that to happen. They thought that people would make Jesus the King of the Jews. The Romans already had a king. So the Jewish leaders thought that the Romans would get angry and take away all their freedom. They decided that Jesus should die. If Jesus were dead, then the Romans would not destroy the Jewish nation.

Jesus knew what the Jewish leaders were saying about him. He knew that they planned to kill him. So he left the area of Jerusalem. He knew that it was not yet time for him to die.

Instead, Jesus traveled to a different area to teach the people there. We can read in God's story about some of the things that Jesus taught. Mark wrote about one day when some people brought their children to Jesus.

MARK 10:13-16

> ¹³ One day some parents brought their children to Jesus so he could touch and bless them. But the disciples scolded the parents for bothering him.
>
> ¹⁴ When Jesus saw what was happening, he was angry with his disciples. He said to them, "Let the children come to me. Don't stop them! For the Kingdom of God belongs to those who are like these children. ¹⁵ I tell you the truth, anyone who doesn't receive the Kingdom of God like a child will never enter it."
>
> ¹⁶ Then he took the children in his arms and placed his hands on their heads and blessed them.

At that time, people brought their children to religious teachers. They wanted these men to put their hands on the children's heads. They wanted them to ask God to help their children. So that is why some people brought their children to Jesus. They thought of him as a Rabbi or Jewish religious teacher. They wanted him to ask God to help their children.

The disciples of Jesus did not want the people to bring their children to Jesus. They thought he had more important things to do. The disciples told the people to take their children away. But Jesus reprimanded his disciples. He said they should let the little children come to him. He used the children as an example. He said that people should come to God just like little children. He said that if

HIS STORY: THE RESCUE

they did not come to God that way, then they could not come at all. But what did he mean?

Jesus meant that people should love and trust God because he is their Father. They should have faith in God, just like a little child has faith in his father and mother. They should listen to what God says and trust him to take care of them. A little child knows that they need someone to take care of them. So Jesus was saying that people should love and trust God just like that. God is the one who made people. So God has authority over people's lives. God loves people and they can trust him to take care of them. God wants a very close relationship with people, just like a Father has with his child.

Mark wrote that Jesus took each child in his arms. Then he put his hand on their head and blessed[221] each one.

Soon after, Jesus was leaving to go to Jerusalem. A man ran up to speak to him. He knelt[222] down in front of Jesus and said, *"Good Teacher, what must I do to inherit[223] eternal life?"*

MARK 10:17-24

17 As Jesus was starting out on his way to Jerusalem, a man came running up to him, knelt down, and asked, "Good Teacher, what must I do to inherit eternal life?"

18 "Why do you call me good?" Jesus asked. "Only God is truly good. 19 But to answer your question, you know the commandments: 'You must not murder. You must not commit adultery. You must not steal. You must not testify falsely. You must not cheat anyone. Honor your father and mother.'"

20 "Teacher," the man replied, "I've obeyed all these commandments since I was young."

21 Looking at the man, Jesus felt genuine love for him. "There is still one thing you haven't done," he told him. "Go and sell all your possessions and give the money to the poor, and you will have treasure in heaven. Then come, follow me."

22 At this the man's face fell, and he went away sad, for he had many possessions.

23 Jesus looked around and said to his disciples, "How hard it is for the rich to enter the Kingdom of God!" 24 This amazed

---
221. **blessed** - he asked God to take care of them
222. **knelt** - went down on his knees
223. **inherit** - to get money, property or something from someone else after they die

SESSION 20: JESUS BROUGHT A MAN BACK TO LIFE

them. But Jesus said again, "Dear children, it is very hard to enter the Kingdom of God.

Jesus asked the man, *"Why do you call me good? Only God is truly good."*

Jesus knew what this man was thinking. God always knows everything that people are thinking. This man was a rich man. He was also a man who tried to follow all of God's laws. Jesus wanted the man to know that people cannot follow all of God's laws. He wanted this man to understand the truth about himself and about God.

The man thought that Jesus was just a religious teacher. He didn't know that Jesus was the Son of God. So when the man called Jesus *"Good Teacher"* he was saying that he thought that people can be good. But Jesus told him that only God is good. He meant that only God is perfect and that people are never perfect. Jesus talked about some of God's laws – about not killing anyone, not committing adultery, not stealing, not lying, and showing honor to your father and mother. God gave those laws to show people that they can't be perfect all the time. It is impossible to follow God's perfect laws. Jesus wanted this man to understand that.

But the man said to Jesus that he had always obeyed all of God's laws. Jesus loved this man. He wanted him to understand that it is impossible for a person to be perfect. Only God is perfect. So Jesus told the man that he should give all his money and things to poor[224] people. Then Jesus said that the man should follow him. The man was a rich man, and he did not want to give away all his things. The man went away very sad.

Jesus had told the man to give away all his things. He wanted the man to see that he had not followed all of God's laws. He was a rich man and other people were poor. So he had not cared for other people as much as he had cared for himself. He had disobeyed one of God's laws.

A little bit later, Mark wrote about another time that Jesus talked about God's laws. Jesus was answering a question from some religious experts. Jesus talked about which are the most important of God's laws.

MARK 12:30,31

[30] And you must love the Lord your God with all your heart, all your soul, all your mind, and all your strength.' [31] The second is equally important: 'Love your neighbor as yourself.' No other commandment is greater than these."

---
224. **poor** - not having very much money to live

HIS STORY: THE RESCUE

The man thought that by following all of God's laws he could save himself. Jesus wanted him to see that wasn't possible. So he told him to do something that he knew the man would find hard to do. He wanted the man to know that God's laws are perfect and that people cannot follow them. The man could not do anything to save himself. Only God is perfect. The man needed to understand that he needed God to save him.

After the man left, Jesus said something to his disciples. He said it was very hard for rich people to enter the kingdom of God. Jesus meant that many rich people feel very happy with themselves. They have money and they have power. They can decide what they want to do. They tell other people what to do. It is very hard for people like that to come to God like little children. To *enter the Kingdom of God* means to understand that God is the one who takes care of you. He is the one who has authority over you. He is the only one who can rescue you. Jesus said that it is hard for rich people to understand that they need God to save them and to take care of them.

1. Why did the Jewish religious leaders want to kill Jesus?
2. Did Mary and Martha understand who Jesus really was?
3. What lesson did Jesus teach about when he was with the little children?
4. Why did Jesus say that it is hard for rich people to enter the kingdom of God?

SESSION 21

JESUS CAME INTO JERUSALEM AND WAS ARRESTED BY HIS ENEMIES

Now God's story tells us about some things that happened to Jesus. Jesus and his disciples were on their way to Jerusalem. Mark wrote about what happened. Jesus was doing the work of God. Because Jesus was God, he knew everything that was going to happen. Everything that was going to happen to Jesus was part of God's rescue plan.

MARK 11:1-10

¹ As Jesus and his disciples approached Jerusalem, they came to the towns of Bethphage and Bethany on the Mount of Olives. Jesus sent two of them on ahead. ² "Go into that village over there," he told them. "As soon as you enter it, you will see a young donkey tied there that no one has ever ridden. Untie it and bring it here. ³ If anyone asks, 'What are you doing?' just say, 'The Lord needs it and will return it soon.'"

⁴ The two disciples left and found the colt standing in the street, tied outside the front door. ⁵ As they were untying it, some bystanders demanded, "What are you doing, untying that colt?" ⁶ They said what Jesus had told them to say, and they were permitted to take it. ⁷ Then they brought the colt to

HIS STORY: THE RESCUE

Jesus and threw their garments over it, and he sat on it.

⁸ Many in the crowd spread their garments on the road ahead of him, and others spread leafy branches they had cut in the fields. ⁹ Jesus was in the center of the procession, and the people all around him were shouting,

"Praise God!
Blessings on the one who comes in the name of the Lord!
¹⁰ Blessings on the coming Kingdom of our ancestor David!
Praise God in highest heaven!"

Jesus and the disciples came close to Jerusalem. When they were near the Mount of Olives, Jesus sent two of his disciples to get a young donkey.²²⁵ Jesus said they would find it tied up in a village just ahead. The disciples went to find the donkey and it was there, just like Jesus said it would be. They brought it back to him, and he sat on it. Then Jesus rode the donkey into Jerusalem.

Many people had seen the amazing things that Jesus had done. So they came to see him. They thought that he was the promised Messiah. They thought that he would rule as King of the Jews. They *spread their garments*²²⁶ *on the road ahead of him* and also some branches from the trees. This was to show that they thought Jesus was a king. They shouted out to him and thanked God for sending their king.

Many years earlier, God's prophet Zechariah had written that this would happen. He said that the King would ride into Jerusalem on a young donkey.

ZECHARIAH 9:9

⁹ Rejoice, O people of Zion!
Shout in triumph, O people of Jerusalem!
Look, your king is coming to you.
He is righteous and victorious,
yet he is humble, riding on a donkey—
riding on a donkey's colt.

The Jewish religious leaders were very worried. They did not want people to follow Jesus. They wanted to arrest and kill him while he was in Jerusalem. But it was Passover. There were crowds of people in Jerusalem. The religious leaders

---

225. **donkey** - an animal that looks like a horse, but with long ears; it is used for riding and for carrying things
226. **garments** - coats and robes - outer clothing

SESSION 21: JESUS CAME INTO JERUSALEM AND WAS ARRESTED BY HIS ENEMIES

thought that the crowds would get angry if they arrested Jesus. So they decided to wait until after the time of the Passover celebration.

¹ It was now two days before Passover and the Festival of Unleavened Bread. The leading priests and the teachers of religious law were still looking for an opportunity to capture Jesus secretly and kill him. ² "But not during the Passover celebration," they agreed, "or the people may riot."

Judas Iscariot was there in Jerusalem too. He was the disciple that Jesus said would betray him.

¹⁰ Then Judas Iscariot, one of the twelve disciples, went to the leading priests to arrange to betray Jesus to them.

Judas went to the Jewish religious leaders. He said that he could get Jesus for them. He could tell them when and where it would be easy for them to arrest Jesus. They were very happy that Judas wanted to help them. They agreed to pay Judas in silver money. Matthew wrote that the money was 30 silver coins. Many years before, King David wrote about the Messiah. He said that a close friend would betray him.

⁹ Even my best friend, the one I trusted completely, the one who shared my food, has turned against me.

Jesus and the disciples were in Jerusalem. They needed to find a place to eat the Passover meal together. A lamb had to be killed and then they would eat it together. The disciples asked Jesus where they could eat together.

¹² On the first day of the Festival of Unleavened Bread, when the Passover lamb is sacrificed, Jesus' disciples asked him, "Where do you want us to go to prepare the Passover meal for you?"

¹³ So Jesus sent two of them into Jerusalem with these instructions: "As you go into the city, a man carrying a pitcher of water will meet you. Follow him. ¹⁴ At the house he enters, say to the owner, 'The Teacher asks: Where is the guest room where I can eat the Passover meal with my disciples?' ¹⁵ He will take you upstairs to a large room that is already set up. That

HIS STORY: THE RESCUE

is where you should prepare our meal." [16] So the two disciples went into the city and found everything just as Jesus had said, and they prepared the Passover meal there.

[17] In the evening Jesus arrived with the Twelve. [18] As they were at the table eating, Jesus said, "I tell you the truth, one of you eating with me here will betray me."

[19] Greatly distressed, each one asked in turn, "Am I the one?"

[20] He replied, "It is one of you twelve who is eating from this bowl with me. [21] For the Son of Man must die, as the Scriptures declared long ago. But how terrible it will be for the one who betrays him. It would be far better for that man if he had never been born!"

[22] As they were eating, Jesus took some bread and blessed it. Then he broke it in pieces and gave it to the disciples, saying, "Take it, for this is my body."

[23] And he took a cup of wine and gave thanks to God for it. He gave it to them, and they all drank from it. [24] And he said to them, "This is my blood, which confirms the covenant between God and his people. It is poured out as a sacrifice for many. [25] I tell you the truth, I will not drink wine again until the day I drink it new in the Kingdom of God."

[26] Then they sang a hymn and went out to the Mount of Olives.

Jesus told his disciples to go into the city. He told them to find a man who was carrying a water pitcher.[227] He told them to follow that man. They went into the city and found a man with a pitcher of water and they followed him. The man showed them a room that was ready. It happened just like Jesus said it would. So the disciples went to the room and got everything ready for the Passover meal.

In the evening, Jesus and the other disciples were in the room. They started to eat the Passover meal together. While they were eating, Jesus said something to them. He said that one of them who was there eating with him would betray him. The disciples heard what Jesus said and they were very distressed.[228] They all began to ask Jesus if they were the one who would betray him.

Jesus told the disciples that it was one of them who would betray him. But he said, *"For the Son of Man must die, as the Scriptures declared long ago."* Jesus

---

227. **pitcher** - a large container for water
228. **distressed** - they were very upset and worried

SESSION 21: JESUS CAME INTO JERUSALEM AND WAS ARRESTED BY HIS ENEMIES

knew that it was close to the time that he would die. He knew that he would have to die. God always does what he says he will do. It had been written about in God's story and Jesus knew it would happen. But he said something about the man who would betray him. He said it would be better for that man if he had never been born. Jesus knew that it was Judas who was going to betray him.

Jesus picked up some bread that was there as part of the Passover meal. Jesus blessed it. That means he spoke to God his Father and thanked him for it. Then Jesus broke the bread into pieces. He gave the pieces to his disciples. Then he said to them, *"Take it, for this is my body."* Jesus was saying that his body would be broken just like the bread had been broken.

Then Jesus picked up a cup of wine from the table. He thanked God for it. Then he passed it to his disciples so they could drink some of it. He said that the wine was his blood that *confirms the covenant*[229] *between God and his people.* Jesus said that his blood would be poured out for many people. Jesus was talking about the work that God had left for him to do. His body would be broken and his blood would be poured out. That would happen to establish the covenant. The covenant was the agreement that God made with the Israelites when they said that they could follow all of God's laws. Jesus was saying that he would die so that the agreement between God and all people would be made right.

Jesus and the disciples sang songs of praise to God. Then they went out to the Mount of Olives, which was very close to Jerusalem.

Mark wrote about what happened next. Jesus and the disciples went to an area known as Gat-Shemanim. That name means 'oil press' in the Hebrew language. In English, we call it *Gethsemane*. It was a quiet area outside the city where olive trees grew.

MARK 14:32-52

> 32 They went to the olive grove called Gethsemane, and Jesus said, "Sit here while I go and pray." 33 He took Peter, James, and John with him, and he became deeply troubled and distressed. 34 He told them, "My soul is crushed with grief to the point of death. Stay here and keep watch with me."

---

229. covenant - an agreement between two people or groups of people

HIS STORY: THE RESCUE

35 He went on a little farther and fell to the ground. He prayed that, if it were possible, the awful hour awaiting him might pass him by. 36 "Abba, Father," he cried out, "everything is possible for you. Please take this cup of suffering away from me. Yet I want your will to be done, not mine."

37 Then he returned and found the disciples asleep. He said to Peter, "Simon, are you asleep? Couldn't you watch with me even one hour? 38 Keep watch and pray, so that you will not give in to temptation. For the spirit is willing, but the body is weak."

39 Then Jesus left them again and prayed the same prayer as before. 40 When he returned to them again, he found them sleeping, for they couldn't keep their eyes open. And they didn't know what to say.

41 When he returned to them the third time, he said, "Go ahead and sleep. Have your rest. But no—the time has come. The Son of Man is betrayed into the hands of sinners. 42 Up, let's be going. Look, my betrayer is here!"

43 And immediately, even as Jesus said this, Judas, one of the twelve disciples, arrived with a crowd of men armed with swords and clubs. They had been sent by the leading priests, the teachers of religious law, and the elders. 44 The traitor, Judas, had given them a prearranged signal: "You will know which one to arrest when I greet him with a kiss. Then you can take him away under guard." 45 As soon as they arrived, Judas walked up to Jesus. "Rabbi!" he exclaimed, and gave him the kiss.

46 Then the others grabbed Jesus and arrested him. 47 But one of the men with Jesus pulled out his sword and struck the high priest's slave, slashing off his ear.

48 Jesus asked them, "Am I some dangerous revolutionary, that you come with swords and clubs to arrest me? 49 Why didn't you arrest me in the Temple? I was there among you teaching every day. But these things are happening to fulfill what the Scriptures say about me."

50 Then all his disciples deserted him and ran away. 51 One young man following behind was clothed only in a long linen shirt. When the mob tried to grab him, 52 he slipped out of his shirt and ran away naked.

SESSION 21: JESUS CAME INTO JERUSALEM AND WAS ARRESTED BY HIS ENEMIES

Jesus knew that the time when he would die was near. He went to the quiet area of Gethsemane to talk to God. He took his disciples with him. Jesus told them to sit down while he went to pray. Then he asked Peter, James and John to join him while he prayed.

Jesus talked to Peter, James and John. He told them *"My soul is crushed with grief to the point of death."* Jesus knew that he was going to die soon. He knew how he would die and he knew everything that would happen. He knew that he was the Lamb of God who would pay for the sins of the whole world. God the Father would have to punish him for the sins of the whole world. Knowing this was very, very hard for Jesus. Jesus said that it was so hard for him to think about that he felt like he would die. He asked Peter, James and John to stay there and to stay awake.[230] Then he went a little way away from them. He fell down with his face to the ground.

Jesus spoke to his Father. He said, *"Abba, Father, everything is possible for you. Please take this cup of suffering away from me. Yet I want your will to be done, not mine."* Jesus is the Son of God. He knew that God could save him from having to die. At first, he asked God to take away the suffering he would have to go through. He used the example of having to drink something from a cup. And he asked God to take the cup away from him. He was talking about all the terrible things he would have to go through. But Jesus also knew about God's rescue plan for all people. So he said to his Father that he would do what God wanted him to do. He knew it would be a terrible time for him. But he wanted to do the work that God had for him to do. He knew that God understood how hard it was for him.

Jesus told the disciples to stay awake, but they fell asleep. Jesus went to speak to them three times. Each time he went over to them, they were asleep. The third time he went to them, he told them to wake up. He said that the man who would betray him was near.

Judas had come. He had a group of men with him. These men worked for the Jewish religious leaders. They had *swords and clubs.*[231] Judas had told these men that he would show them which man was Jesus. He said that Jesus would be the man that he kissed. To kiss someone on the cheek was a common greeting[232] at that time. So Judas walked up to Jesus and said *"Rabbi."* Then he kissed Jesus.

---

230. **awake** - not sleeping
231. **club** - a heavy piece of wood for hitting people
232. **greeting** - something that you do when you meet someone

HIS STORY: THE RESCUE

The men with Judas saw which man he had kissed. So now they knew who Jesus was. They arrested Jesus and held on to him. One of the men standing there took out his sword. He cut off the ear of the slave of the high priest. When Luke wrote about this, he said that Jesus healed the slave's ear. Then Jesus asked why the men needed swords to come and arrest him. He said that they could have arrested him when he was in the temple. He knew that they wanted to arrest him in a quiet place. They didn't want a lot of people to see what they were doing. Jesus said, *"But these things are happening to fulfill what the Scriptures say about me."* He meant that God's story had told that this would happen. So it would happen.

All the disciples ran away into the darkness. Jesus was left alone with the people who wanted to kill him.

Peter ran away with the other disciples. But he followed the men who took Jesus. They took Jesus to the house of the high priest in Jerusalem. Peter stayed outside the house. Peter was in the courtyard[233] of the house.

MARK 14:53-65

53 They took Jesus to the high priest's home where the leading priests, the elders, and the teachers of religious law had gathered. 54 Meanwhile, Peter followed him at a distance and went right into the high priest's courtyard. There he sat with the guards, warming himself by the fire.

55 Inside, the leading priests and the entire high council were trying to find evidence against Jesus, so they could put him to death. But they couldn't find any. 56 Many false witnesses spoke against him, but they contradicted each other. 57 Finally, some men stood up and gave this false testimony: 58 "We heard him say, 'I will destroy this Temple made with human hands, and in three days I will build another, made without human hands.'"
59 But even then they didn't get their stories straight!

60 Then the high priest stood up before the others and asked Jesus, "Well, aren't you going to answer these charges? What do you have to say for yourself?" 61 But Jesus was silent and made no reply. Then the high priest asked him, "Are you the Messiah, the Son of the Blessed One?"

62 Jesus said, "I am. And you will see the Son of Man seated in the place of power at God's right hand and coming on the clouds of heaven."

---

233. courtyard - an area outside a large house that has walls around it but no roof

SESSION 21: JESUS CAME INTO JERUSALEM AND WAS ARRESTED BY HIS ENEMIES

> ⁶³ Then the high priest tore his clothing to show his horror and said, "Why do we need other witnesses? ⁶⁴ You have all heard his blasphemy. What is your verdict?"
>
> "Guilty!" they all cried. "He deserves to die!"
>
> ⁶⁵ Then some of them began to spit at him, and they blindfolded him and beat him with their fists. "Prophesy to us," they jeered. And the guards slapped him as they took him away.

Inside the house, the Jewish religious leaders were meeting together. They were trying to find someone to give testimony²³⁴ against Jesus. That meant that they wanted someone to give evidence²³⁵ against him. They wanted to find someone who would say that Jesus had done something that was against the law. Then they could kill him.

God's story says that they could not find any evidence against Jesus. Many people came to speak against him, but what one person said did not agree with what another person said. So the chief priest spoke to Jesus. He asked Jesus if he had any answer to the things that people were saying about him. But Jesus kept silent²³⁶ and he did not answer.

Many years before, David wrote about the Messiah. He talked about the false witnesses²³⁷ who would speak against him.

PSALMS 27:12

> ¹² Do not let me fall into their hands.
> For they accuse me of things I've never done;
> with every breath they threaten me with violence.

Then the high priest asked Jesus, *"Are you the Messiah, the Son of the Blessed One?"* He was asking Jesus if he was the Messiah, the Son of God. Jesus answered, *"I am,"* and he said that one day they would see him sitting in a place of power and authority beside God. The high priest said that this was *blasphemy*. Blasphemy is when a person says something untrue about God. They thought that what Jesus said was not true. God's law says that people must not blaspheme against God. So the high priest asked all the Jewish religious leaders what should happen to Jesus. They all said that Jesus should die for saying things that were blasphemy.

---

234. **give testimony** - to speak in a court of law about something that you say is true
235. **evidence** - someone to say that Jesus had done something very wrong so that they could kill him
236. **silent** - quiet, not making any noise, not speaking
237. **false witnesses** - people who say they have seen something when they have not seen it

HIS STORY: THE RESCUE

Then some of them spat on Jesus. They put a blindfold[238] on him. They hit him and said that he should *prophecy*. Prophecy means to speak the words of God. They were making a joke about Jesus. They did not really believe that he was the Son of God or that he could prophecy.

God's prophet Isaiah wrote many years before that this would happen to the Messiah.

ISAIAH 50:6

⁶ I offered my back to those who beat me
and my cheeks to those who pulled out my beard.
I did not hide my face
from mockery and spitting.

The Romans were the people who ran the government[239] at that time. So they were the only ones who could kill criminals.[240] The Jewish leaders had to ask the Romans to kill Jesus. The next morning, they took Jesus to Pilate. Pilate was the Roman governor.[241]

MARK 15:1-20

¹ Very early in the morning the leading priests, the elders, and the teachers of religious law—the entire high council—met to discuss their next step. They bound Jesus, led him away, and took him to Pilate, the Roman governor.

² Pilate asked Jesus, "Are you the king of the Jews?"

Jesus replied, "You have said it."

³ Then the leading priests kept accusing him of many crimes, ⁴ and Pilate asked him, "Aren't you going to answer them? What about all these charges they are bringing against you?" ⁵ But Jesus said nothing, much to Pilate's surprise.

⁶ Now it was the governor's custom each year during the Passover celebration to release one prisoner—anyone the people requested. ⁷ One of the prisoners at that time was Barabbas, a revolutionary who had committed murder in an uprising. ⁸ The crowd went to Pilate and asked him to release a prisoner as usual.

⁹ "Would you like me to release to you this 'King of the Jews'?" Pilate asked. ¹⁰ (For he realized by now that the leading

---

238. **blindfold** - a piece of cloth tied over someone's eyes so they can't see
239. **government** - the group of people with the authority to run a country or state
240. **criminals** - people who have broken the law
241. **governor** - the leader of the government in an area

SESSION 21: JESUS CAME INTO JERUSALEM AND WAS ARRESTED BY HIS ENEMIES

priests had arrested Jesus out of envy.) ¹¹ But at this point the leading priests stirred up the crowd to demand the release of Barabbas instead of Jesus. ¹² Pilate asked them, "Then what should I do with this man you call the king of the Jews?"

¹³ They shouted back, "Crucify him!"

¹⁴ "Why?" Pilate demanded. "What crime has he committed?"

But the mob roared even louder, "Crucify him!"

¹⁵ So to pacify the crowd, Pilate released Barabbas to them. He ordered Jesus flogged with a lead-tipped whip, then turned him over to the Roman soldiers to be crucified.

¹⁶ The soldiers took Jesus into the courtyard of the governor's headquarters (called the Praetorium) and called out the entire regiment. ¹⁷ They dressed him in a purple robe, and they wove thorn branches into a crown and put it on his head. ¹⁸ Then they saluted him and taunted, "Hail! King of the Jews!" ¹⁹ And they struck him on the head with a reed stick, spit on him, and dropped to their knees in mock worship. ²⁰ When they were finally tired of mocking him, they took off the purple robe and put his own clothes on him again. Then they led him away to be crucified.

Pilate asked Jesus, *"Are you the king of the Jews?"* Jesus answered, *"You have said it."* Jesus was saying that he was the King of the Jews. He said that because he is the true King of God's people. Jesus knew that many people did not know who he really was. And he knew that many people did not understand about the Messiah. They thought that the Messiah would be a great king for the Jewish nation. But Jesus knew that his work would be different.

The chief priests accused²⁴² him of many things. Pilate was amazed that Jesus did not answer the people who were accusing him. God's prophet Isaiah had written about this many years earlier.

ISAIAH 53:7

⁷ He was oppressed and treated harshly,
yet he never said a word.
He was led like a lamb to the slaughter.
And as a sheep is silent before the shearers,
he did not open his mouth.

---

242. **accused** - to accuse someone means to say that they have done something bad

HIS STORY: THE RESCUE

Isaiah said that the Messiah would be *oppressed and treated harshly*. That means that he would suffer and other people would hurt him. But he would be silent. Isaiah used the example of a lamb going to be killed and of a sheep going to have its wool cut. Lambs and sheep are quiet and don't make any noise at those times.

God's story says that Pilate knew that Jesus had not done anything wrong. Pilate knew that the Jewish religious leaders wanted to kill Jesus. He knew that it was because of *envy*. Envy is when you want something that someone else has. Some people wanted Jesus as their leader. So the Jewish leaders were worried that Jesus would take away the power that they had over the people.

Each year at the time of Passover, the Roman governor would release[243] one prisoner.[244] So the crowd came up and asked Pilate to release someone. Pilate asked them if they wanted him to release the King of the Jews. Pilate did not believe that Jesus was really the king. He said that because that is who Jesus said he was.

Just a few days before, the people had seen Jesus ride into Jerusalem. They thought he was the Messiah. They thought he would become a great ruler . But now he had been arrested. So now many people did not think he could be the Messiah. They thought the Messiah would be very powerful. They thought that the Messiah would come to rule as a king, not to be arrested. The chief priests and the crowd asked Pilate to release another prisoner. The one they wanted to release was a criminal called Barabbas.

Then Pilate asked the crowd, *"Then what should I do with this man you call the king of the Jews?"* The crowd shouted that Jesus should be crucified. The Romans at that time killed people by crucifying them. They made a cross out of large pieces of wood. Then they stood the cross up. They put nails through the hands and the feet of the person they wanted to kill. Then they would leave the person on the cross until they died. Sometimes the person would live for many days before they died. They killed very bad criminals and their enemies in this way. They crucified people in places where many people could walk by and see them.

About seven hundred years before, God's prophet Isaiah wrote about the Messiah. He said that people would despise and reject him. That means that they would hate him and turn away from him.

---

243. **release** - let him go free
244. **prisoner** - a person who is locked up in prison or in jail

SESSION 21: JESUS CAME INTO JERUSALEM AND WAS ARRESTED BY HIS ENEMIES

ISAIAH 53:3

³ He was despised and rejected—
a man of sorrows, acquainted with deepest grief.
We turned our backs on him and looked the other way.
He was despised, and we did not care.

Pilate wanted to keep the crowd happy. He wanted the Jewish religious leaders to be happy with him too. So he released Barabbas. Then he said that Jesus should be flogged.[245] After that, Pilate gave Jesus to the Roman soldiers[246] to be crucified.

The Roman soldiers took him to their meeting place. They called all the soldiers together and they mocked him. Mocked means to make cruel jokes. They joked because he had said that he was the King of the Jews. They put a purple robe, or cloak, on him. Purple is the color that kings wear. Then they made a crown out of branches with thorns.[247] They put the crown of thorns on his head. They bowed down before him and said *"Hail! King of the Jews!"* They hit him and spat on him. Then they took Jesus, the Son of God, away to be crucified.

1. When Jesus rode into Jerusalem, who did the crowd think that he was?
2. What did people think that the Messiah had come to do?
3. When Jesus was talking to his Father in Gethsemane, what did he say? Why did he say that?
4. Could Jesus have saved himself if he had wanted to?

---

245. **flogged** - to beat someone with a whip or stick
246. **soldiers** - men who are in the army
247. **thorns** - spikes on a plant or tree

SESSION 22

JESUS WAS CRUCIFIED, BURIED AND RAISED FROM THE DEAD

The Roman soldiers took Jesus through Jerusalem. They made Jesus carry the heavy wooden cross that they would nail him to. They started to walk to where the crucifixion would take place. Jesus had been beaten very badly so he would have been very weak. It would have been very hard for him to carry the cross.

MARK 15:21

²¹ A passerby named Simon, who was from Cyrene, was coming in from the countryside just then, and the soldiers forced him to carry Jesus' cross. (Simon was the father of Alexander and Rufus.)

The soldiers saw a man passing by. His name was Simon. He was from Cyrene, which is in modern-day Libya. The soldiers asked Simon to carry the cross for Jesus, and so Simon carried the cross. By now, a large crowd was following them. Some of the people were Jesus' family and friends. They did not have to go too far to reach the place. It was just outside the city walls.

MARK 15:22,23

²² And they brought Jesus to a place called Golgotha (which means "Place of the Skull"). ²³ They offered him wine drugged with myrrh, but he refused it.

225

HIS STORY: THE RESCUE

The place was called Golgotha. It means 'place of the skull' in the Aramaic language. Some people say it was a hill that looked like a skull.[248] Sometimes, English Bibles use the name Calvary for that place. The Romans crucified people in that place because it was near the city. Many people walked past there. The Romans wanted many people to see what happened to people who broke their laws.

When they arrived, some people tried to give Jesus a drink. It was *wine drugged with myrrh*. Myrrh was nice smelling gum that came from a tree. When people drank it, they felt less pain. The women in Jerusalem made it to help people who were going to be crucified. But Jesus did not want to drink it.

MARK 15:24,25

²⁴ Then the soldiers nailed him to the cross. They divided his clothes and threw dice to decide who would get each piece. ²⁵ It was nine o'clock in the morning when they crucified him.

At 9 o'clock in the morning, the Roman soldiers crucified Jesus. First, they took off all of his clothes. God's story says that they were throwing dice to see who would get each bit of his clothing. Then they crucified Jesus by hammering[249] long metal spikes through his hands and feet. They left him hanging on the wooden cross.

David had written about this many years before in one of his Psalms about the Messiah. David was the King of Israel but also a prophet who wrote down the words of God. God knew everything that would happen to his Son.

PSALMS 22:16-18

¹⁶ My enemies surround me like a pack of dogs;
an evil gang closes in on me.
They have pierced my hands and feet.
¹⁷ I can count all my bones.
My enemies stare at me and gloat.
¹⁸ They divide my garments among themselves
and throw dice for my clothing.

When the Romans crucified criminals, they would put a sign up near them. The sign said what law the criminal had broken. Then everyone could see why that person was being crucified. But Jesus was not a criminal. He had not broken any law. So the sign that the Romans put near Jesus said *The King of the Jews*. It said

---

248. **skull** - the big bone inside the head
249. **hammering** - to hit something with a hammer; a hammer is a tool for putting nails in things

SESSION 22: JESUS WAS CRUCIFIED, BURIED AND RAISED FROM THE DEAD

that because that was who Jesus said he was. That was the charge[250] that the Jews had brought against Jesus. They did not believe that he was the King of the Jews. They had seen all the amazing things he had done, but they still did not believe he was who he said he was.

> [26] A sign announced the charge against him. It read, "The King of the Jews."
> MARK 15:26

Jesus was hanging on the cross. Everyone in that area could see him. This was just what Jesus had said would happen. Remember when Jesus was talking to the Pharisee, Nicodemus? Jesus said that he would be lifted up just like Moses had lifted up the bronze snake. When the Israelites looked at that bronze snake, they would not die from the bites of the poisonous snakes. Now Jesus was hanging high on a cross. That was what he meant when he told Nicodemus that he would be *lifted up*.

> [27] Two revolutionaries were crucified with him, one on his right and one on his left.
> MARK 15:27

On either side of Jesus was a man who had also been crucified. One of them started to scoff[251] at Jesus.

> [39] One of the criminals hanging beside him scoffed, "So you're the Messiah, are you? Prove it by saving yourself—and us, too, while you're at it!"
> LUKE 23:39-43
>
> [40] But the other criminal protested, "Don't you fear God even when you have been sentenced to die? [41] We deserve to die for our crimes, but this man hasn't done anything wrong." [42] Then he said, "Jesus, remember me when you come into your Kingdom."
>
> [43] And Jesus replied, "I assure you, today you will be with me in paradise."

---
250. **charge** - in a law court, a charge is the thing people say someone has done to break the law
251. **scoff** - to call out bad things about someone to show that you do not respect or like them

HIS STORY: THE RESCUE

These two men were criminals. They had broken the law and so they were being crucified. One of them did not believe that Jesus was the Son of God. He said that if Jesus was really the Messiah then he should save himself and save them too. But the other criminal reprimanded him. He said that it was right that they were being punished. They had broken the law. But he said that Jesus had not done anything wrong. Then he spoke to Jesus. He said, *"remember me when you come into your Kingdom"*. This man did believe that Jesus was the Messiah. He knew that Jesus was the rightful king. Jesus knew that this man believed that he was the Son of God. This man also knew that he was a sinner. He knew that only God could save him. So Jesus told him that later that day, he would be with Jesus in paradise.[252] After that man had died, he would go to be with Jesus in heaven.

God's prophet, Isaiah, had written some things about Jesus many years before. He wrote that Jesus would be *counted among the rebels*. That means that he would be grouped with people who were criminals.

ISAIAH 53:12

¹² I will give him the honors of a victorious soldier,
because he exposed himself to death.
He was counted among the rebels.
He bore the sins of many and interceded for rebels.

Mark wrote about the people passing by on the road where Jesus was hanging on the cross. Many people were mocking[253] Jesus. Mark described what some of the Jewish religious leaders called out to Jesus.

MARK 15:31,32

³¹ The leading priests and teachers of religious law also mocked Jesus. "He saved others," they scoffed, "but he can't save himself! ³² Let this Messiah, this King of Israel, come down from the cross so we can see it and believe him!" Even the men who were crucified with Jesus ridiculed him.

They called out to Jesus that he should save himself and come down from the cross. They did not believe that Jesus was the Messiah. They *ridiculed* him. They were joking about how he said that he was the King of the Jews. They said he should save himself just like he saved other people. Jesus could have saved himself. He was the Son of God and so he could do anything. But he did not

---

252. **paradise** - another name for heaven
253. **mocking** - making fun of someone or something in a cruel or bad way

SESSION 22: JESUS WAS CRUCIFIED, BURIED AND RAISED FROM THE DEAD

save himself. And God loves his Son in every way. God could have saved his Son. But God did not save him.

Jesus was nailed to the cross at nine in the morning. At noon, in the middle of the day, Jesus was still hanging on the cross.

³³ At noon, darkness fell across the whole land until three o'clock.

MARK 15:33

Mark wrote that from 12 noon until 3 pm, *darkness fell across the whole land.* God made it dark at that time. He did that to show what was happening to Jesus. God had turned away from his Son.

Many thousands of years before, Adam and Eve had turned away from God. Ever since then, people had been born into the world of sin and death. They were separated from God. People could not just come to God in the way that they wanted to come. That would not be a true way to do things because people were separated from God. So after Adam and Eve, all people were born and grew old and then their bodies died. After their bodies died, they were separated from God forever. Each person who was born after Adam and Eve was like this.

Only the people who came to God in the way that he said – by killing animals – could come to him. People had to kill animals to show that they knew what the truth was. They were showing that they knew that they were sinners, separated from God. They knew that they should die for their sins. So they had to kill animals to show that they knew that only God could save them. But they sinned over and over again. And so they had to kill animals over and over again. The blood of the animals did not pay for their sin. It was just a sign that they knew the truth about their real relationship with God. God wanted them to know that there had to be death as the payment for sin. God knew that in the future, there would be a final payment for sin.

God is perfect. He always does what is right. He always does things that are real and true. That is who God is. He never does things that are wrong. He never does things that are not true. So God had to have a real and a true relationship with people. The truth is that people are separated from God because of their sin. Since Adam and Eve, people have been born outside the garden. They are born into the world of sin and death. They can never be perfect like God is perfect. They can never return to the garden. People cannot fix their broken relationship with God. Only God can do that.

HIS STORY: THE RESCUE

God loves people even though they turn away from him. He loves people even though they sin and disobey his perfect laws. God wants to rescue people so they do not have to be separate from him forever. He wants to make a way for people to come back to him. God promised that he would do that. He said that a man would come who would defeat Satan. A Rescuer would come. He would pay for the sins of the whole world – once and for all time.

So God chose another man to take Adam's place. This man was Jesus. Jesus was the Son of God. He was not the same as other people. He was God, so he was not born as a sinner like all other people were. He did not disobey God. He did not turn away from God. He was perfect, just like God is perfect. God chose his Son to be born as a real man. He did that so that Jesus could live and die as a real man too. God chose his Son Jesus to die for the sins of the whole world.

So when Jesus was hanging on the cross, it went dark for three hours. God did that to show that he was turning away from Jesus. Jesus was the Lamb of God. He took on the payment for the sins of all people. He was dying to pay for those sins. So God turned away from Jesus because Jesus was carrying the sins of all people. This was a terrible time for God and for Jesus. God had to turn away from his Son who he loved so much. And Jesus had to be alone at a time when he needed his Father very much. His Father, God, had turned away from him. God had to turn away because Jesus was paying for all of the sins of the world as if they were his own. Jesus was separated from God because he was dying to pay for the sins of all people. God showed what a terrible time it was by making the sky go dark.

When it was 3 o'clock in the afternoon, Jesus called out to his Father. His Father had turned away from him so he called out to him. He needed his Father at this time of terrible pain and suffering. He used the Aramaic language, so the people there did not understand what he was saying. They thought he was calling out to God's prophet, Elijah.

MARK 15:34-37

³⁴ Then at three o'clock Jesus called out with a loud voice, "Eloi, Eloi, lema sabachthani?" which means "My God, my God, why have you abandoned me?"

³⁵ Some of the bystanders misunderstood and thought he was calling for the prophet Elijah. ³⁶ One of them ran and filled a sponge with sour wine, holding it up to him on a reed stick so he could drink. "Wait!" he said. "Let's see whether Elijah comes to take him down!"

³⁷ Then Jesus uttered another loud cry and breathed his last.

SESSION 22: JESUS WAS CRUCIFIED, BURIED AND RAISED FROM THE DEAD

Jesus called out loudly and then he died. Jesus died because he wanted to die. He could have saved himself, but he did not. He knew that he had to die to rescue the people of the world. John wrote the words that Jesus called out when he died.

JOHN 19:30

> ³⁰ When Jesus had tasted it, he said, "It is finished!" Then he bowed his head and gave up his spirit.

Jesus said, *"It is finished!"* He meant that the payment for the world's sin had been made. God's great plan to rescue people that he had started so long ago was now finished. A way had been made for people to come to God. This was what God had planned to do. He wanted to have a real, true and close relationship with people. So Jesus, God's Son, took on the sins of all people. And he died to pay for those sins for all time. That is why Jesus said it was finished. He had made the payment for sin that fixed the relationship between God and people forever. Mark described something that happened right at the time that Jesus died.

MARK 15:38

> ³⁸ And the curtain in the sanctuary of the Temple was torn in two, from top to bottom.

Remember that there was a thick, heavy curtain hanging in the temple? It divided the two rooms inside the temple: the Holy Place and the Most Holy Place. The Most Holy Place was where God stayed among his people. Only the high priest could go in there once each year to sprinkle the blood of animals on the top of the Ark of the Covenant. If any other person went in there, they would die.

But now, Jesus had made the ultimate²⁵⁴ sacrifice for sin. Because he did that, people were free to come to God at any time. God's story says that the curtain was torn from the top to the bottom. God was showing that he was the one who tore the curtain. Now there was nothing separating God from the people. Jesus had made the final payment for sin. Remember when Jesus was eating the Passover meal with his disciples? He said to his disciples that his blood "*confirms the covenant between God and his people.*" He meant that he would die and his blood would be shed. And because of that, the agreement between God and people would be made right. And that is what happened. God tore

---

254. **ultimate** - final and complete

HIS STORY: THE RESCUE

the curtain in the temple to show that the agreement had been fulfilled or completed - finished.

Jesus died on a Friday. The next day was the Jewish Sabbath, when no work could be done. The Sabbath started at sunset on Friday.

MARK 15:42

⁴² This all happened on Friday, the day of preparation, the day before the Sabbath.

It was nearly the Sabbath day. So the body of Jesus had to be put into a tomb before the Sabbath began. There was a rich man called Joseph from a village called Arimathea. He was a member of the Jewish council or Sanhedrin. Joseph believed that Jesus was the Messiah. He was a disciple of Jesus but he did not tell anyone. He was afraid of what the Jews would do to him if they knew.

MARK 15:43-47

⁴³ Joseph of Arimathea took a risk and went to Pilate and asked for Jesus' body. (Joseph was an honored member of the high council, and he was waiting for the Kingdom of God to come.) ⁴⁴ Pilate couldn't believe that Jesus was already dead, so he called for the Roman officer and asked if he had died yet. ⁴⁵ The officer confirmed that Jesus was dead, so Pilate told Joseph he could have the body. ⁴⁶ Joseph bought a long sheet of linen cloth. Then he took Jesus' body down from the cross, wrapped it in the cloth, and laid it in a tomb that had been carved out of the rock. Then he rolled a stone in front of the entrance. ⁴⁷ Mary Magdalene and Mary the mother of Joseph saw where Jesus' body was laid.

Joseph went to Pilate to ask for the body of Jesus. Pilate was surprised that Jesus was already dead. So he checked with a centurion and he found out that Jesus had died. Then Pilate gave the body of Jesus to Joseph. Joseph wrapped the body in *linen cloth*. This was cloth that cost a lot of money. He put the body in a tomb and put a large flat stone over the door of the tomb. This stone was put there so that no people or animals could touch it. It was very heavy and hard to open. Some women, who were followers of Jesus, were there watching the tomb.

John also wrote about what happened to the body of Jesus after he died. He wrote that Nicodemus helped Joseph with the body. Nicodemus was the Pharisee who had come to talk to Jesus at night. He was also part of the Jewish high council. Nicodemus helped Joseph to take the body down from the cross. He brought

SESSION 22: JESUS WAS CRUCIFIED, BURIED AND RAISED FROM THE DEAD

myrrh[255] and aloe.[256] These were nice smelling spices that cost a lot of money. Nicodemus helped Joseph to wrap the body with the cloth and the spices. Then he helped Joseph to put the body in the tomb.

JOHN 19:38-42

 38 Afterward Joseph of Arimathea, who had been a secret disciple of Jesus (because he feared the Jewish leaders), asked Pilate for permission to take down Jesus' body. When Pilate gave permission, Joseph came and took the body away. 39 With him came Nicodemus, the man who had come to Jesus at night. He brought about seventy-five pounds of perfumed ointment made from myrrh and aloes. 40 Following Jewish burial custom, they wrapped Jesus' body with the spices in long sheets of linen cloth. 41 The place of crucifixion was near a garden, where there was a new tomb, never used before. 42 And so, because it was the day of preparation for the Jewish Passover and since the tomb was close at hand, they laid Jesus there.

They did not have much time to put the body in the tomb. The Sabbath was going to start soon. So they put the body in a tomb close to where Jesus had been crucified. The tomb belonged to Joseph. He had not used it yet. Many years earlier, Isaiah had written that the Messiah would be put in the tomb of a rich man.

ISAIAH 53:9

 9 He had done no wrong
 and had never deceived anyone.
 But he was buried like a criminal;
 he was put in a rich man's grave.

After the Sabbath had ended, three women went to the tomb. It was very early on Sunday morning. These women were Mary Magdalene, Mary the mother of James, and Salome. Mark wrote before that they had also been there when Jesus was crucified. They went to the tomb to put spices on the body of Jesus.

MARK 16:1-5

 1 Saturday evening, when the Sabbath ended, Mary Magdalene, Mary the mother of James, and Salome went out and purchased burial spices so they could anoint Jesus' body. 2 Very early on Sunday morning, just at sunrise, they went to

---

255. **myrrh** - nice smelling gum that comes from a tree
256. **aloe** - nice smelling gum that is dried and made into perfume or incense

HIS STORY: THE RESCUE

> the tomb. ³ On the way they were asking each other, "Who will roll away the stone for us from the entrance to the tomb?" ⁴ But as they arrived, they looked up and saw that the stone, which was very large, had already been rolled aside.
>
> ⁵ When they entered the tomb, they saw a young man clothed in a white robe sitting on the right side. The women were shocked,

The women were on their way to the tomb. They thought about who would help them to move the heavy stone that was over the door of the tomb. But when they got there, the stone was gone. So they went inside the tomb. They saw a young man dressed in a white robe sitting there. This young man was one of God's spirit messengers, an angel. He had presented himself in human form to speak to them. Luke and John wrote about this too. They said that there were two angels there. Mark only talked about one, probably because only one angel spoke to the women.

MARK 16:6-8

> ⁶ but the angel said, "Don't be alarmed. You are looking for Jesus of Nazareth, who was crucified. He isn't here! He is risen from the dead! Look, this is where they laid his body. ⁷ Now go and tell his disciples, including Peter, that Jesus is going ahead of you to Galilee. You will see him there, just as he told you before he died."
>
> ⁸ The women fled from the tomb, trembling and bewildered, and they said nothing to anyone because they were too frightened.

The women were very amazed and afraid. The angel told them not to be alarmed.²⁵⁷ He knew that they were looking for Jesus from Nazareth who had been crucified. He told them that Jesus was not there because he had risen from the dead. He showed them the place where the body had been placed. But there was no body there. The angel told the women to go and speak to the disciples. He said that they should tell the disciples that Jesus was going ahead of them to Galilee. The angel said that the disciples should go and meet Jesus there. He said, *"You will see him there, just as he told you before he died."* The angel wanted them to remember that Jesus had told the disciples that he would die and rise again.

---

257. **alarmed** - to be amazed and afraid

SESSION 22: JESUS WAS CRUCIFIED, BURIED AND RAISED FROM THE DEAD

The women ran from the tomb. They were shaking because they were so surprised and amazed. They did not talk to anyone as they went. But Luke wrote that they went to talk to the disciples. They did what the angel had told them to do.

LUKE 24:8-12

> 8 Then they remembered that he had said this. 9 So they rushed back from the tomb to tell his eleven disciples—and everyone else—what had happened. 10 It was Mary Magdalene, Joanna, Mary the mother of James, and several other women who told the apostles what had happened. 11 But the story sounded like nonsense to the men, so they didn't believe it. 12 However, Peter jumped up and ran to the tomb to look. Stooping, he peered in and saw the empty linen wrappings; then he went home again, wondering what had happened.

Later, Jesus appeared[258] to many people. He showed himself to Mary Magdalene, to some other men who were walking, and to his disciples.

MARK 16:9-14

> 9 After Jesus rose from the dead early on Sunday morning, the first person who saw him was Mary Magdalene, the woman from whom he had cast out seven demons. 10 She went to the disciples, who were grieving and weeping, and told them what had happened. 11 But when she told them that Jesus was alive and she had seen him, they didn't believe her.
>
> 12 Afterward he appeared in a different form to two of his followers who were walking from Jerusalem into the country. 13 They rushed back to tell the others, but no one believed them.
>
> 14 Still later he appeared to the eleven disciples as they were eating together. He rebuked them for their stubborn unbelief because they refused to believe those who had seen him after he had been raised from the dead.

Then the disciples walked with Jesus to Bethany. God's story tells us that when they were in Bethany, God took Jesus up to heaven. Jesus had finished his work, so he went back to be with his Father. That is where he is today.

---

258. **appeared** - showed himself to them

HIS STORY: THE RESCUE

MARK 16:19

¹⁹ When the Lord Jesus had finished talking with them, he was taken up into heaven and sat down in the place of honor at God's right hand.

On the cross, Jesus took on all the sins of all people. God turned his back on Jesus and judged him for our sins. God judged Jesus and passed sentence[259] on him. That sentence was death. Jesus died to pay for the sins of all the people of the world. Jesus did that and then God brought him back to life. God was showing that he accepted the payment that Jesus had made. The sentence was over. The full and final payment for the sins of all people had been made.

1. How did God's prophets know what would happen to Jesus?
2. Why did God have to turn away from Jesus when he was dying on the cross?
3. What did Jesus mean when he said "It is finished"?
4. Who raised Jesus from the dead?
5. Can people do anything at all to pay for their own sins and save themselves?

---

259. **passed sentence** - when a judge tells someone what their punishment will be

OUR PLACE IN HIS STORY

We have been following God's story from the very beginning. We have heard about the things that God has said and done from the beginning of time. Now, in the last part of this book, we are going to think about our place in God's story. Every person is a part of God's great rescue story and that includes us. God wants every person to know the story of what he has said and done. That is why he made sure that it was written down clearly in the Bible. He wants people to know the true story. He wants people to be able to know him and to have a real relationship with him.

We will first look back at what has happened in the story so far. Then, we will look forward to the rest of God's story as it is written in the Bible.

It is *His Story* because he is God, the Creator. He made the heavens and the earth. He is the only One who can tell the true story of everything. He chose people to write down his true story in the Bible. The people that he chose wrote down his words and his thoughts and wrote about the things that he did.

God loves people and he wants to work with people. From the beginning of time when God created everything, God's story has been about his relationships with human beings – with people just like us. God made people in his image. He wanted people to be able to have a relationship with him. He wanted them to know him and to love him. He gave Adam and Eve a real part to play and real

HIS STORY: THE RESCUE

work to do. Adam and Eve were created by God to be his people. They had a real and true relationship with God, their Father.

All people are descendants of Adam and Eve. We come from them. So because we come from them, it's like we were there too, in the garden of Eden with God. That's who we were in God's story.

But then everything changed. Adam and Eve turned away from God. They became sinners. When they became sinners, that meant that all people who were born after them were also sinners. That means you and me. We are the people who turn away from the truth and from God, we are the people who follow God's Enemy. We are the group who needed to be rescued by God. Each of us has turned his own way. God's prophet, Isaiah, wrote about this in the first part of Isaiah Chapter 53 verse 6.

⁶ All of us, like sheep, have strayed away.
We have left God's paths to follow our own.

ISAIAH 53:6A

We needed to be rescued from sin, from death, and from the power of God's Enemy. We had only one hope – the One that God promised would come to defeat His Enemy. And He did come, as we've heard. But let's read what the second half of that verse in Isaiah says.

⁶ All of us, like sheep, have strayed away.
We have left God's paths to follow our own.
Yet the Lord laid on him
the sins of us all.

ISAIAH 53:6

It says, "*Yet the Lord laid on him the sins of us all.*" Jesus was punished for all of our sins. We have heard how that happened. Jesus, God's Son, is also a part of God's Story. God sent him to rescue us.

As we have followed God's story from the beginning, we have heard about many different people. We have heard the stories of some of the things that happened to them. The different stories we have heard as part of God's great story are real. They happened in real places to real people. God put them there in his real story to help us to understand ourselves and to understand him. He made them happen and he made sure that they were written down in the Bible for us to read. He wants us to know how he sees us.

Just like Cain and Abel, we were born outside of the garden. We had no way to get back to God. We were the people who were cut off from God. After people were put outside of the garden, they could only come to God by killing an animal each time. We no longer need to do that because Jesus died for us. God accepted the sacrifice that Jesus made for our sins. So now we can go and speak to God at any time.

We are no longer cut off or separated from God. We are no longer outside. We have been brought back into the relationship with God that Adam and Eve enjoyed while they lived inside the garden. We can go to God and ask him to guide us or help us. We can talk with him about whatever we want to talk to him about. God wants us to do that. He wants to be our Guide and our Helper in life.

We were also like the people in the time of Noah. It was like we were outside of the boat. We did not know or care that God's judgment was coming. But if we have listened to Him and have believed the things that he has said, then we have been rescued. When Jesus was on earth, he said that he is the only way, the only door. The boat that Noah built had only one door to get inside. Just like that, Jesus is the one way to reach God. If we believe in Him, then it is like we have gone through the one door. When Jesus was hanging on the cross, he took God's judgment for our sin on himself. God was pleased with that payment and so he will never judge Jesus again. So if we have faith in Him, it's like we are inside the boat. The flood of God's judgment is raining down outside, but we are safe. We are the people inside the ark, the rescued people.

Remember the promises that God made to Abraham? He said that through Abraham and his son all the nations of the earth would be blessed. He said that Abraham would have more descendants than all the stars in the sky. Abraham's human descendants are the Israelites. But his spiritual[260] descendants are all those people who have been rescued. They are all the people who have been saved through the Promised One who came. If we have put our faith in Jesus, and we understand that there is nothing that we can do to save ourselves, then we are the descendants of Abraham. We have been blessed. We have become God's people as well.

Abraham's grandson, Jacob, had a dream one night. He saw a set of stairs reaching from heaven down to earth. Before, we had no way to reach God. But Jesus made a way. Jesus is like that set of stairs that Jacob saw in his dream. Now

---

260. **spiritual** - something that is not physical but it is real and it involves God's Spirit

HIS STORY: THE RESCUE

we can go to God to speak to him. We have a real and true relationship with God because of Jesus.

Later in the story, we heard about the children of Israel in Egypt. They were slaves of the Pharaoh of Egypt. We were also slaves of an evil ruler. Satan is the evil ruler of this world. We were slaves and we could not escape. But God sent Moses to lead the children of Israel out of slavery. And he also sent his son, Jesus, to save us.

After God rescued the Israelites from Egypt, they reached the Red Sea. Pharaoh and his army were coming. They had no way to escape. But God used his servant Moses to make a path through the water. Just like that, he used his servant Jesus to make a path for us. It is like we are on the other side of the sea and we are safe. Our enemy has been defeated.

Later on, in the wilderness, poisonous snakes were biting the Israelites. God told Moses to make a bronze serpent and to put it up high on a pole. When someone was bitten they could look at the bronze serpent and be healed. It is like we have been bitten by sin and death. But if we have looked at Jesus hanging on the cross with faith, then we are now healed.

And then in God's story, we learned about Jesus coming to earth. When he was baptized, God said, *"This is my dearly loved Son, who brings me great joy."* Right after that, Jesus entered the wilderness for 40 days. Jesus was weak from hunger when Satan came and tried to trick him. Satan tried to make him sin. But Jesus was not like Adam and Eve. He wanted to obey only his Father and carry out God's rescue plan. He did not listen to Satan. Jesus answered Satan with God's Word. Jesus showed how a person can relate to God the Father. He showed how to know him and love him.

Jesus also showed his power over storms. He could heal people who were sick, and people who were blind. He could bring dead people back to life. He could tell evil spirits what to do and then they did it. He is the Creator, God.

Jesus is God, and he died for us. When he died on the cross, he defeated sin, death and Satan. He said, *"It is finished"* and then the big curtain in the temple was torn from top to bottom. Because of him, we can go to God any time we want. We are no longer cut off from the Most Holy Place of God. We do not have to make sacrifices to God. We do not need human priests to help us to reach God. We are God's people. While we are on this earth, we will continue to sin, but God does not look at our sin or judge us for it. When God looks at us, he sees his perfect Son who has already carried our sin for us.

The rest of the Story

Now we have looked back at how we are a part of God's wonderful story. But what comes next? When Jesus died, was buried and rose again, God's great rescue plan was finished. However, not everything is finished. As people who have put our faith in Jesus, we have already been rescued. But the world is still the same as it was after Adam and Eve disobeyed God. Satan is still the ruler of the world. Sin is still here. Death is all around us. We still find that we have to live with sin and with pain.

It was the same way for the disciples and other followers of Jesus. They believed that he was the Messiah, the Christ. They had come to understand that his death was needed to pay for sin. They had seen Jesus die and then rise again to life. But then Jesus returned to his Father in heaven. And the people who had been the enemies of Jesus were their enemies too. The Jewish religious leaders were angry with the disciples and followers of Jesus. And his followers were only a few people, a small group. They had to live with sin and with other problems. What would happen in the future? What were God's plans? How would his story continue? How would it end?

Jesus had created a new agreement with God through his death on the cross. But what did that mean for the followers of Jesus as they continued to live their lives? The relationship between God and people had been restored,[261] but how would he guide them? How should they speak to him? How should they relate to each other? What work should they do? How should they relate to people who did not yet know about him? All their questions could be answered, but first they had to believe something very, very important that Jesus had told them.

John wrote down what Jesus had promised not long before he died.

JOHN 14:16-19

¹⁶ And I will ask the Father, and he will give you another Advocate, who will never leave you. ¹⁷ He is the Holy Spirit, who leads into all truth. The world cannot receive him, because it isn't looking for him and doesn't recognize him. But you know him, because he lives with you now and later will be in you.

---

261. **restored** - made new again

HIS STORY: THE RESCUE

> 18 No, I will not abandon you as orphans—I will come to you.
> 19 Soon the world will no longer see me, but you will see me. Since I live, you also will live.

Jesus knew that his followers would be afraid and alone after he left the earth. But Jesus promised that he would not leave them alone like *orphans*.[262] He said that he would ask his Father to send the third One who is also God – the Spirit. Because he is a Spirit, no one would see him. Other people would not even know he was here. But Jesus said that he would come and he would live in all those people who had put their faith in Jesus. He would be Jesus' representative[263] here on earth.

Jesus also called God's Spirit a *Advocate* and "*the Holy Spirit who leads into all truth.*" He called the Spirit those names because this would remind the followers of Jesus of all the things that Jesus had taught them. It would remind them what Jesus was like. In that way, the Spirit would help them to tell others about Jesus. John described what Jesus said about this.

JOHN 15:26,27

> 26 "But I will send you the Advocate—the Spirit of truth. He will come to you from the Father and will testify all about me.
> 27 And you must also testify about me because you have been with me from the beginning of my ministry.

Testify means to speak about something. Jesus also said that the Spirit of truth would have the work of guiding the followers of Jesus into *all truth*.

JOHN 16:13

> 13 When the Spirit of truth comes, he will guide you into all truth. He will not speak on his own but will tell you what he has heard. He will tell you about the future.

Jesus meant that God's Spirit would be there ready to answer their questions. He would help them to know about God. He would teach them how to live under the new agreement. He would show them how they should live as God's children on the earth. He would show them what God wanted. And he would help them know how to live in a way that pleased God.

---

262. **orphans** - children who don't have a father and mother to take care of them
263. **representative** - someone who speaks the words or does the work of someone else

OUR PLACE IN HIS STORY

Jesus also said that the Spirit would *"tell you about the future."* God's story was going to keep going, and they were part of the story. Noah, Abraham, Isaac, Jacob, David and many others before them were part of his story. Now Peter, James, John, Andrew and others were going to be part of God's story, too.

God's Spirit was going to show the apostles the rest of God's rescue plan. Jesus had defeated Satan, sin and death. Now his followers would be the ones to tell people about that so that they could be rescued too. This is what would happen from that time on, right through history, and it is still happening today.

Just before Jesus was taken by God back to heaven, he left the apostles with some very important work to do.

MATTHEW
28:18-20

¹⁸ Jesus came and told his disciples, "I have been given all authority in heaven and on earth. ¹⁹ Therefore, go and make disciples of all the nations, baptizing them in the name of the Father and the Son and the Holy Spirit. ²⁰ Teach these new disciples to obey all the commands I have given you. And be sure of this: I am with you always, even to the end of the age."

Jesus told the apostles to help other people to understand that they needed to be rescued from Satan and sin. Their work would be to help others to know that Jesus had come to rescue them. They should help others become his followers, or disciples, as well.

In the rest of the New Testament, the apostles wrote down the story of how God's Spirit came and gave them the strength to do this work. It tells the story of how the good news about Jesus was shared. It started in Jerusalem, then spread to other areas of Israel and into other nations. It went out to people who spoke other languages. And now it has come to us today. If we are Jesus' followers, then this is also our work.

We have God's Spirit living in us too. We know the truth that he gave to the apostles that they wrote down for us with his guidance. Satan has been working hard ever since, trying to stop the good news about Jesus and the rescue from going out. But he can never win. Sin still exists, but when the followers of Jesus read his words in the Bible and listen to the Spirit, they can please God. We can be his witnesses.²⁶⁴ We can help others to follow him.

---

264. **witnesses** - people who tell others about what they have seen or what they know to be true

HIS STORY: THE RESCUE

Later in his story, God teaches us how to work together. He tells us how to come together as groups of his children. We can understand how to worship him together. We can help each other to follow him better.

And just as Jesus said would happen, God's Spirit taught the apostles many things about the future. They wrote these things down for us to read in the Bible. We can read it and know God's plan for his children who die. And we can understand that Jesus will come again. He will defeat Satan once and for all. He will finish the rule of sin and death. This is part of his story too. We are part of *His Story*.

DEFINITIONS FOR SOME WORDS USED IN THIS BOOK

ability - to be able to do something

accepted - he took it

accused - to accuse someone means to say that they have done something bad

adopted - to take another person's child and bring it up as your own

agreement - for two people or groups of people to say that they promise to do the things that the agreement says they will do

alarmed - to be amazed and afraid

allowed - something that is OK to do and it is not wrong to do it

aloe - nice smelling gum that is dried and made into perfume or incense

amazed - to be very very surprised about something you see

ancestor - people in our family who have lived before us

appeared - showed himself to them

arrested - put into prison or gaol

ashamed - to feel sad about something you have done. To want to hide because you did something bad

astounded - very, very surprised and amazed

authority - the power or right to give orders and to have other people obey those orders

awake - not sleeping

baptize - to put someone under water and then bring them up out of the water again. It is a sign for other people to see that the person agrees with God that they are a sinner and that they need him to save them

basic - the starting point or the foundation (for all the other rules)

battle - in wars or fights

beginning - the start

betray - to help someone's enemies to catch or hurt them

birthright - all the things that would belong to the first son after his father died. It was also the blessing that the father would give to the oldest son to say that he would be the head of the family

bitter - very difficult and unhappy

blame - to say that someone or something is why something happened

blessed - he asked God to take care of them

blindfold - a piece of cloth tied over someone's eyes so they can't see

boils - inflamed pus-filled swellings on the skin

border - the outside edge of something

HIS STORY: THE RESCUE

boundary - a line that marks an area
brass - a yellow metal made up of copper and zinc
calf - a young cow
calm - quiet and peaceful and still
camels - large hairy animals with long necks and long legs that can live in very dry places
camped - set up a place to stay for a short time
carved - to cut into something with something sharp to leave a deep mark
cave - a room inside a stone area under the ground or next to a cliff
celebration - a time when people get together to remember something good that has happened
chant - a song or saying that people think will make things happen if they say it
charge - in a law court, a charge is the thing people say someone has done to break the law
chariot - a small cart with two wheels that was pulled along by horses
chief - the leaders
choice - to have to do one thing or another thing, to decide between two things
clearly - so it is easy to understand
cloth - material or fabric that clothes are made out of
club - a heavy piece of wood for hitting people
commandment - a rule from God that must be obeyed
commit adultery - sex between a married person and someone who is not their husband or wife
community - a group of people living together in the same area
companion - someone who spends time with you, and helps you
complain - to say that you are not happy about something or to say bad things about someone because of something they have done
contract - something that is written down that two people or groups of people agree to
convulsion - to fall on the ground and have your body shake without being able to stop it
courtyard - an area outside a large house that has walls around it but no roof
covenant - an agreement between two people or groups of people
covered - the water was over the top of all the earth
Creator - the one who created, or made everything
creatures - living things that God made
criminals - people who have broken the law
crowd - a very, very large group of people
curse - to hurt or do harm to someone
curtain - a piece of material held at the top to make a screen
dazzling - so bright that it is hard to look at
debt - something that you owe to someone else and have to pay back
decide - to think about what you are going to do
decorate - to make something look better by adding pictures or paint or curtains to it
defeat - to win over someone else in a fight or competition; to overcome or beat

DEFINITIONS FOR SOME WORDS USED IN THIS BOOK

defeated - to be the one to lose in a fight

defile - to make something dirty or not acceptable to God

descendants - any people in your family who are born and live after you

desert - a very dry place with no water

deserve - to earn something by something you have done

destroy - to kill, to ruin, or to end something so that it isn't there any more

difficult - not easy

disasters - sudden events that cause great damage or loss of life

disciples - the men who were close followers of Jesus

disobey - not obey. Not do what someone says to do

distressed - they were very upset and worried

divorce - a legal ruling by a judge or court to break a marriage agreement

donkey - an animal that looks like a horse, but with long ears. People use it for riding on and for carrying things

dove - a bird that is a sign of peace

education - getting school and learning

energy - power that makes things happen

engaged - promised to be married to someone

enjoy - to like doing something or seeing something

equips - prepares someone for a task or for work they have to do

escape - to get away from something

establishes - to make something strong so that it cannot change again

eternal - something that goes on forever and does not stop

evening - the time at the end of the day, from about 6pm until bed time

everlasting - something that lasts forever

evidence - someone to say that Jesus had done something very wrong so that they could kill him

exactly - he told them every small detail

exist - for something to be there

explained - to tell about something and what it really means

failed - were not able to do something

faith - when someone believes that the things that God says are true

false - not real or true

false witnesses - people who say they have seen something when they have not seen it

famous - known about by many people

favourite - the one that he likes the most

festival - a time when people get together to remember something good that has happened

fig - a kind of tree

flogged - to beat someone with a whip or stick

followers - people who follow someone else. Follow means to listen to them and to be with them and to believe what they say

HIS STORY: THE RESCUE

foreign - a land that was not their own land
forgave - said that they did not have to pay for something they had done wrong
forgiven - to be made free of a debt that you owe to someone else for doing something wrong to them
furniture - things for people to use in a room, like tables, chairs and lamps
future - the time after now
garments - coats and robes - outer clothing
generation - a set of members of a family that are alive at the same time. The time in a family when children are born, grow up and have children of their own
generations - all of the people born or living at about the same time
giant - a huge, very tall man
give testimony - to speak in a court of law about something that you say is true
glorify - for people to see who Jesus really is and to praise and worship him for it
gnats - small flies like mosquitos
gods - we write the name of the true God with a big "G" but false gods with a small "g"
gospel - God's good news about who Jesus really is
government - the group of people with the authority to run a country or state
governor - the leader for the government in an area
grace - when God loves people or forgives people or saves people when they have not done anything themselves to earn it or get it
grains - food that people get from plants like wheat and rice
graze - eat the grass
greeting - something that you do when you meet someone
hail - pieces of ice that fall like rain
hammering - to hit something with a hammer. A hammer is a tool for putting in nails.
head - the leader
heal - to make someone well again
heaven - a real place where God's story says that God is
Hebrew - people that are descended from Jacob, the grandson of Abraham
holy place - a place set apart for God
honest - to speak the truth and not to hide anything
honor - to give someone love and respect for something they have done
horrible - very bad or unpleasant
huge - very, very big
hunter - someone who goes out to find and kill animals to eat
idol - something that people make out of metal or wood that they worship as a god
ignore - To act like you don't know about something. To do nothing about something
impossible - something that can not be done
inherit - to get money, property or something from someone else after they die
instructions - directions or orders about how to do something

DEFINITIONS FOR SOME WORDS USED IN THIS BOOK

Jewish religious experts - people who know all the rules and laws of the Jews
judged - to be told how you will be punished or rewarded for what you have done
justice - to be fair and true
justified - to be put into a right relationship with God again
kingdom - an area and a group of people who are ruled by one king
knelt - went down on his knees
knowledge - all the things that people know
lambs - young sheep
layer - a sheet of something that can be thick or thin
lentils - small beans that come from a plant and can be dried and then eaten
listen - to choose to agree with someone and follow what they say
loaves - pieces of bread that are shaped and baked and then cut up for eating
locusts - large flying grasshoppers that eat plants
melted - heated the gold so they could make another shape out of it
merciful - showing forgiveness to someone who you have the power to punish or harm
mercy - love or forgiveness shown to someone when you could harm them
message - something written or said by one person to tell something to another person
messenger - a person who tells things to people for someone else
misuse - to use something in the wrong way
mocking - making fun of someone or something in a cruel or bad way
mourned - to feel sorry because of the death of someone
murder - the killing of one human being by another
musician - someone who plays music and writes songs
myrrh - nice smelling gum that comes from a tree
nation - a large group of people who all come from one ancestor
nephew - the son of your brother or sister
nostrils - nose holes for breathing
obey - to follow what someone says
offering - animals or anything that a person brings as a gift to God
orphans - children who don't have a father and mother to take care of them
overlooking - from the top you can see over the whole land
palace - a large and beautiful building where a king or ruler lives
paradise - another name for heaven
passed sentence - when a judge tells someone what their punishment will be
physical - flesh and blood bodies
pillar - something that is tall and that stands up from the ground
pitcher - a large container for water
plagues - things that happen to cause damage or sickness to many people
poisonous - something with poison in it that can kill people

HIS STORY: THE RESCUE

poor - not having very much money to live
pour - to tip a liquid over something
prayed - to pray means to talk to God about something
preaching - to teach a group of people things about God
pregnant - going to have a baby
prepared - to be ready for something
priest - someone who helps other people to worship God
prisoner - a person who is locked up in prison or in gaol
promise - to say that you will do something
prophets - teachers or speakers of the words of God
protection - to keep safe from harm or injury
provide - to give something
province - an area at that time that had a Roman governor
punishment - something bad done to someone because they did a wrong thing
rainbow - an arch of many colours that can be seen in the sky
ram - a male sheep
rape - to force someone to have sex when they don't want to
rebels - people who rebel or turn away from the truth and from God
region - a large area with many countries and people groups
reign - to rule as a king
reject - to not listen to someone, to not like or love someone, to not agree with someone or to say that what someone says is wrong
relationship - the way in which two or more people are connected or linked together
release - let him go free
repent - to agree with God that you have sinned against him
representative - someone who speaks the words or does the work of someone else
reprimand - to tell someone to stop what they are doing
rescue - to save someone from danger or death
Rescuer - the One who saves people or rescues people
restored - made new again
resurrection - to come to life again after being dead
righteousness - to live and speak in the right way or in a true way
rough - the sea had a lot of waves going up and down and from side to side
rowed - pushed the boat along with paddles or oars
sacrifice - to kill an animal or to give something else as an offering to God
sailors - people who travel on the water in boats
scoff - to call out bad things about someone to show that you do not respect or like them
scribes - Jewish religious leaders who were experts in Jewish law
separate - to move one thing away from another thing

DEFINITIONS FOR SOME WORDS USED IN THIS BOOK

separated - to be apart from, or away from something
serpent - a snake
servant - a person who does work for someone else
shed - when blood is 'shed' it means that blood flows out of someone's body
shepherd - someone who takes care of sheep
shore - the edge of a sea or lake
shouted - called out in a loud voice
shrub - small plant
silent - quiet, not making any noise, not speaking
sin - means to go against what God has said, to disobey God
sink - fill up with water and go down under the water
skull - the big bone inside the head
slaves - people who have to work for other people without being paid
slept with - had sex with
soldiers - men who are in the army
soon - in a short amount of time
splendor - very big and beautiful and rich
spiritual - something that is not physical but it is real and it involves God's Spirit
sprinkle - to cover something with small drops (of the blood)
sprouted - started to grow
staff - a pole made of wood that Moses carried with him
starve - to die because you don't have any food to eat
storms - when there is very strong wind and high waves
strangers - people that do not belong somewhere, that are not in their own place
strict - a strong law that should not be broken or disobeyed
subdue - to bring under control
suffer - to have something bad or painful or harmful happen to you
sulphur - a yellow powder found in rocks and in dirt. It can burn
surprised - to see something that you do not expect to see
tax collector - someone who has the work of getting money for the government from people
telescope - a thing to look through so we can see very, very far away
temporary - something that is only for a short amount of time
terrible - a very, very bad thing. Something that makes you very afraid
terrified - very, very afraid
territories - areas of land that are ruled by a state or country
tested - tried it to see if it was real or not
thieves - people who take things that belong to other people
thorns - spikes on a plant or tree
together - to be with each other. To be close to one another

HIS STORY: THE RESCUE

tomb - a stone room where dead bodies are put. A big stone is put at the door to close it
transformed - to change very much
trapped - having no way to escape
tribe - a group of people who have the same language and culture and come from the same ancestors
trick - a clever act to make someone do something you want them to do
trusted - he believed what God said was true and that God would always do the best thing
twins - two children born at the same birth
ultimate - final and complete
unblemished - flawless or perfect in every way
universe - all of outer space. All the stars and all the planets
valuable - things that are worth a lot of money
vegetables - food that comes from plants like carrots, potatoes and onions
virgin - someone who has never had sex
waiting - to stay somewhere until a later time
warlike - they often fought wars against other groups of people
wickedness - to do very bad or evil things
wilderness - an area where there are no people living and no farming
witnesses - people who tell others about what they have seen or what they know to be true
womb - the place in a woman's body where a baby grows before it is born
wonderful - something very good that makes us very happy when we see it
worried - thought something bad would happen
worse - when something is not as good as it was before
worship - to show love for God, to enjoy God, to talk about how good God is and to thank him for all he has done
wrapped - to put material or cloth all over and around something
young - babies or offspring

For more resources visit accesstruth.com
info@accesstruth.com

www.ingramcontent.com/pod-product-compliance
Lightning Source LLC
Chambersburg PA
CBHW060419010526
44118CB00017B/2276